# A SECRET GRIEF

# A SECRET GRIEF

## A MEMOIR

## NATALIE SCOTT

PEPPER PRESS

PEPPER PRESS

First published in 2025 by Pepper Press, an imprint of Fair Play Publishing

PO Box 4101, Balgowlah Heights, NSW 2093, Australia

www.fairplaypublishing.com.au

ISBN: 978-1-923236-33-2

ISBN: 978-1-923236-34-9 (ePub)

© Natalie Scott 2025

The moral rights of the author have been asserted.

All rights reserved. Except as permitted under the *Australian Copyright Act 1968* (for example, a fair dealing for the purposes of study, research, criticism or review), no part of this book may be reproduced, stored in a retrieval system, communicated or transmitted in any form or by any means without prior written permission from the Publisher.

Cover design and typesetting by Amy Mack.

This work depicts actual events in the author's life as truthfully as recollection permits and/or can be verified by research. Occasionally, dialogue consistent with the character or nature of the person speaking has been supplemented. All persons are actual individuals; there are no composite characters. The names of some individuals have been changed to respect their privacy.

All inquiries should be made to the Publisher via hello@fairplaypublishing.com.au

 A catalogue record for this book is available from the National Library of Australia

# 1

'Drink,' was her command in a smooth voice, yet a voice with a scratch. 'Drink your milk.'

And I drank. Trapped in the highchair, with small hands, I levered up the blue and white mug that had my initial—N—elaborately twirled with blue roses the colour of a winter sea.

Swallowing, swallowing, gasping and swallowing, I would smell the milk, the cloudy whiteness of it like paste. I'd come to know there was another rose. At the bottom. Just one, but identical. I'd never seen a real blue rose then. Nor since.

'Drink your milk.'

Is memory ungrateful? I don't know.

Time sweeps on.

∽

IN THE VAGUENESS of a cold May day, sharp below were wind-chopped waves the colour of the winter sea. Above, from our ledge, their patterns were never complete as they broke below in a world which had fallen away. Somehow, I knew that if I leaned out, I would lean out into nothing.

Nina stood behind me, the soft stuff on my viyella skirt pressed against my legs. Four pearl buttons like frosted sweets marched down the smocked bodice on my skinny chest.

'Natasha,' she said, 'look up.'

I widened my eyes and obeyed. What was happening? How to understand at four? Two birds flitted in the air, one chirped and swayed before, protectively it seemed, the second bird slipped closer, fluttered alongside it till, wings unfolded, they both dropped, then rose again, before disappearing. Head stretched back, my mother's hands were light on my shoulders.

'Don't look down now,' she was saying, but I did. Edged on the ledge, the toes of my small shoes were scuffed by the rough track we'd followed to get here; a track between honeycombs of sandstone, with other rocks weathered to the colour of prunes. Earlier, up ahead of me, below the navy pleats of the dress she wore which sheered rhythmically from her spare, girlish body—right, left, again—had she pranced on heels like knives?

Arriving, she pushed me to lead.

'Am I the queen of the castle?'

With a ragged tone, but calm gesture, she said, 'Why not?'

Why not? Two words which can haunt me still.

Motives are beyond a four-year-old's comprehension. But what was my mother's motive, a motive I couldn't recognise, let alone label if I was that child again?

No, I've no wish to revisit or re-hear some sad, inner tune of that far-off time. Yet on occasions, sharp-edged sounds: like mewling gulls or snarling water ... and sights: blue, stuffed pillows of waves bursting with feathers of foam ... and scents: saltiness that pinches like lemons, and '*Joy*', marketed as the world's costliest perfume, can fill me with a dread not consciously experienced back then. There was no frozen helplessness, but hearing her breathe, perhaps my mother underwent some hum of anxiety. But having been subjected to her previous anxieties, did I just conclude that this too would pass?

That little girl—the version of myself once—caught on that Australian clifftop under a sombre sky, cupped her hands to her mouth, swallowing screams.

The way a foal is nudged to its feet, her knees were nudged from behind. Rocked forward. Gravel grated to shift minimally under the small shoes buttoned across insteps. Her mother's vivid face bent to her cheek, brushing it with puckered lips. Close and sweet '*Joy*' spread between them, a nebulous veil.

Next there was a pause, before slowly the long fingers uncaged that child's shoulders, then ... a split moment's pressure from her mother's palms on her back. In seconds, she could be a doll dangling jointlessly adrift in the muttering sea below.

DID my eyelids blink down only to flick open to a sky circling above? My spine clutched against her stomach, her arms were taut straps of flesh; and like one body, she drew us both back, retreating from that cliff edge. Who knows, were the pupils of her eyes dark with fright? At the enormity of what she might have done? Unhinged, extinguishing her child's life? Following that child, and ending her own?

She spun me about and, lips stretched into her dress, my face pushed into her, while in a vexed reality I felt her gulp, then pant like a hurt animal. When I heard her sobs, I was ready with sobs of my own, to fling my arms about her, scrabbling my fingers to feel through her dress the bones of the corset she had no need to wear. A flesh-coloured thing, very occasionally I'd seen it hung over a 'boudoir' chair in my parents' bedroom; a room where, staring at nothing, my mother would lengthily brush her hair. A room I was not encouraged to enter where, off and away in her mind, she was not to be disturbed.

THREADS OF AWFULNESS—AN aloneness scarily experienced, if they jittered through me in any sense, they flashed on in an instant. Snapped; they were gone and this hostile world shaded to become our world, my mother's and mine. She was speaking —saying something to me but the words whisked away in a wind that came up like the sweep of a broom. Behind us, leaves on stunted shrubs bent and bobbled. Beyond a ridge, bulks of clouds began to form.

Sounds like beetles clacked, shimmering together with strands of dry grass and the whispering sea.

'Natasha,' she said, and as she held my hand tight, I felt her tremble. Wisps of her dark hair had come unpinned and, eyebrows notched together over her pale face, she was searching mine as if trying to discover something. What? Some form of certainty? A promising future for herself? For me, her only child? Now, years on, I only suppose that perhaps she found a glimpse of herself, as I did grow to resemble her in some ways. But parents, do we know them at all?

'Natasha ...'

For a tormentingly long time, we stood there. She was saying my name again into my hair, her breath quavery and warm.

Yet I wasn't warm. 'Cold,' I said, 'cold.'

She shivered as if the cold just touched her. Then, forever able to surprise me, my mother laughed, and even if only a gasp of a laugh, it was still a laugh. I laughed.

'And hungry?' she asked and this thought took centre stage in my mind. I nodded, licking my lips.

'Caramel ice-cream cake?' my mother said enticingly. 'Like that? At Cahill's?' she pointed. Cahill's was a chain of restaurants, with white-starched cloths and frilly-capped and aproned waitresses in black.

'And humbugs?'

I jiggled my toes. Humbugs were a treat; black and white sugar spun together, twisted and skeined. Mouth-watering and suckable. My saliva was juicy in my mouth.

'Yes.'

THAT NIGHT, when casually with no sense of prying, my father asked where I was that day with my mother, 'Up, up on rocks,' I said, reaching high. 'In the sky.'

'Go on.'

'Near standing on the sea,' I elaborated. Momentarily crumbling, his face ashen, a vein fluttered under one of his eyes.

'Near standing on the sea,' he repeated.

So today, forced to resort to fragments mystifyingly stored in my memory, how do I put into words, words that were never said. Was his silence strength? Why not?

Why not let go of the past, let it slide away and drain off into a sea of forgetfulness? A winter-blue sea. Cover the surface with thick wads: mattresses of weed and kelp rocking and see-sawing in the footlessness of waves. A montage of fish in a world of anemones, bladder-wrack tough with rubbery tissue, dead-men finger sponges and sea monsters. Never dangle a wrist or ankle below a mirror of water to be entwined by bangles of weed, shackled and dragged down. At all costs, keep your head above water.

Inevitably, you become the person you are. Who needs a high or low tide? Some things can be absorbed from a manageable distance, yet if I run from them, memory runs with me.

## 2

I had a stern paternal grandmother; the only survivor of a quartet of grandparents who had contributed genes but no living monument or characteristics to be observed by a child.

Hannah Ross—'Ross' in a generation shortened from Rosovsky—was not only large but formidable. Bombazine-bosomed, her throat encased, no, slotted with high lace, she was high-haired and most times in my presence, high-hatted with the addition of chooky feathers that shone like a March fly's wings. There was a smell about her that I later learned was the smell of gardenias. And this matriarch was perfumed for more than a summer's day. For an end of summer's day, when clouds would gather and boom with thunder.

They were terrible days when she came to visit. My mother dressed us in our Sunday best—me with very white socks—and she vigorously brushed my hair, tying it back with an ironed ribbon. She took more trouble than usual with the flowers which tumbled into vases and decked our rooms, and she used her best china. With an all-consuming belief that my father, on whom Hannah Ross doted, had erred in the choice of his wife, there was no woman worthy of her darling son. What's more he'd fallen trap to a beautiful woman in whose shadow her own daughter, my aunt, paled.

So, my grandmother was not set on approving me; her own daughter's daughter, Marina, was the apple of her eye. A month my junior, and the second of her granddaughters to grace the planet, Marina was the star.

Needless to say, my mother did not welcome my grandmother's visits. She was like an ancient adversary with her rituals and battles, who saw to it that she divided my father's loyalties and demanded sacrifices.

Enthroned, she would beckon me closer. Imperiously.

'Natasha,' she'd narrow her eyes that were the colour of slate, then chin raised, pinch in her mouth and extend fingers encrusted with diamonds. Hannah was born in Holland to a diamond merchant, and there was evidence in the brooches of graded stones which blinked from the inevitable black of her tailored jackets. Relieved by white or coffee-coloured blouses, pearls too habitually nested on that stretch of concealed flesh. Her only flesh that I ever saw was her face, hands, and occasionally her wrists, so I concluded that she was different from me.

'Closer child,' came the instruction, and at my reluctance she would bend creakily forward, droop her torso almost to her knees and clap a jewelled hand to each of my cheeks. I'd feel the gold jointing the pads of her fingers when she was intent on holding me captive for inspection.

What did she see? Not Marina, her favourite, but my mother's daughter with my mouth squashed to a tight tomato, nose thrown out of shape, and huge eyes in a young face straining not to cry in fright and miserable outrage.

When at last released and poised to flee, I was then subjected to the ritual of afternoon tea and put through the endurance of behaving properly. 'Behaving properly' meant not spilling anything, answering only when spoken to, knees together and no fidgeting with the napkin spread to cover my tightly held lap. If my mother and I were unspoken allies on these occasions, there was one awful day when she betrayed me.

'Natasha, go and wait at the gate for your grandmother.' Then a pause, followed by a sharp intake of breath. 'Kiss her cheek if she offers it.' Did she wince? 'Escort her through the garden.' Escort? Only later did I learn what 'escort' meant. 'Do not run ahead!'

With no hovering angel present to take care of me under splashed shadows of leaves from a plane tree, I swung on the gate, dragged a toe on the path, and kicked off again. She would arrive by taxi if unable to commandeer someone to deliver her to us.

There was always the elaborate cake she could be counted on to bring in its coronation tin, Their Majesties in profile, crowns set on authoritatively held heads. And with lofty patronage, each cake she brought us could have been iced with letters to spell out: 'My son's wife is an indifferent cook.'

True, my mother preferred reading to baking, but other than in my grandmother's mind, we did not go hungry. 'Wholesome' rather than 'fussy' was my mother Nina's kitchen credo. Cherry-topped sponge, honey cream roll, apple strudel, even Madeira wine. My hand was slapped away should I reach for a piece of anything before being invited to do so. While wordless, my mother would stab at a slice with her cake fork, push it round her plate and give the impression that as much as a crumb would choke her.

The blue morning was now a yellow afternoon and next door but one, my friend Gwennie lived in her house nestled among trees too, where hens laid eggs in a wired area behind Mr. Hunt's shed. I could hear Gwennie's sharp-toothed dog barking, which usually meant that Gwennie and her mother were out, and her brothers at school. My status was 'only child'.

Engrossed, my fingers were on the latch on the gate. I was clacking it up, down, up, down, up. Fuelled with what must have been a sense of righteousness, I waited, knowing what was expected of me. Yet when I heard the car drive up, I didn't raise my head to look at it. Or her. Was I practising a furtive smile directed at tracking ants near my feet?

'Hello, girlie,' called the driver, one foot on the running board of his polished Rover. The slug of a cigarette held fast to his lower lip, and his eyebrows were grey caterpillars. 'Here's the dear old lady. Nanna.'

Nanna! I'd never called her that and peremptorily my grandmother was ordering me: 'Don't just stand there child.'

I bit my lip. Where should I stand? She fixed a gimlet eye on me from a face more creased in strong sunlight and more unkissable than usual, but should she offer a floury cheek, I knew what must be done; submit.

'Gotta kiss for me as well?' the driver asked. A kiss for him! Appalled, my tongue went furry, or something.

'Get off with you, Eric,' she sounded almost playful, a spasm of a laugh biting into the creases. She appeared to save her smiles for other people. 'She won't remember you. No, no, don't give her the tin,' and her handbag was adjusted, sliding towards one elbow. 'This child very likely will drop it,' and Their Majesties were delivered into my grandmother's outstretched hands.

Obedient to instructions, I held the gate open and the black galleon of Hannah Ross sailed through, though not before summoning: 'Be back here at four, if you will, Eric. Four o'clock sharp.'

''Righty-hoh,' he replied with a neat sniff before waving.

'Natasha. Fasten the gate. Securely.' So I did, though securely against what? I didn't care because freed and up on my toes, I was off. Off up the driveway, arms scooping the air, my hair a black rope flying out from my head.

'Where is she? Where IS your grandmother?' Touched by indoor shadows, holding herself tall inside our front door with its panels of stained-glass waratahs to each side, the austerity of my mother's voice was enfolding like smoke. Grey and acrid, it was smoke I wanted to push away. Why? The sting of it? I didn't know.

A hand lifted to shade her eyes. 'WHERE IS SHE?'

The tongue in my mouth wasn't there. I tried, but dumb, pulses tapping my throat, I couldn't frame an answer. I couldn't even tell my mother that my grandmother—greeted and dutifully kissed—right now was sailing with her waddle towards us and the house. With Their Majesties.

If my mother's nerves twitched, mine fizzed. Something was unfixably wrong. 'WHERE IS SHE?'

Her smell of gardenias the warning, she arrived sheened with sweat; Brunhilde on the warpath, bent on blood. My blood I imagined after she transferred Their Majesties into the keeping of a livid daughter-in-law, whose eyes resembled glass.

'Your impossible child,' my grandmother's hum rose to a shout to my mother. 'Your impossible child!'

Hot tears burned inside me, but filled with her hate words, I continued to flee in fear.

'Come in, please come in,' my mother said as she put her lips together in a smile. She stood aside before, with an operatic sigh, Hannah Ross huffily obliged. But the episode was not over.

Miserable, we waited for further punishment—scalding words, stabbing comparisons with Marina, the dimple-kneed-sweeter-than-sugar star with her unnerving ability to please, and I understood enough to know it was useless trying to squeeze a sign of fondness from Hannah Ross for me. At last seated, the tray with a jug of lemon barley water at her side, her glass up-ended then replenished, my grandmother boomed: 'She's been taught no manners.'

'Manners ...' my mother echoed.

'Yes, manners. Proper behaviour,' she emphasised, as her voice rose in satisfied indignation.

'But ...'

'There are no buts,' she said, before adding 'my dear,' acidly. 'She must be sent to the bathroom. For the entire afternoon.'

'I think that ...' began my mother.

'Don't think. She must be taught to respect her elders.' She cleared her throat and proclaimed: 'In this modern world of ours, I move with the times. Never can it be laid at my door that I am left behind.'

Modern! I didn't understand the concept, but this ogre saying things I didn't want us to hear would have been as modern as Methuselah; a woman on whose insistence mirrors were covered during a storm should lightning strike, sewing was set aside, and knives during a meal were replaced by spoons.

'I do think,' my mother began again, bravely I thought, 'that we can explain your grievance to Natasha.' Her glance fell on me. 'She will ...'

'She will what?'

'Understand.'

'Mend her ways is what's required.' Her resolve, along with her voice, did not falter. 'Take my word for it, punishment makes for a faster learner and an afternoon in the bathroom will prove me right. She ... '

'No,' I said, and for a second, I had a sense of obscure satisfaction. 'NO!'

'Did you tell me NO?'

Shaken by my audacity, blood seething, I rushed to my mother, snatched up her hand, and nosed it like a cat.

My grandmother creaked into action with a vigour I'd never witnessed. As she rose to her feet with a snarl of rage, fright whined in my head. Brunhilde towered over me, veins throbbing in her forehead, her face a mottled red. Bees seemingly stung my ear. Things in the room—chairs, our nest of stork-legged tables, the bowl of roses, a vase with sweet peas—seemingly went crooked, then hung topsy turvy. Distorted. Feeling the heat of her face on mine, I couldn't squirm free as I was pulled from the room, her breath a set of low and hard bellows.

'Muuummmy!' I screamed wild with fright, 'Mummmy!' That beseeching maternal noun. The hall was like a long burrow to another world.

Opened quietly enough, the door slammed; an enamel-handled door on a cold white bathroom. Funereal diamonds of black tiles half way between the floor and ceiling ran around each wall, creating a mourning frieze.

# 3

My spells of doubt dispersed. Had the rooms been aired, the smell of gardenias blown away? No, I was excited when Gwennie was invited to play the following day after my grandmother visited. Was my mother contrite as she promised us something special for lunch? Lemonade too, and I felt the bubbles detonate in my throat.

Gwennie, so pink and pretty, whose jelly eyes I saw as lovely—so big they seemed to wobble in her face. Today her lolly-like curls were a bit floppy, which made me conclude that the previous night she hadn't been forced to sleep with her hair in rags. Mrs. Hunt was given to parting Gwennie's hair into strands before each strand was sausaged tight in a strip of cloth to writhe overnight. Sectioned, she slept in huge discomfort; it was curious because her mother doted on Gwennie, she loved her. But with Mrs. Hunt's own hair straight as a poker and captive under a hairnet, I guess she couldn't know what she put Gwennie through.

'What'll we play?'

'You choose,' I said, with Gwennie the guest.

'Red Indians and I'll be Hiawatha,' Gwennie pronounced, too often subjected to a menial role with her brothers. Brothers who had cap guns.

When Gwennie and I were together, our relationship tended to reshape her and free of interference, we did things OUR way. Our china-faced dolls could take on roles as soldiers or shipwrecked sailors when we immersed them in water. However, Gwennie often favoured playing mothers and fathers, though I didn't.

Purposefully, Gwennie declared she would be a mother when she grew up and would ask: 'What do you want to be?'

My answer seemed to astonish her. 'When I grow up I want to be a grown-up person.'

'How do we play that?' Gwennie asked. Not sure, we reverted to her game. There was also a memorable occasion when Gwennie was not perfect. She told a lie—a whopper.

'I'll be the mother and you be the father, like always,' Gwennie stated and set about making the marital bed from cushions and a tartan rug on one of our verandahs. Both the Hunt and Ross houses had one verandah meshed against flies, mozzies and moths.

Outside, the sunlight was broken up by touches of leaves, the green of a creeper, and pink bougainvillea. Our space arranged among our toys to Gwennie's satisfaction, we stretched out side by side. And, as always, if I agreed to her game, Gwennie took the conversational lead.

'Now, Dad,' began Gwennie in her serious voice, 'it's time for new shoes for the boys.' She sat up, wiggling a finger at me. 'The rate those feet grow is astounding.'

'Is it?' I had no knowledge of boys' feet.

'And new socks, dear. I can't keep up with the darning. What with boiling up and bottling the jam.' Mrs. Hunt was a jam maker, and we were regular recipients of plum or quince sealed in Vegemite jars.

'Well, Dad?' Gwennie faced me, scowling. 'You're supposed to say: '*Yes dear*'.'

'Why?'

'Because that's what Dads say.'

Did they? I could have been peering over a very high and private wall. What's more, we were only moments away from the fact that Gwennie could tell lies.

'Right, dear. I'll go shopping in town tomorrow. Now,' Gwennie wriggled back on the bed, 'call the kids in for a cuddle.'

'WHAT!'

Non-plussed, Gwennie repeated her request. 'Call the kids in for a cuddle. Like always.'

'Like always,' I said, anxiety eating into my reply. My echo was a whisper.

Yes,' Gwennie propped herself on one elbow, her expression arching as she surveyed me. 'EVERY morning. EVERY day.'

In a blurred way, perhaps this was the first time I came to acknowledge a separateness from Gwennie. I wanted to cry. Or run away. There was a limit to what I was able to accommodate. Mothers and fathers did not call kids—their children —into their bed. To be cuddled!

'You're telling a 'normous-awful lie.'

'Am not.'

'Are.'

'Am not.' Angel-like, Gwennie was caught between indignation and disbelief at my inexperience of the world.

Fingers twitching at my sides, then breathing fast, I was trapped between a thudding heart and monumental disbelief, followed by cold anger.

GWENNIE WAS six months older and her birthday was due. Her present from me was something I was not keen to give up—cut-out dolls with cardboard clothes for Gwennie to dress them in—a full wardrobe from pyjamas to overcoat with tabs to fold back at the shoulders. The 'best dress' was striped.

Her party was to be at a beach, and when I asked Gwennie how beaches came to be beaches, she didn't know either. Her party was to be a picnic at Newport under a tarpaulin festooned with crepe paper and pink balloons.

Pink was also Mrs. Hunt's choice for Gwennie: dress, socks, ribbons plus of course, pink icing and candles for the cake. She'd also knitted her daughter a pink bathing suit—a cossie—which would weigh to Gwennie's knees with water when the obligatory hour passed after we gobbled the food and were let loose to wallow in the surf.

Blocks of ice as big as babies were collected at the local ice-works then wrapped in hessian bags to keep strawberry ice cream unmelted, and the raspberry syrup cool. Gwennie was a summer child.

My mother's hesitation in accepting the invitation was not Mr. Hunt at the wheel of his rackety Oldsmobile, but Mrs. Hunt's disregard of the sun.

'All the kids'll need cold tea leaves on burned shoulders next day,' a Hunt aunt was prompted to predict, clicking her tongue to the roof of her mouth. 'They'll be sore and ... '

'And?' Gwennie and I begged, because earlier hadn't she amazed us with the possibility that skins can shrivel and brains can fry?

'And?' again, breathless.

'And your skin'll peel off like tissue paper.'

Mrs. Hunt, who tended to forget exact references—she read it somewhere or heard it on the wireless—suggested this did the skin a heap of good in the long run. Her tone was confident. 'Trims it off like fat from a chop. Promotes a fine healthy growth.'

My mother disagreed. I was to keep a hat on all day IN AND OUT OF THE WATER, and wear a blouse under my cossie. Worse, a Hunt aunt was enlisted to slap gelatinous cream on my nose which smelled disgusting, a cross between mothballs and fish.

Finally, it was agreed that I could go. Yet I came close to prohibiting myself, as well as close to testing the boundaries of friendship between my family and the Hunts.

Left with me while preparations were at full tilt for the following day, and clomping around in an old pair of her mother's high-heels she brought with her, Gwennie sighed at the torture that had overtaken her at bedtime the previous night to produce her birthday curls. Seemingly to bounce on her head with a life of their own!

I shaped my words into hard little squares, sure of my reason, and sure her mother would see it my way too. 'Gwennie, do you want rags in your hair? The curls?'

'No.'

'You sure?'

We exchanged a consenting glance. 'Yes.' And she kicked off Mrs. Hunt's old shoes to look levelly at me.

'Cross your heart and spit and hope to die.'

Gwennie performed the crossing of heart, spitting and hoping to die ritual and I made straight for my mother's sewing basket. Awkward but purposeful, with her 'best' scissors I set to it. Snip, snip, snip. Pulling each curl out straight, Mrs. Hunt's chosen ringlets could have been jumping with joy off Gwennie's head to heap at our feet.

What was left were crimps of hair looped on her scalp like little shells. I wanted to see them in the water at Newport, where she might be lucky enough to have them investigated by fish. Gwennie hoped for a tiddler of a goldfish. I hoped for something striped and red-eyed. How innocent!

Discovery came when we were three-quarters through, with a few corkscrews still bobbing to her shoulders.

Mrs. Hunt and my mother stood in the doorway, a hit-and-miss line of lipstick streaking towards Mrs. Hunt's chin. The 'best' scissors fell to the lino, splayed out dagger-like. Partners in calamity, Gwennie and I linked hands as steel fingers flew out from a larger hand, and tugged at a hank of MY hair.

'I ... I ... I...' I stuttered. Or was I pleading, because all I could focus on was shadowed fat under Gwennie's mother's chin? 'I ... I ...I ...' I tried again, my mother waving aside any forming words and, her mouth puffed to protest, Gwennie too was ignored.

I don't know who completed Gwennie's haircut, but do remember the misery when it came to me that I could be excluded from the birthday party. A pariah, when the rest went to Newport. Slapping waves became mountains pounding to shore, shark fins sliced towards the beach where Gwennie and I planned to gather shells in our buckets, and thread them on lengths of fishing lines later.

If my mother was silent and touchy for the rest of the day, my father was disapproving when told that night. A frown between his eyes, but in my favour, his paw of a hand was straying over my hair, smoothing fly-away strands.

# 4

My father. Marcus.

If shafts of light slipped in and out of his darkness, he adored his wife. Besotted by her from their first meeting, something must have flung itself open in his chest and it stayed open to her all his life.

Athletic, above medium height, eyes a shaded green, upper lip moustached, with an easy grin he'd parked his Harley Davidson by the clipped hedge, alongside Harry Beecham's motorbike. Smoothing his fair hair flat, then pocketing his goggles in his leather coat and belting it tighter, he strode up the drive. In the gathering dusk, there was no intimation that fate paused, waiting in the over-furnished rooms of the family of his friend, Paul Bayson.

Damask curtains, genoa velvet chairs, glass-fronted china cabinets, a lacquered screen with perpendicular mountains, willows and a foreground of kiminoed girls coying with fans, all laid out on a patterned wall-to-wall.

Laughter reached out through the open windows. Squeals from a group of girls, and there she was, Paul's sister's weekend guest. In a cream dress with yellow hip sash, seed pearls gleamed on her throat in the light from tasselled lamps. A face pale as paper, her large brown eyes were framed by dark hair cut abruptly to the ears, flapper style. Tentatively, she extended a hand to him which did not throb in his.

'How do you do?'

'How do you do?' came the reply.

No casual 'Hi' back then. Unaware that her 'How do you do?' might —or might not—be imparting some secret in his mind, which seemed to vibrate with a kind of recognition. If such things are possible.

'Nina,' someone called, and she went to the kitchen to help convoy supper to the table: curried eggs, chicken vol-au-vents, cheese straws, custard tarts, trifle and lemon meringue pie.

Did Marcus need a second drink—tea or something stronger—to dislodge a lump in his throat? Was he watchful, turning reproachful eyes on all other males in the room who took up her attention? Later, nonchalantly, did he thank Paul's family, his grin broadening when plans were made for a picnic?

Sunday week?

'Yippee,' a Marcus expression. 'YIPPEE!' He kicked the Harley Davidson into action. He revved, then revved again, exhaust fumes flying up into the shadows, trailing out warrior-like behind him.

DURING THE FOLLOWING DAYS, Marcus Ross guarded fragments of that night, that meeting: her eyes, cheekbones and mouth slanting with smiles as cucumber-cool she offered food while he juggled his glass, plate and cake fork. He just avoided trampling one narrow foot into the pattern of the carpet, his apology strangled. The pearl necklace she wore, the music of her voice; even if he heard only a few bars. She was not like other girls.

He scowled, and, thinking of her, might have been possessed.

Emotional excesses? Couldn't help it; and fingers clenched in palms, he laughed.

Were Nina's affections already engaged? His heart crashed about in his chest. Paul, who believed that life was to be seized and squeezed into an acceptable shape, should know. He'd quiz him after the

Monday lecture, when, with Harry Beecham, the third of their trio schooled together, all three to graduate at the same time, habitually they'd lean into a sandstone wall and smoke. But muttering through gritted teeth, he hesitated. Nina, he sensed, was guarded. Unpredictable.

So the days thrummed on gloomily, the nights distant with stars till Sunday week dawned. Innocent times!

Marcus rode his Harley Davidson, with carrot-haired Jim as pillion, and Paul astride his smaller Velocette, with Harry following. Maggie, Paul's sister, was able to borrow her father's Oldsmobile which, on Mrs. Bayson's insistence, the girls of the family were taught to drive as well as the boys. Maggie was the first to learn— except to cope with reverse— now she was finally competent and covering fewer miles. A Vauxhall completed the party. The first rendezvous was the G.P.O. at Martin Place, and the second south at Audley in the Royal National Park where the water splashed over the causeway.

'Got your puncture kit?' Paul grinned. 'They'll have a spare, as well as half a dozen girls to push 'em up the hills,' and the girls, smiling and admiring each other, looked up in a wild sort of way, wailing. One, Dorothy, whose body seemed to resemble a seal, slapped a red-nailed hand to her head and grunted.

Eyes slitted, tongue hard under his lip, Marcus directed his gaze to Nina, reassuring himself she was there. Martin Place, the Cenotaph, the clock on the G.P.O. about to strike, trams with high steps and varnished seats trundling down George Street to Circular Quay, they were all fast translating to somewhere more than a locality.

Nina wore blue with a white sailor collar. A cardigan slung over her shoulders, she clutched a stitched-cloth hat, a scarf twined on one wrist to anchor the hat in a wind. Everything she wore looked intentional. The sun beamed down, warming him. Chasms of silence separated them; should he address her directly, he risked shouting, so he said nothing. Yet Marcus was convinced that what would come to matter between them for the moment was invisible, still mysterious.

Everything went well, apart from a pair of screeching magpies and his embarrassment while he couldn't keep everyone's name in his head.

The Elaines, the Dorothys, the Rosalies, the Myras–just one of each but their faces smudged together.

Cricket bat at the ready for sneaky bowlers or tossing the ball, and later lolling over sandwiches set out on rugs spread under casuarinas, it wasn't the pickling light that muddled him. Nor the bursts of early cicadas, shrill after how many years underground? Soberly, he chose to dilute the beer and drink shandies, because homeward bound with foot to the accelerator, he might push the Harley's speedo too high. Nina, he noted, was composed, her legs folded as she leaned on one arm, wrinkled her nose against insects, and pursed her lips at ideas that surfaced; some argued and hotly discussed.

A walk by the river was suggested and stiff-legged, hands thrust in his pockets, Marcus frowned and manoeuvred to reach her side. The water spreading downstream from the causeway had bronzed in the light. The bush was tangy and lush with spring. Their feet kicked up the smell of grass, ferns, and it exploded in Marcus' head that he'd never find anyone like her again.

He must not ask.

The river bent into an elbow and the bank sloped more. Pockets of grass grew longer among spindles of weed and thickened vegetation.

'Watch out for snakes,' someone warned and Nina sniffed.

'Anaconda or a cobra?' she asked, head tilted, and her tone sarcastic.

'You can't tell us snakes don't frighten you.'

Nina gave a pointed sigh. 'I grew up in the country, so ...' She swung away.

'So? When you were little? A kid?' asked Paul.

She gazed into the distance before her eyes snapped back into focus. 'What gives a little kid a point of view is,' and if she examined him with tight attention, her expression might have been raw, 'what surrounds that little kid.'

Drenched in the late sun, the trees above were still. Later it occurred to Marcus that he should have shied away but he didn't.

'Where?' he asked. 'Which part?'

Nina turned to face him, turned away. 'My part,' she said, walking on, and his mouth flooded with words, but he let them drown.

Elaine, Dorothy, Rosalie and Myra were lingering at the rear when with no warning, a pair of magpies swooped down with ugly squawks. Earlier, a greedy bunch of them had strutted close-by while they ate.

'Big, black and white,' carrot-haired Jim declared as he munched. 'They remind me of my teaching nuns. Especially old Sister Magpie Miserabilis. Nasty,' he snorted. 'Beady-eyes, too much chin, she'd watch some poor little bugger in short pants every move before she whacked into him.' Paul also contributed the fact that magpies were known to take the eye out of a baby sheep.

'Crikey, what's that?'

Screams curdled the air. Behind them, one of the boys flapped maniacally to protect one of the girls from a second attack. Who? Rosalie, who clutched her head and moaned. Seconds ago, her ears glinted with diamante studs, now one was spotted with blood.

'Get off!' was shouted, 'get off!' The attacker retreated to a stump nearby.

Then Nina was racing back. Her hat whipped off, her hair loosened and freed. Marcus noticed a wildness in her voice. 'Rosalie, Rosalie, are you all right?'

'Yeees,' Rosalie replied, shaken. She took Nina's extended hat, yanked it down helmet-like and rocked while someone raced to the river to sluice a handkerchief to clean off the blood.

'That rotten bird should be shot.'

'No,' said Nina. 'They only attack when they're nesting.' Her features tightened, almost as if part of her hurt. 'Or to protect their young.'

A blade of grass between his teeth, Jim turned to Nina and sort of smirk- grinned. 'Would you attack to protect your young?' Maybe it was flippant, but Marcus' heart took off. It raced.

## 5

Did each of my parents need the protection of the other as safeguards to life? As weeks passed and they drew nearer, Nina—playful, almost flirtatious—could make a move forward, then abruptly retreat.

In differing ways, did they suspect each meeting was not to be the last? Caught in attraction, soon to generate deeper feelings? Love?

But enmeshed, something in her would surface if never break through, and while respecting her reticence, baffled, he didn't understand why and with an unnerving ability to withdraw, she held back. Was he too serious too soon?

But he'd anchored her attention; so for the moment, he was willing to surrender to the barriers she imposed, her eyes full of intricacies he couldn't read. She was preoccupied, but with what? Was she on the edge, waiting to jump? He burned to know, as well as to insulate her against hurt, realising she didn't suspect how extraordinary she was.

But even if her steps were slow, she teetered towards both love and affection with this man who was to become my father.

With a belief in reason—he was an engineer—he was also fun, a significance Nina must have grasped, just as she must have grasped his willingness to protect her. His interests were defined by his work, along with cricket, swimming and surfing. Optimistic about natural resources, Marcus wanted to invent an engine to run on boosted water, not oil. Simmering in his head, the idea to give it a go had a strong appeal.

Despite Hannah Ross' diamonds and the substantial estate that came to her in widowhood, Marcus had limited cash at his disposal. Hannah was of the school that kept purse strings tight, extremely tight. Her husband was a generous man and his genes, not Hannah's, were evident in their son who was open-handed with what he earned. And popular. He was 'Marcus Superbus' to friends. Concerned and in the main cheerful, he hated to hurt people, which inevitably could happen, but no shadows or awful things dogged his steps or dragged him down. Nina recognised that.

Tram rides to Centennial Park, Watsons Bay, ferry rides to Manly, Nina's bathing suit neck-to-knee, they swam at Bondi or Coogee, where offshore waves crashed against Wedding Cake Island. Tennis, and did she like to dance? Yes, and they danced at Paddington Town Hall, The Trocadero. Happy together at free museums, occasionally there were seats at concerts—the Theatre Royal and The Tivoli—and, like their contemporaries, they window-shopped, walked, and when Nina could reach for his hand, she would wrap her fingers round his as if never to release it or release him. Once they went to the races and won twenty pounds! Though the enormity of twenty pounds tempted them, they zig-zagged away, not chancing such luck again.

At the Easter Show with the huge 'District' displays of rural produce and wealth, they sat across a small terrazzo table for lunch, their fingertips touching till the food and a pot of coffee arrived. Next were the ring events: cattle drafting, sheep penned, horse judging, jumping and dressage that Nina absorbed in her indistinct past. Marcus absorbed it with her.

'Nina?'

'Mmm ...' but it seemed she'd not heard and obscurely, gradually, he would become aware that underlining their linked lives, she lapsed into herself at times. Nina could become shreddingly apart.

That day the sky was blue, the sun hot but not too hot and the noise on every side was holiday noise—cheering, chattering, eating, distant screams and thrills. From the Big Dipper and the Roller Coaster, while in the main ring harnesses jingled, hooves tapped and pounded prize cattle lowed.

In the early evening in sideshow alley, Marcus scored a pair of plaster angels and hoop-la-ed a silver kewpie doll which, arms linked, they agreed should be given to a small girl whose eyes devoured the glitter of it at the tram stop.

The mother was incredulous. 'You don't really mean to part with it? 'I really do,' Nina replied, but not the angels. They each kept one.

# 6

'Paulie,' hands busy with her hair, Maggie walked ahead of him down the hall to her brother's room. 'Paulie,' she called, 'Marcus is here.'

There was no reply, but from another part of the house came her mother's voice. 'Paul phoned, he's running late,' followed by a clatter as Mrs. Bayson dropped something.

'You all right, Mum?'

'Yes, dear.' A pause. 'Take Marcus out to the verandah.' Was she aware, or simply guessing her daughter's eagerness to do so? 'Keep him entertained.'

The verandah was an oasis of potted geraniums, begonias and pansies. At one end, a pyramid shaped from chicken wire was threaded through with ivy. To its right hung baskets of maidenhair.

'Sit down.' Maggie patted the seat beside her on the swinging lounge. 'Marcus, you've clipped your moustache,' she murmured coquettishly, fleetingly brushing it with her fingertips before crossing her legs. They were good legs, she knew to arch as she straightened a stocking seam before setting a foot to kick them into motion.

If he had the feeling he should play the fool, he only managed: 'Err, yes.'

Not completely naïve, he recognised Maggie's ploys as head back, breasts heaving, she simpered. Paul's sister! He shook his head and cleared it. She was just that—Paul's sister—a friend, and he saw no reason to inch away, sidling along the cretonne-cushioned seat. But was she bent on teasing out something more when she sent them swinging faster? Faster towards what?

'What do the other girls think? Dorothy, Myra?' Maggie smiled knowingly. 'Nina?'

Nina! 'Don't suppose she's noticed,' he replied.

'Go on.' Maggie pouted, her eyebrows resembling her mother more than she would have believed. Pretty, yes, but lacking Nina's features, Nina's flair. 'Go on,' Maggie repeated, wheedling as she ran a hand up and over her own arm; Maggie, who should have scaled down any expectations of him. 'Go on.'

Marcus flattened his hair. If she wanted him to explain himself, he was relieved she didn't ask again. Noisily, Mrs. Bayson arrived, like an older Maggie with something of a driven look. Heavy lidded. Tray in hand, she noted Maggie, fetching in her skimpy green blouse and paisley skirt.

'Stay where you are, no need to get up,' she directed Marcus and rattled frosted glasses against a jug. 'You two must be thirsty.'

'Thanks, Mrs. Bayson.'

She scrutinised his face and her daughter's. What did she hope to see in this sunny afternoon light? Hoisting back her shoulders, she gave the impression she held nothing close to her chest apart from the wish to slake their thirst.

'This ginger beer is my mother's recipe. And her mother's before her. Would you like to stay for a meal; cold lamb, salad, potatoes, stewed pears?'

'Thanks Mrs. Bayson, but not tonight.'

'Another time,' she peered at him, then briefly at her daughter, before wrinkling her nose and leaving. She withdrew into shadowed Bayson territory, closing the door behind her.

Marcus heard Maggie heave a sigh and waited. Predictably, she began to chatter. About Paul, their gang of friends, a movie, then Nina.

'I hope we'll always be friends,' Maggie, who was no sourpuss, went on. 'Nina and me. All three of us.'

Was she resigned?

'Yep,' replied my father, and so it went, in future years proving to be true.

'Marcus?'

'Ummh?' Palms spread on his thighs and confused, a shower of needles filled his head for if Maggie fostered hopes of an intimacy between them, this was her fantasy. Yet something critical now occurred to him and he laughed, then coughed.

There was no spite in Maggie's voice even as a frown pinched between her eyes. 'You know, Nina's thorny,' Maggie registered and my father listened. 'Fragile too.'

FRAGILE? A month later, my father had a haircut and then proposed. No indecision, no circling, he was sure. And their lives having converged, if Marcus had thrown her over the pommel, spurred on his horse and pounded off with her, Nina may well have been thrilled.

Now as he paced step to step with her, no other woman existed. Captivated, he felt complete; far from fragile. Actual, real.

He was returning her to the small place she shared with two flatmates in Elizabeth Bay. Classic-featured Lily was soon to elope with Victor Jagoda and settle seventy miles south on the coast. Plainer, rounder Rowena, forever sustained by late night snacks, was to make a spectacular match within a year.

Wedged close against a pocket-sized park, overshadowed by the spread of a fig tree and with no view of the nearby harbour, the flat was far from awful if far from luxurious. Two flights up, with kipper-colour paint, three beds on a worn carpet but only two wardrobes, one maple dressing table and the bathroom on the landing, they lived in shabby discomfort and managed to meet the rent.

There was a density to the night. An unseen bird chittered, giving off what might have been a prompt. With the scent of honeysuckle from the railed patch of garden, what Nina must have smelled were the violets he bought her earlier from a flower stall in Martin Place. Did my mother gasp? Her lips move feebly? Her face collapse as if the bones crumbled?

Unscripted, if not lost for words, Marcus hung on her answer.

'Nina?' They stood at the gate. Coned light fell from the street lamp at the corner which swung in a breeze, stirring high fig leaves. They didn't move towards the front door. What more could he say? Did her name crowd out everything? He kissed her hair, placed a hand behind her neck and when she looked up to him—but still with no answer—he bent his chin down to her. For moments that seemed like centuries, they stood nose to nose. The whites of her eyes very white, her upturned eyes huge. Marcus took a deep breath, then exhaled.

When Nina closed her eyes, was this to prevent him seeing into them? Into her? Withholding something unshareable?

'Nina?'

'Yes,' my mother said. And again with emphasis: 'Yes!' She was fully alive to him now. 'Yes' might have been a secret filled with positive things.

After all, don't most of us shape and colour our landscapes with personal needs when we want to believe we can convert the world to our terms?

# 7

My mother, Nina Alicya, was the third daughter born to a family where above all, a son was desired. Sophya, Annya, Nina. The birth of a brother, Michael Nicholas, was to follow in precisely one year, their mother's face forever tenderly turned to him, his progress watched over with unalloyed pleasure; three charming, small girls to fade into the background.

The background? It was lodged awkwardly between Russian, English and an Australian influence. It would appear weird in the extreme today.

Redolent with echoes of czarist Russia, though far from poor, Nikolai Lazarev, my maternal grandfather, was not obliged to do work he didn't wish to do. I don't know if he worked at all. Perhaps he oversaw his rural property, likely only overseeing managers, capable country men, while he pursued interests in his library, whatever they might have been.

These grandfathers of mine never met in Europe. In fact, they never met during their lifetimes, but both were Russian. Both died before Nina and Marcus met. Light years before I was born.

Briefly residing in Paris, numbering among a million refugees who fled the Russian revolution and its aftermath, they were émigrés—

exiles. However, branches of both families had remained behind; the smoke of war smothering households of tragic aunts and cousins, relatives incapable of leaving, or those who chose to stay.

Divorced not only by distance but from the atrocities of the revolution, Nikolai Lazarev's world of etiquette, dowries and entitlements, was gone, though some family wealth was salvaged.

Not so for my paternal grandfather. Sergei Rosovsky was to be numbered among the waiters, taxi drivers and shadowy extras who swelled crowd scenes in French cinema, polishing their thinning boots as their suits grew shabby, his old certainties gone. Yet fate was to take a sidestep before it beamed his way in the form of a diamond merchant's daughter from Amsterdam. Wed to Hannah, his dreams focused on America as an earthly paradise; the giant propellers of an ocean liner churning them across the Atlantic to New York. Thrilling as it proved to be, they found this new world extreme, and with the means to seek further passage, they crossed the world again. In due course their two children—Marcus and his sister, Adele—were born in Australia.

Australia was also my maternal grandfather's destination. Whether destiny or destination, taking the decision to quit Paris and what he came to see could become a ghetto of émigré life, Nikolai believed that Europe was dancing on a volcano. With numbers of his fellow Russians forced to quit the expense of Paris for Berlin, many left to reunite with family in Prague, London, Shanghai and an America that Sergei Rosovsky and his wife Hannah spurned.

Tracking westwards again from Paris, Nikolai's bride was English— gentle Alice, the mother-to-be of three daughters and their son, Michael Nicholas. With wind plastering blonde tresses over her blue eyes and mouth on deck at her husband's side, if she had misgivings as the cliffs of Dover receded, she left no diary, no record. Repressed, oppressed? Who knows? Uprooted, perhaps her reality was random. Or, more simply, not an easy reality, shrinking from a light— a life—which to her eyes put hard edges on everything? Where she felt she might cry her heart dry?

Here I must confess that to me much of Nina's life, and in particular her childhood, is no more than a partly opened book. She volunteered little; so some of what I write is real, combined with possibilities, which makes for unknown details, gaps, and a confusion like that which exists with anyone else's life. Besides, my mother was a secretive woman; certainly towards me. I have no reason to distort or change the past but, cursed or blessed by my imagination, my writing to some extent may prove a way to understand Nina. And myself.

Privy to bits of information told, retold or overheard, there is also the evidence of photographs, evidence of things like jewellery along with poignant affirmations of wealth and social preoccupations. One is an exquisite small silver case for visiting cards. Visiting cards! It's lined with ivory and has a tiny silver pencil to record a message. Engraved with Nina's initials, there is also the date. On my mother's sixth birthday, it must have been reckoned an appropriate gift for her.

Twenty miles from a station and an infrequent, lumbering train, Nina's life was lived in a sharpness of light and space: blues, greys and gritty browns. Alien trees planted between garden beds, gums rose beyond a tennis court then a creek, from which rough-throated birds, if not birdsong, began to jar her mother Alice's ears less as time went on. Beyond, further home paddocks fanned away to an unforgiving landscape; acre upon acre to sway under summer heat. Then, iced by distance, chillingly winter swept about the homestead, stables, tackroom and outbuildings, the cold turning small fingers blue. Seasonally, the shearing shed vibrated with action and sunburnt men in flannel shirts; city visitors an occasional rarity.

What a curiosity they must have been in the Australian countryside.

Did their father continue having thoughts of Russia? Or suppress them? Button-booted and with frilled lace on 'their best', the girls' pinafores were as crisp as wafers. The children's pony cart was led by a groom, and a sequence of French governesses were imported over the years, their father's belief that every educated Russian was to speak French. Photographed, the little girls held china dolls, their brother a miniature fishing rod. Michael Nicholas progressed from nursery dresses to sailor suits, the latter to foretell his grim future at twelve.

Nina and her sisters were schooled in formal subjects and to play piano, create and perform small theatricals, paint, sing and embroider.

It's unlikely they learned to cook or mix mud pies. But these girls were also wild, with thighs clasped to their ponies' ribs, long hair streaming. Riding was a pursuit their father encouraged. Bright and able to devise codes to use between themselves, doubtless they formulated childish answers to the puzzles imposed by their elders. Hardly an underprivileged childhood of that time. Or any time.

There were rules to be broken at a child's peril: speaking to your father before spoken to, mumbling, or worse, overlooking a 'please' or 'thank you', or 'may I? Reprimanded by words which could drop like icicles and at times be scalding, there was no contender for the crown, Nikolai Lazarev was an absolute ruler. Repressed, oppressed, a witch's brew for any child.

To titter in his presence was unthinkable, rebellion punishable, a misdemeanour, if not quite a crime. Not too bad, not unbearable, was his wife. If she was forced to a world of daydreams—or melancholy—trying to remember why she married him, she at least loved her children, even if moodily. Their beds were turned down by a maid at night. Tucked in, dutifully she kissed them one by one, silencing any clamour for more with a movement of her hand. She was a mother whose own life was defined by her relationship with Nikolai, her sole thread to spin her back to her former life.

But unjust and undeserved shadows hovered, making ready to stitch themselves to four small backs. With autumn thinning to winter, Nina was almost eight when tragedy approached; it crossed the wide verandahs and knocked at the door. Uninvited. Within days, another dawn swelled the sky, the nursery and the school room. Their world changed. Their mother was dead.

Bolts of black cloth were dispatched in haste from store to sewing room, a machine pedalled and mourning garments for four children —the eldest twelve— were made within hours. Being country children, they must have witnessed animals die, but their mother! Pretty and alive, then suddenly prone in a box, her face pallid by candlelight, her long-fingered hands inert, crossed on her breast in death. This mother exited their lives with horses bearing her away to a deep trench on the hilltop visible from the house. Within hours, her grave was ringed by a chain fence to ensure no sheep or cattle trod her further down.

Being expected to behave with stoicism, the solemn mourning rituals of that time would have traumatised any child. When the silver-framed photographs of Alice were stowed—if temporarily—from sight, it was only when Michael Nicolas wailed for his mother that their father relented and acknowledged both the boy and his sisters' distress. Four children who had learned not to cry easily.

Once a year, a photographer had been summoned from the city with his paraphernalia of camera gear and collapsible backdrops—landscapes, seascapes and formal gardens—each child was given one photographic portrait of their mother as a keepsake. Nina's? Alice with hair upswept, staring into the camera as she stood against a sketched balustrade, a collar of pearls at her throat.

It left a tragic vacuum in their lives. Nikolai, too, began to absent himself from home, travelling to Melbourne and an expanding White Russian community. Never to consider himself irresponsible, further staff were installed and if his children relished more freedom, a dutiful welcome was expected from them on his return. What's more, Nikolai had plans to introduce his daughters to Melbourne society and a dame of the old school; a tyrannical matchmaker with proven results. Michael Nicholas at twelve was to leave them, enrolled as a midshipman in the Australian Navy.

But a selectively heedless second tragedy was to stalk their lives. As irrefutable as it was cruel, Nikolai's three youngest had to learn to predict nothing, and be sure of nothing. Sophya, the first-born before Annya, and Nina's eldest sister_affectionate, quarrelsome, fair-minded and fun—who, though motherless herself, had somehow become part-surrogate mother to Alice's brood, took cold. It was the treacherous outbreak of what came to be known as the Great Flu. It developed into pneumonia, and Sophya slipped out of her life and theirs. Quitting them to take residence alongside their mother on the hill.

Why in my mind's eye do I see Nina unclasp the little brass lock of her beloved sister's diary? Where, through tears, Nina is shaking her 'goodbye' before she turns the tiny key, and hurls it into the creek, watched by birds with leathery wings.

Were they the leathery wings that bore Nikolai south again? Although there was no official declaration of war, soon my grandfather was under siege. A man of fortune, a wealthy widower in his prime— my grandfather set for scrutiny as a good catch. How customs have changed. But in drawing rooms, tea rooms with ornamental palms in brass pots and theatre foyers, Nikolai Lazarev, could have cupped hands to his mouth, megaphone-like, and shouted: 'Here I am, ripe to be fooled by the worst possible candidate for further matrimony—step-motherhood.'

Outrageous. If families hold long shadows, then why, why, why hadn't there been someone to somehow reveal to him the insult that was Clara Sibbald. Remember the blood ties and the three children in the Antipodes? Why was it that Alice's ghost was not present and prepared to reach out to suffocate Nikolai when this woman applied? With spectres, wraiths and many a phantom immune to distance, though globally apart? Why didn't Alice's forebears pick up the scent? Stir in their celestial fields divided by hedge rows and village greens? Surface from a Britannic underworld? Or Nikolai's restless Russians come shrieking south to Australia from the steppes?

A widow with two dependents—Stanley and Winifred—Clara Sibbald assumed an expression of maternal piety. Faux Madonna, her face was tight, her eyes suspicious and she had a voice able to saw through closed doors. Giddily intent on accessing Nikolai's wealth, ensnaring him was paramount as she struggled to show her better side, which was to change dramatically once under his roof. Sheened by power once she became his lawful wife, Nikolai's needy offspring were to be targeted with antipathy and spite. She managed the household by using iron control.

Half in fear, and half in excitement with the hope of affection, Alice's two daughters and her young son had prepared to first meet her and hers, who revealed themselves not only to be nasty, but vacuous, with daffodil-coloured teeth, Nina observed! Wide-eyed and hand in hand, Annya and Nina at once recognised the threat they faced while with his young features screwed tight, Michael Nicholas stood aghast at their mother's replacement. Pudding-faced and rouged, her hair was an improbable black against a parrot-green shawl. His prepared little greeting caught in his throat like a stone.

'Hello,' his sisters managed, and pulling back from even accidental contact, Nina baulked in rage towards this woman, their father's wife. Also towards their father, who whether gullible or fiendishly stupid, in Clara Sibbald had provided a woman seemingly happiest when they were upset.

Clara proved to be the wicked stepmother from hell that Annya, Nina and Michael Nicolas should never have met. Nor the staff: housekeeper, governess and maids, who were all agape at Nikolai's choice. Except between themselves, there were no comforting words—they were aware that intervention on the children's behalf meant dismissal. How had it come to this? Deceitful and deceiving, her voice as harsh as a rock to Alice's brood whom she was set on disinheriting, yet this same voice honeyed for Nikolai. Living under the same roof, even if a large roof, above it the sky arched in a vast scowl.

At sixteen and with an ardent wish to become a doctor, Annya escaped to train as a nurse. This choice housed and fed her in the nurses' quarters of a city teaching hospital.

Astonishingly, Michael Nicholas began life at sea at twelve. A midshipman, he was housed and fed by the Royal Australian Navy on land or afloat.

Nina? Constantly provoked, brooding but powerless against her father and her circumstances, Nina was sixteen before she flew the coop. She went to the city where with Annya's help—and the more worldly friends Annya had made—she sought out the photographer who had recorded their younger lives.

Untrained, impractical Nina had no useful qualifications, but she was artistic, so he employed her. As an assistant? A dark room roustabout? No, to tint the portraits of the wealthy families he photographed.

# 8

With regrets—but small regrets—Marcus traded the Harley Davidson for a secondhand Austin; green and upholstered in red with a dicky seat and dented mudguards. Marcus was twenty-six, Nina twenty-one.

The day dawned in quilted clouds, then cleared. Wedding ceremony, wedding breakfast and speeches over, the cake poised on four little pillars then cut, Nina changed from her bridal gown to her powder-blue 'going-away' dress, with matching cloche and dove-skin gloves. A disapproving Hannah Ross wore black and her spectacular diamonds, her only concession to the occasion a plum-coloured hat. Having vainly attempted to persuade her son that if he'd wait there was the strong possibility she could arrange a more advantageous match, which she maintained for as long as decorum and the rules allowed.

However, her misguided son had declared: 'Nina is the woman I love. I will love her all my life.'

'Well,' was the sole, loaded word Hannah was to emit as a suitably tortured sound. 'Well!' She was forced to accept the disagreement between herself and her son, and direct her energy on uncovering a proper son-in-law for her prominent-toothed daughter, Adele. Shiftily, she eyed her son's best man Paul Bayson, and his groomsman, Harry Beecham. She tightened her lips.

Promising she supposed, so she questioned herself; should she press for introductions? No. Prospects, limitations? No. They may not fit.

'Try to catch it. Try,' Hannah could not hold back from urging Adele forward when, with cheeks bright, Nina made ready to throw her wedding bouquet. Up on their toes, excitement among the young spinsters leapt to fever pitch; for those moments, they were members of a select club. Wheeee ... up went the ribboned roses to be caught by Nina's sister, Annya, who while forever courted, was not to marry; a bridesmaid, never a bride. It was agreed she'd make a gorgeous arm-piece for some lucky man. Maybe Annya was too choosy or maybe he never appeared. Michael Nicholas, the bride's young brother, cabled congratulations from the current ship on which he served somewhere at sea.

Showered with good wishes and rice, Marcus took his bride in his arms. With one foot on the running board, he spun her into the passenger seat, exposing her lace-hemmed petticoat and blue garter. Hoisting himself up beside her and jubilant, he squeezed the horn, and gave Paul the nod.

'Here goes,' Paul snapped fingers to a salute before cranking the engine, with Harry Beecham bracing if needed to push. Beside him, lovely Lily's Victor—his hair slicked back with Vaseline—leapt in the air and shouted a Polish blessing. A string of tins clanked below a 'JUST MARRIED' sign which Paul's sister, Maggie, had helped paint on cardboard. She was now pressing a thumb hard to her teeth.

The Austin backfired. And again to cheers. Then Marcus eased the sleeves of his suit, and my parents were on their way to the Carrington Hotel at Katoomba, the romance and grandeur of the Blue Mountains being a popular choice for honeymooners back then. They'd embarked on marriage with its many pitches and pulses, the great and small events. Did Marcus change my mother at all? I guess they changed each other. A bit. Part of marriage does that. The following year, Nina was pregnant, the gourd that was her stomach containing me.

## A Secret Grief

WAS it my reluctance to leave her womb and a protracted labour of two days that determined my mother never to risk a repeat? Many people equate an only child with a spoilt child, a lonely child, a lucky child, a precocious child, a this or that child. Why? We get up in the morning and go to bed at night the same as the rest.

Years on, I came across the existential view: '*There's the freedom to recreate yourself*', but conceived then born, one must wait. With little choice, mother and child attune to each other and each other's flaws. Told that I screamed for the first year of my life—who knows what babies hear and see?—and with their faces blotched red, baby gums exposed, mouth pitched in squalls of protest, but against what? And invariably with the rider: '*Your poor mother, poor pet.*'

What finished my screaming? Who knows and while it's not unreasonable that Nina ached for me to stop, only once did my father—wretched with feelings I refuse to examine—cajolingly extract from her hands a pillow that she suspended over me. No, she didn't panic, snuff me out, nor, bowing to some inner fear, let me slither under the weight of my bath water. So did she exercise a frightful calm? Struggle for control? Exist outside herself?

Box-Brownie black-and-whites give the lie to this with evidence of my parents' social life. In small squares, my parents are corralled in numerous gardens, tennis courts and beach holidays with friends. Laughing, at what? There too is the cane pram which held me; maybe not in the foreground but neither was it not there, while forever in the foreground was Marcus unashamedly adoring Nina, and Nina graciously accepting her due.

In the twists of living, lives don't run in straight lines, they never have; and if anxiety fingered me young, I was not distanced from what passed as normality, except that in a normal family a child perhaps has continuous and secure access to a mother. Theorists may declare that, though not unworkable without this continuous and secure access, a child remains starved no matter how well fed. Do we miss what we don't have? With our pasts built into us by ancestors, we all have a special grounding, a history particular to us. I believe I was my father's pride and joy. His second pride and joy. Number two.

When school was on the horizon, with a mid-year birthday I wasn't held back. 'She's ready,' authoritative Nina said against any opposition. Hadn't she taught me to read? Taught me letters coiling into words? Were these early reading lessons calculatedly instigated to ensure she was less interrupted in her own reading; *The Little Classics Vol. 1–10* occupying the shelf above my bed? Or did my mother just wish to endow me with a love of words?

Love! Words conveying ideas were not the only bonus. My father was pleased when he returned at night, but there was something more which, along with my mother's perfume, I came to label 'joy'. Who would have guessed I was poised on the rim of another world that first time she called: 'Come here. Sit beside me. Closer,' and I wriggled absurdly close. Close enough to see that her lips were pinker, her teeth larger and whiter, exposed in an easier smile.

With only the belief or disbelief available to the young, I believe I retain images of that day: an egg-yolk sun, fuzzy-warm air. Marigolds bunched in a wide-necked vase, oranges in a bowl on a table under a window through which branches of a tree hung with pods. Above all, the thick-paged alphabet book with its pictures clasped on Nina's knees as she leaned back into the support of the chair where the lessons took place.

Never in my parents' bedroom; a room where I was rarely invited: spacious with its lace-covered bed, casement window, padded pelmets, chintz-upholstered window seat, both wardrobes and my mother's dressing table with hinged mirrors and secret drawers. Here too was an ottoman box—a hollow day-bed with storage space—filled, I was certain, with further secrets, and where as a prodigious reader, routinely my mother took her 'afternoon escape'.

Marigolds, poppies, roses— seasonal flowers—in those months some days she'd reach forward to settle my skirt when it rucked up to my thighs, inspect my nails, and tuck a strand of hair behind one ear. Other gestures to become familiar were to do with her strings of beads when she fingered one of two favourites; the amber-like swollen drops of honey, and the crystal-like ice linked between tiny silver balls.

Near to make-believe in my memory, I wonder if deep inside I guessed this couldn't last. It would seem not; because as my reading improved, surely I would have had the cunning to learn slowly to spin out this doting time.

Instead, I learned fast, too fast, but how was I to think that through? Maybe it was true, maybe not. To the child I was, her praise was magic like the words which formed stories of cats, dogs, farmyards, fairies and giants. Fantasies.

Then the time to start school arrived. Ambivalent, excited but stung by alarm, the uniform was green and hung beside the blouse was the panama hat with elastic under the chin. New, regulation shoes stood in my cupboard alongside a boxed pair for 'best', which were red.

I couldn't finish dinner the night before I started; I even refused ice cream.

'Bedtime,' my father yodelled before piggy-backing me off to my room, then having pressed his lips to my forehead, again at my demand, he tucked me in. I couldn't sleep.

'Natasha,' Nina's expression was foreboding, but on Marcus' suggestion, indulgent this once as she flattened the pages on her thighs. She had agreed to read to me. 'No,' she said, 'no *Little Match Girl*, tonight. Yes, if you want it, *The Witch of the North, the Witch of the West and the Witch of Wonder Hill*.' Eight o'clock struck, and leaving a warm hollow where she sat on my bed, she snapped off the light at the last strike.

Clutching my nightdress above my knees, and fearful of being scolded but more fearful of school, I crept the length of the hall, my shadow elongating the nearer I moved to the sitting room with its curtains drawn against the night. Teeth rabbiting, underfoot the hall runner was knobbly and my breath was sharp enough to have drilled holes in the air.

'Nina, you must ...'

Feet cold and body hot, I watched my father's hands droop between his knees.

'No. YOU must. Be reasonable.' His tone was stubbornly rational.

Pleading? From where I hung at the door, cheek against wood, I watched the shape of my mother as she stooped.

'Nina, every mother takes her child to the first day of school.'

Gathered behind my eyes, my head swelled with tears, and when she turned I was able to see her face—her huge eyes glossy brown with bluish whites. The moment seemed endless; and even if I wanted to bolt back to bed and bury my head, I stood paralysed.

'Nina ...'

Her shoulders folded in and, frail, my mother opened her palms in what was either a beseeching or dismissive gesture before she swayed with exhaustion.

'Nina, my Nina.' Sorrow bit into my father but, arms latticed hard against her ribs, my mother's mouth was pulled tight; barricaded against words.

# 9

Mental snapshots accumulate. Ginger sunlight, and the three of us up early on what was to be a big day, with a new key to turn.

Helping me dress, straightening my collar, patting the pleats of my uniform, then making ribbons stiff on my plaited hair was a mother at odds with my mother of last night. She held me at arm's length, and appeared to approve what she saw. Me!

'Lovely,' she murmured, causing my heart to jump and sink at the same time, because if was hungry for her approval, I had it now. Next, she said: 'There's a surprise,' flashing a smile. 'Marcus thought you should arrive in style on your first day'

'What?'

Then hearing 'toot-a-toot-toot', I craned forward and raced to the door.

Handsome as a pirate, astride the saddle of a borrowed Norton motorbike and in his leather coat, my father raised an eyebrow and bared his teeth. Attached to the Norton was a sidecar, a merry-go-round gondola with a brass handle on its door.

'Hop in,' he called.

With an uncharacteristic lapse to tenderness and a laugh, my mother hugged me to her bones. Uncaring, she squashed my school hat that was looped by elastic over my wrist, and nuzzled the top of my head. Then kissed it!

'Hop in. Let's not be late.' And Nina nodded my way, to recoil as his foot kicked the Norton's starter. One grunt, then rips of sound.

'Wait, wait,' my mother shouted, her cheeks flushed as if somebody else had taken over in her skin. 'Wait.' She took the steps two at a time, then disappeared to reappear with food for me in a paper bag. Anzac biscuits to be eaten first, egg sandwich and an apple for later in the ant heap of the playground, and two chocolates from a box of Cadbury 'Roses' someone had given her.

The Norton shuddered. My spine tingled and we swept away. Off under spotted trees with low boughs, then on towards the shine of the sea ahead. Before a burst of speed, Marcus beamed down to his pirate's mate. 'Hang on to your hat!'

The school gates yawned open, huge. Dread lunged out from nowhere, and in a sort of fog, I willed myself to be someone else. NOT ME. The pebbled path that was the route in could have been hot coals burning through the soles of my first school shoes. The flat space of the playground seemed like acres dotted by tufts of shrubs, casuarinas and a peppercorn tree. A flagpole flew our flag with its Southern Cross. Behind chicken wire there was a patch of lilies, a sand patch, and further on, a corrugated iron shelter. What was I to shelter from there? And with how many of these gap-toothed kids whose sobs tumbled out like a tide?

Finally, and forcefully, Marcus withdrew his arms and handed me over to a teacher in a dirndl skirt and pink blouse—then stood back stiffly. I had to hate someone. So I hated Gwennie, who should have been standing beside me, hand in hand. I was aggrieved. The Hunts had moved. Not just from their house but from the State to South Australia, and their card at Christmas might as well have been posted from the end of the world. The friendship was gone, but as yet Gwennie hadn't faded, maybe Gwennie had a sorrow like mine.

Marcus was given the final nod. How did I feel? I couldn't tell, but hands jammed in his pockets, my father's face was red. 'Don't go,' I said with a cheep of a sound.

'It's not for long.'

'Don't.'

Marcus pulled a long face. 'As your father, you're stuck with me,' he declared, and someone as tall as a house chimed: 'That's a brave little girl, self-contained.'

Teeth clenched, I didn't cry. Shuffled into line and shoved to the front, then under instruction to hold hands, I can't remember tears; I have always tried not to cry a lot when it showed. But to what extent does a child distinguish an external world from an internal one? Perceive herself in either? Perspectives flatten out.

After a fortnight at school, with my tight-plaited hair and no protection, my head was infested. Nits. Paraffin and the opal scum it left on the rinsing water proved to be ineffective treatments, and repeated treatments were useless.

'Nothing else for it,' Nina was told at the chemist shop after applications from something blue in a bottle and use of the fine comb for tearing strands of hair and scraping my skull failed too.

'Cut it off.'

From hair tapping my shoulders on Saturday morning, by Saturday midday, there was no more than a thatch above my ears. Earlier, there'd been a climb up into the barber's chair, and a towel was clipped round my neck. Camera held to his chest, Marcus duly recorded the event. Nina was nearby, one hand on the rope of the garden swing, with furrowed grass tracked under it.

'Smile,' Marcus said, snapping the Kodak box. Then: 'Keep smiling, there's a good girl,' he crooned before he leant over and fingered my woolly dark crown; it was all that was left. Next, he was solemn, pacing back a step as he stroked his jaw and frowned. 'I do declare, we've swapped a daughter for a son.' He paused. 'A little boy.'

No further shutter clicked, but in a crevice in my brain, I recorded my mother as she stepped to him, her shoulders cramped, the fence behind them iced by blue hydrangeas. Blue for a boy! Nina laid a hand on his shoulder, drew a shaky breath. A sigh? Signifying what? Regret? Her large eyes were hooded. Bleak?

Mine blinked. Did they want to be rid of me? Find a proper boy? A fresh gust of misery, and high in the sky, earlier cavorting lamb and piglet clouds now lay flat, unpromising and gone. My parents, too, began to recede, and I was frightened; somehow decimated, cut in half. They seemed far away, and along with the cloud animals, would they disappear into slits of blue sky? Distraught, with ribs heaving, I fingered the blunt ends of my hair.

Was this the genesis of what was to become a wandering pain? Is what is unconscious, unchangeable, something impossible to track down or understand? Incapable of articulating what squirmed through my head, stones I tried to swallow jabbed the length of my neck; my voice box was gone.

They didn't want me. They wanted a boy.

Then: 'Daddy,' I croaked out; yearning to huddle into him.

'Yes?'

Plaintive, I hoped he wouldn't dare ask if the cat had my tongue. Archie had been our cat. Black and supposed to be lucky, but hadn't Archie been given away?

Did they suppose I felt nothing? Who knows? Both true and incomplete, can memory be trusted? Perhaps this was the first time my mind learned to keep its secrets from itself.

ANOTHER FORTNIGHT PASSED—MY first month of school—and the next day I opened my eyes to a strange white room. A sink with a tap over it squatted in one corner, and there were two straight chairs by an Ali Baba wicker basket with a lid. Outside, something emitted a low hum. My head swarmed. Casting my eyes up under weighted lids, the frothy dome of a mosquito net bunched above the bed. I guess I had been prepared but had not properly taken it in; I did not want to. My throat was a narrow wall painted with glue, which stung.

## A Secret Grief

Where was I? Wearing striped pyjamas! I breathed in smells, neither good nor bad, but excessively clean—hospital smells. Sunlight fluttered in through a window. I turned my head, and there neatly on a third chair sat Nina, her lashes shadowed on her face. Putting aside his newspaper, Marcus now edged closer, laid my hand like a fish in his, and shook the fish bones of my wrist up and down.

Words spread around me: 'Tonsils out. You've been brave. As much ice cream as you want. And lemonade,' which was promptly poured into a glass with a straw. Marcus perched on the bed, I sipped, faltered and sipped, but swallowing hurt, and open-mouthed, the gaps would have shown in my teeth.

Nina rummaged in her bag. When she spoke, she sounded too bright. 'Want to see what I, we, have for you?'

Yes, I did, but a yowl from a bed opposite halted her. The girl in that bed retched, missed the basin, and then came her high-pitched screams. My mother rattled the bedside bell while my father patted my hand, forehead netted with lines.

A nurse bustled in followed by a white-veiled sister making hushing sounds. 'We'll soon get you cleaned up, and fresh pyjamas. You'll be right as rain, pet.'

My back arched in dismay, and uneasily smiling, my father began, 'Nina.'

'Oh, yes,' and bag on her lap, she groped around inside it and produced the tissue-wrapped box.

The sister left, and the nurse cleaned, changed, and settled the girl. Pretty and pert-nosed, she crossed to my bed, her shoes squeaking on the linoleum. 'Are we feeling better?' she said to me.

My father ran both hands through his hair, winked my way, and answered for me. 'Sore throat but otherwise fine.'

Stroking my cheek, she gave him a coquettish smile, then turned to Nina. 'Oooh, a pressie. Let's guess what. A fire engine? A Dinky toy truck?' Then blinking eyelashes: 'He resembles you, he does,' she told my mother before she goggled at me. Nina stared from a face suddenly starched.

'You're a lovely little boy,' the nurse said.

The present? A bangle that was slipped over my fingers and held as stiff as sticks to my wrist. Twelve-carat gold, it had been given to Nina when she was my age, five.

## 10

It is said that our eyes employ about seventy per cent of our sense receptors, so the imagination has to be a chancy recall. A memory is a record of a person's experience of an event, not a record of the event itself, and in my childhood, little seemed to stay safely the way it should. Just as my hand had to fall from Gwennie's, the friendship was swallowed up by distance not of our making.

What pictures hang on the walls of my gallery when five? Nina in steepled heels, silk stockings with seams, and chic hats with veils. Walking between my parents, one hand pulled high to my tall father's hand. Me seated in the sidecar holding an umbrella with both hands when it rained, and squealing kids from my class who begged for a ride. Marcus in his shed, shavings curling from a plane when he carpentered a doll's house I didn't want, and a billy cart that I did. My mother, not always easy: wringing her hands a bit, her headaches, her wintry smiles. All of which increasingly I began to feel was my fault, that I should have been able to prevent. Purple-faced Marcus is blowing up an inner tube, with a rope attached to tow me in and out of the surf. Again at the beach, close on my parents' heels, vainly trying to fit my footsteps to Nina's by lengthening mine. Long green waves throwing spray beach-wards, wondering if the blue sea ever went flat like the blue sky. Nina's presents, which were always something-and-a-book. My parents' friends, their parties when fitful surges of sound reached through to me, their regular card nights with titbits from 'supper' put aside under a doily if I stayed in bed, and the tang of cigarettes filtering through to my room.

The smells of summer, autumn, winter, and spring under pink layered skies, dove or rat-grey, the burgundy and orange sunsets, velvety air, and air-like ice, along with the fruity smell of our old dog Horace, then dachshund Gus, who memorably chewed one of my grandmother's kid gloves. Christmas, the hinge of the year, and Cracker Night in June: sparklers, tom-thumbs, Catherine wheels and our bonfire—a rhumba of flames.

Everything can change, and you don't know why. Searching for links rarely works. However, when told at a baffled seven-nearing-eight that I was to be sent away to school, this made no sense.

Was I to go away for a few days? As long as a week? 'No. Boarding school means ...,' and it was spelled out.

Boarding school, which in a detached, unreal way did and didn't sink in— before a screaming demand tore to the ceiling. 'WHY?' (My screaming demand.)

Why was my life to be swept out of shape? My eyes boiled.

'Natasha, ' Marcus' voice dropped, and stretching out his legs, he crossed them at the ankles.

There was no unquestioning acceptance; all I could do was try to scream myself out of uncertainty. 'WHY?' Jangly, awful. 'WHY?'

'Natasha, ' His expression sobered by alarm, he sighed through his nose. If, accompanied by my mother, they'd been inspected by the school as the parents of a prospective student, I didn't know. A child's freedom to choose was non-existent. 'Listen to me.'

'WHY?'

Behind him stood Nina, one hand fiddling a cameo brooch she wore on a green dress, a handkerchief gripped in the other.

Gaze intent, he rolled his lips back from his teeth in flicks of a smile which came and went before he pulled me onto his knee. 'Why? Because we only have you; you're an only child.' An only child! If there were more children, Marcus and Nina might have had? Didn't their phantom progeny a sister or a brother for me? 'Please,' he was saying, and I suppose I nodded through a sadness and an awfulness that plummeted down from nowhere I knew, nowhere I'd been before.

Half turning, Marcus exchanged a glance with my mother before turning back to me. And Nina, who might have been on the point of saying something, left us then, quitting the room. Indifferent to my misery? A door closed, and soon we heard her at the piano, then falter, while in my mind's eye I saw her face tight, and her eyes unnaturally bright, the way it was when she sat to a difficult piece, her long fingers embroidering difficult sounds. Or—as in a far-off future, I came to suspect—at times when she wasn't capable of loving her child enough. In an emptiness of dejection, impatient with her child's daily presence, when her voice suggested concern, but a concern that possibly was false.

'Listen to what I have to say,' my father was at pains to enunciate. Buying time? 'Listen carefully. Because you're an only child, you can't always have someone to play with. We want you,' he laid emphasis, 'to have friends your own age. Companions. To grow up with other children.'

'No!'

'Natasha, to acquire a degree of independence.'

Independence! I didn't know, but Marcus must have known that humans take longer to become independent than any other species on earth. Next, his arms linked to construct a circle around me that I wanted to last forever, underlined by the smell of him. 'I promise you that away at school in the country ...' he began.

The country! There'd been the promise of safety in his closeness; a cross-your-heart-and-hope-to-die trust, but my bafflement swung to deep resentment. Had I only lived in a game where I trusted that he loved me? With no impermanence, no separation, and where he came home to me every night? Hot, boiling hot, I tasted a taste like tar. He was cruel; with awful hide-and-seek tricks, and I refused to hear, let alone absorb, what he was saying to me.

I exploded. 'I hate you. HATE YOU, a million more hates than I hate

Gwennie!' Rigid and betrayed, I burst out from a safety taken for granted all my life.

This was no ordinary unhappiness. Never had I thought of hating him, and my fury was enough to bring Nina back; both of them stung to the edge of tears, her skin waxy, Marcus mottled, both in shock. Bewildered, I had to run. Where? Familiar rooms, and did I undergo a sense of moving outside time? Then 'yap, yap …' Gus brought me back. Gus, whom I'd always sneak into my bed, but his kennel was too small for the two of us. Besides, I knew dogs weren't four-legged children with fur.

'Natasha,' Unstitched by her distanced voice from where she stood in the frame of the doorway—only feet away—I was unravelling in a collapsing world, a rag doll with the stuffing oozing out. 'Natasha,' my mother wavered, blinking. Attempting a smile, her smile dropped. She covered her mouth with one hand.

'Natasha,' now from my father and my eyes, jammed shut against tears while I longed to be rocked to his chest, held. 'Hate you, hate you!' I spat out, then repeated again in a circularity of hate and grief: 'Always will. Always!'

He groaned but I blocked both ears with tight thumbs and the pitch of my voice rose. 'Always, always,' as if set on stealing something from my father. 'Always. Till the end of the world!

## 11

The doorman at David Jones bowed to my mother, winking at me. 'School outfitting, fifth floor, madam. Take the elevator to the right.'

There's a persistent tug to memory. After she closed the cage of the elevator, a white-gloved woman yodelled: 'First floor ... fabrics, patterns and haberdashery. Second floor ... women's and matrons' wear,' and the door opening onto faces never to be seen again. Fizzy-stomached and clammy-palmed, I was swept up towards another life.

'Which ladies' college, madam?' my mother was asked. 'Yes, madam,' he responded to her reply, and we were allocated a Miss Smithers. With cylindrical kiss curls, rouged cheeks and tape in hand after seating Nina on a gilt-legged chair, she was all attention to the crested list my mother drew from her snakeskin handbag, matched to her snakeskin shoes.

Summer and winter uniforms. 'Do try not to fidget,' my mother stressed intermittently, but I was grumpy. There appeared to be dozens of 'regulation' everythings. Everythings which soberly, with a fixity of purpose, Miss Smithers advised—having outfitted countless growing girls—that my mother take in a larger size. All with that particular new smell; sports tunics, black velveteen and Liberty cotton 'best' dresses, swimmers, top coat, long socks, short stockings—even a suspender belt! But worse, among all this, I was measured for a device which could have come from a medieval torture chamber.

'To ensure good deportment; keep the young lady's shoulders back.'

'What?' my mother began, drawing in her chin when Miss Smithers extruded the arrangement from its tissue-lined box. Wide, padded straps were fitted over and under my arms, and this contraption was then laced together to tighten across my back. Pink—flesh pink—like women's corsets and bent on demonstration, Miss Smithers suggested I slump forwards and relax.

'What?' again from my mother to my 'OUCH' as the straps pinched into my armpits to pull skinny me poker straight, with no dimples of fat, and my arms like plucked wings.

'Is that really necessary?' Nina questioned, a finger to each cheek, only to be told that this was part of the regulation outfit, including cotton summer underpants, wool for winter, and both short and long-sleeved singlets with boat necks that were to be gathered in with ribboned strings, etc., etc.

I'd been compliant long enough. 'I won't wear it. Or singlets with sleeves.'

I didn't stop. 'You never make me,' I charged Nina, and though she agreed, these clothes were added to what was fast becoming a mountainous pile. A pile to which, laboriously, she must stitch the Cash's name-tape-labels ordered in my name. A van, my mother was assured, would deliver them—and more—the following day.

Etc., etc. was to include a tennis racquet, hockey stick, travelling rug and a monogrammed cutlery set, but before this came shoes, which proved the best part of all this. If Nina was beginning to show impatience, I didn't mind waiting because behind me waited a girl with freckles, with her freckled mother in a feather-nest of a hat. Determined not to laugh, we looked at each other, pouted, then sucked in our cheeks to become mouthless and smirked. Maybe she was starting at my school too; I liked this idea, but had to cancel it out, the chance being very remote. However, she was a sage of sorts: 'If you don't want trouble when you get there, pretend to be like everyone else,' she shot my way as I was led off to 'Galoshes'.

'Up you step, young lady,' came the instruction when I stood to face a chest-high box. From above, I looked down through a pair of goggles set into the machine, which x-rayed my feet. In an asymmetrical outline, shoes, socks, skin, muscle and flesh disappeared to reveal skeletal feet. Mine! The only skeletons I'd seen were skeletons of fish. I was so absorbed that turn by turn I wriggled each of my ten toes, hooked then straightened them in everyday shoes, a patent leather pair, sandshoes and ballet slippers, until the fit was pronounced correct.

From there we went to David Jones' tearoom. We had a vanilla milkshake, iced cupcakes topped with silver cashews, and a pot of Earl Grey for Nina, who seemed to frown into her teacup a lot. Then, finally, home by tram.

Our world changes, and a child's consciousness of self is unfathomable to that child. What to do but adapt? Try to adapt even as I continued to argue. Repetitious, my defence was blatant: 'I WON'T GO!' which had to pale to: 'MUST I GO?'

'Yes.' The decision was taken. Irreversible.

'But ...'

Marcus arched over me, holding my chin to ask—and he seemed serious—'Do you have your mother's lack of compromise?'

'What's that?'

He flapped a bit before he took me by the ears. 'Something you'll come to understand one day. In time.'

Time! Time gave me trouble. Time goes on no matter how desperately you want it stopped.

Forced to see there was no choice, I suppose I began to swing between gloom and less gloom. Marcus was optimistic and dedicated to persuading me that there would be heaps of 'fun'. Giggles, games and midnight feasts. My imagination churned.

I avoided his eyes for as long as possible, concentrating on the skeleton of my toes encased in my flesh, plus my toenails.

'How will it be fun,' I prompted, 'how?'

'Midnight feasts? We'll send you parcels of ... let's think ...' Stumbling, visibly pulling himself together, his voice turned boyish. 'Chocolate fudge, fruit cake, tins of toffees.' Full of concern, he leaned close, close enough to be searching for something he didn't seem able to see.

Another prompt. 'Hum bugs?'

'Hum bugs, yes, yes,' and hand clamped to his mouth, he rolled back his eyes. 'Loads, enough to blacken your tongue, and make you sick.'

'Oooh.'

'What's more,' he arched one arm, 'the three of us'll feast like kings come 'Boarders' Weekend' each term when we take you out.'

I peered at him. Were his eyes watering? Tears! I'd never seen my father cry. 'So, quick as a flash you'll come to see that you're in for a wonderful time.'

Unable to maintain my initial rage, emotions jumpy and askew, I fluctuated between gloom and resignation. Then, surprise; an inkling of hope sneaked in. It wafted in like a weather change.

The taxi was ordered for 1 p.m. to take me, my mother and my trunk to Central Railway Station. Each anxious in our separate ways and unhappy that due to the pressure of work, my father was unable to come as well.

Night ruptured, morning dawned and I lay quiet for a while, listening to my house. The day had a dry, savage look; a day which must be shaped. Breakfast, and I stared at the bowl of cereal set before me in the place routinely mine. A treacly-bitter smell in our kitchen; it was not like Nina to burn the toast.

Marcus strode in tying his tie. 'Eat up,' he said, and often having watched him shave, tongue held hard inside his cheek stretching the flesh, I saw there was a raw razor nick.

Always told not to play with my food, I played with it. 'Natasha.'

I could have been a baby trying out sounds. 'Not hungry. Don't want it.'

'At least drink your milk.'

Reluctantly, I drank from my old blue and white mug decorated with 'N', now hair-lined and crazed. Swallowing, gasping and swallowing, I could once again smell the milk, the cloudy whiteness of it like paste.

His breakfast finished, Marcus heaved back his chair, stood balancing weight on both feet while, grimly intent, I elbowed my mug to the table edge, another inch, another—then pushed it.

'Natasha!'

'It's all right, Nina,' his chuckle taut.

'It's her baby mug!' Her hands like white mice, Nina gnawed her knuckles as she regarded the pieces scattered over the floor.

'It's all right,' he repeated, then winked at me. 'No spilled milk.'

Though aware he must leave the house, he gave the impression he was in no hurry with all the time in the world. Then, a background to our lives, the hall clock struck. Parting had arrived. Scared I'd fly apart, inside I went wobbly and when Gus whined at the door and minced around, I rushed to him. Kneeling, I enfolded him in my skirt and thrust our heads together. If only we were to run away, Gus and me. I tipped him out of my lap. The treacly-bitterness in the kitchen was different; converted to a smell of impending loneliness.

'I wish, I wish …' I whispered, emotionally wary.

'Come here,' Marcus hugged me crushingly before he held me at arms' length. If his eyes told of sadness and his ache of need, he pulled me close again to murmur into my hair. 'It's for your protection.'

Breathing noises. But why didn't my father say he loved me, and forever? No, he said, 'Try hard to make it a good time. Wonderful.'

Wonderful?

## 12

Central Station. A huge cave of arrivals and departures buzzed and reverberated, threading towns and cities together, and severing them in turn.

Queues, clocks, porters and imperious announcements that were words from a mammoth mouth; men and women cross-stranded as they came and went. Hapless children, too.

Caught between the dependency of childhood and the new schoolgirl I was forced to become overnight, I was self-conscious. Scared too, which my mother maybe understood because she clamped my hand in hers.

When we found the platform—No. 14—from which the train was to puff its way out of Sydney before heaving up the Blue Mountains, if I wanted flight, I found invisibility. And hesitation as my ticket was clipped at the barrier. My mother's 'Platform Only' ticket was duly inspected. The porter with his trolley went on ahead as we approached the hopping, hooting, giggling and wriggling groups which drifted loose, then re-formed. Any one of them—their uniforms interchangeable—could have been me but wasn't. Identity cancelled; there was no more me!

Advancing in quick steps to match Nina's, my ribs panting under my monogrammed serge blazer, I could have been stumbling with legs in black tubes of rickety stalks, like I was learning to walk. I felt lost among legions of strangers. Part of me wanted to go on, and part to retreat and bolt at breakneck speed to my known life, knowing that this couldn't possibly be.

Then my mother was introducing me to a harried woman in a tweed suit and beret. Cradling a clipboard between her left hand and stomach, with pencil raised, she asked: 'And whom do we have here?' Then mystifyingly: 'Surname?'

'Ross,' Nina spoke for me.

'Aaah,' the woman eased out a husky sigh. 'Quentin,' she flipped a page. 'Ralston, Raymond, Richmond, Ross. N?'

'No, Natasha Ross,' I said.

'Quite so, quite so.'

With an air of privileged well-being, a male parent—squarely built and florid—trained a camera on us like a bazooka. I braced my legs, stiffened and cringed. The whites of my eyes as his targets. When he pressed the button, I expected to be exploded, broken up, an arm, a leg, guts and blood-splattering organs strewn everywhere, mingled with ribboned plaits sliced clean from heads, unseeing glasses in twisted frames, racquets, hockey sticks, spilling cases, and bags of fruit leaking juice. I imagined the teacher with the clipboard bravely throwing herself forward to take the worst of the blast.

Positive that the time for a miracle to save us was gone, feeling began to seep back to me. A trolley with magazines, sweets, and fruit was trundled along the platform and drew nearby. With a nod to me to stay where I stood, Nina approached it and returned with a brown paper bag that she placed in my awkward grasp.

Miss Clark, the teacher who I imagined had thrown herself forward to take the worst of the blast, now took a position of command on a box or something to elevate her above the crowd; her clipboard as protective as chain mail.

'Five minutes,' she was yodelling, 'five minutes, girls.'

'Five minutes! The direction was unmistakable; knelled like a bell of doom. My heart clenched. Five minutes! Then to be cast out, catapulted to the other world. I fought to contain a whimper. Five minutes! Each minute stunting, a sort of agony as it seeped away. My stomach hurt. No one in the universe could have felt as I felt. Shoulders sagging, forlornly I dug my teeth into my lips. Why had Marcus assured me I would be happy in the face of proof to the contrary? I hadn't asked enough for fear of finding out more than I wanted to know. I should have.

'Well,' Was my mother's smile uninvolved?

Girls, shaped and sized in my uniform, were hugging and being hugged by parents and siblings, too. Some girls, parents and siblings were blinking tears. Others wept overtly, clinging to mothers who, hats askew, stooped to clasp and soothe. Fathers with mouths full of teeth smiled, but mothers were more in evidence. En masse, I hated them—these girls with whom I was to be schooled. One at a time might be safer.

Then a whistle blew.

Nina took my face between her hands and tilted it to gaze into my eyes. Strangely to me, hers could have been jumbled with yearning. And good-bye.

'Natasha,' she said, then released me, her voice a rustle of leaves. 'You could well remember this day, always.' She may have sounded loving, yet I felt peculiarly unloved. 'Seven years old and next year eight.'

What? I didn't understand. Was this a code for survival?

'Eight,' she repeated, dragging the word out which to me should have been seven.

'Yes,' I could only clutch the paper bag, wanting to say that I didn't understand, but I didn't say it. Nor did I understand the way, huge-eyed, she was searching my face with something about her that I didn't remember ever seeing before.

The whistle screamed. 'All aboard, all aboard' and in the grit of the station air that ballooned out enveloping the school party, all I could smell was loss. Close by was my mother, somehow with me, yet not; what I felt was ever-changing fragments of shapes and bits of shadows. I might have been peeled off like wallpaper from the rooms that held my almost-eight years; wet wads of the stuff were glued together to make me.

'All aboard.'

Nina kissed me, and my life changed. Giddy-sick, I went onboard, unsure of where I was or who I was. Nudged by someone on my heels, I clambered up the high metal steps of the train. I was not an orphan, a child betrayed by nature, but I felt like one. Clutching for a rail, my fingers were as empty as gloves. I heard the clunk of the carriage door, and it closed.

Pushed forward and shoved again, I found myself in a window seat. The train air was stale with the window only half-raised, so I knelt on the seat, struggling to heave it higher and click it into place. A savage reflection—me—stared back till I had it up.

Motionless, I could have been thrashing in the confined space to bend forwards and lean out above the clustered crowd. To wave goodbye and give a spiritless gesture of departure in this razor-edged air.

*Where was she?* I scanned the faces of stiffly smiling parents, and there she was, wearing deepwater blue and far from drab like most of the mothers in their putty fawns and browns. *If I blinked, would she vanish?* One, two, three, and I blinked, scared to open my eyes to see if she was still there. She was, and coming closer. Nina was elbowing forward with no apology to anyone in her way, her face naked except for the red on her lips.

The whistle curdled my blood as it shrieked again. A shudder ran through the length of the linked carriages, and unfolding caterpillar-like, the train began to move. Everything turned meaningless.

Was this when I began to grow up? I had to. On the rim of another life, did some part of me clatter away and hide like the shards of the broken baby mug?

The train gathered speed and rhythmically began to move faster. Among floating arms at a diminishing distance, there was Nina's floating arm still. Signalling affection? Care? Warmth?

ALONE FOR HOW long in the pack, I couldn't tell. Teachers and prefects were demanding we be seated and stay where we were; one mistress with a heather-mix complexion above a heather-mix jacket was particularly bossy. Lonely among them all, bundled and wordless, I edged back on my seat, paper bag centred in my lap. I needed time to think, and I thought: one day today will end. End END. I must go on believing that. Nothing else.

Someone was tugging at my arm. 'What have you got?'

'Don't know.'

'Let's have a look.'

'No.' I clamped the bag closer and felt something oozing and moist.

'You new?' Needing only disassociation to show on my face, I wanted to push her away with her nosy questions. I didn't. Alarmed by her, if not scared, it was just that my limbs were jelly. Lonely jelly.

Lifting my head which had sunk a bit, I sort of examined her. She looked puffy, a bit red round grey eyes, and the truth dawned. She must be new like me. Swaying nearby, the others seemed to be in ready-made groups or at least pairs.

'Let's have a look,' this girl repeated, her voice fluty as she pointed a finger only inches from my brown paper bag. Had I been in a mood to guess, I would have guessed it contained fruit; my mother was a fanatic for fruit.

It was a bag of red, heart-coloured cherries. A few were bleeding, wounded by my convulsive grasp. Lifting one by its stalk, I rolled it into my mouth and sucked before I broke the skin to taste it and tongue the stone that was as smooth as marble.

Unblinking, she watched me, staring. I wished she wouldn't; I didn't want to give her anything. I wanted them all myself, with the mutinous heaviness clouding down. Still, she kept on staring, steadily watching my mouth, beyond the bounds of any convention I'd known, and words I didn't want to say were about to escape. I wish I'd never been taught words, a wish I was to relive often in the years ahead.

'Want one.' It wasn't really a question. My voice was deadpan and flat.

She smiled, and that's when I saw her face wasn't angular like mine but round. Dimpled. When we became friends, I'd see her dimples often linked by a grin, but there was circling about to be done first.

'I'll eat the squashed ones,' she proposed, which was a generous offer. 'They're your cherries,' she said, and my sense of loss and anger subsided. A bit.

Looking back, our attachment sprouted then. We'd find much to talk about when less inhibited and less shy.

'Cherries, cherries,' somebody sang, somebody with syrupy eyes. Then seniors—big girls with big greedy leers—stood over us. A posse.

'They're hers,' said my acquaintance—we weren't friends yet—but to no avail.

'They're mine!' I shouted, with cheeks burning, my timidity gone. 'They're mine.'

'They're hers, they're mine, hers, mine,' they mimicked, and there was no way to stop them. My brown paper bag was seized and emptied, and the ugliest bully had the effrontery to spit stones in my lap. Her heart and face icy. I don't belong here, I wanted to wail.

With a focused determination that was to stand her in good stead in the wake of future injustices, the dimpled girl swore. With the venom of practice, she could have turned the air blue. A further surprise was to discover that not only was she Church of England, but a clergyman's daughter, one of six, an afterthought by five years. No wonder she knew so much.

Tears not easily shed—and rarely in public—created a bond between us; my eyes became a bit red like hers, and puffy too.

Her name was Celia Sale, a name without significance to me before she said that Celia was Latin for 'heaven'. What also occurred to me, but later, was that with R and S—Ross and Sale—we stood a chance of being alphabetically teamed, maybe for things like monitor duty or baths. The idea of communal baths sent shivers up me. We might need each other. No, it was likely we would.

Through the windows, the land bent and we bent with it on railway tracks leading on like metal snakes. There were goods yards, tight houses with fingers of land, and through widening suburbs we slanted up, down, and up again. A low, layered sunlight glanced through buildings, flattened open spaces, and mirrored trees in rivers and lakes. And inexorably, as we sped on, I tried to keep my head blank.

Just as well; and just as well it did not occur to me that, shaking into my bones, the rhythmic rumble of the train would continue on for a further seven years.

Stations we passed meant nothing; I wasn't up on geography. Or weather patterns, as eerily and unseasonally, the sky clouded over to gloomy grey. What felt like hours later, we were marshalled out onto a platform while guards in uniforms with lamps shouted: 'Valley 'eights, Valley 'eights.' It seemed that at Valley Heights the mountain gradient increased, and while coal was shovelled, water hissed, and the train was linked to a second engine to take the strain, we were told to stretch our legs.

Stretch our legs? What? A torture of a terrible kind?

But Celia knew. In creamy diction, she informed not only me but a clutch of other 'news', including one poor thing who was labelled 'Madelaine Brown', which made me grateful not to have just been parcelled up, tagged and despatched like her. Who knows what lies behind nice-sounding names?

Spacing her words, Celia informed us: 'We're supposed to walk up and down this damn platform, till the damn engines are joined. Worse, at double pace come winter term,' she shuddered. 'To stop the blood freezing in our veins.'

Three of her five sisters, earlier pupils, had demystified 'Valley 'eights' for her, including possibly a million other bewildering things to set us humming with fright and downright misery.

'Valley 'eight, all aboard,' and the whistle sounded inexpressibly melancholy.

Finally disgorged from the two-headed train and freed like beetles, we were mustered, counted, counted again, and ticked off the list, which convinced Celia someone had gone missing. But no, we must have been the full complement to crocodile away in a queer, weaving sort of walk through what was known as 'The Village'. It contained a post office-bank, a garage, a general store, and old hands pointed out the one shop of consequence: 'The Mrs. Jenkins' Sweet

Shop', where Saturday mornings we were able to spend our pocket money.

A wind had blown up, and inside my uniform I shivered. Out of nowhere came the thought of the regulation singlets, with sleeves which I'd cut off as soon as I could lay hands on a pair of scissors. I'd never worn singlets, let alone with sleeves. Certain they'd itch, and only suitable for old ladies, I ground my toe into the path as the crocodile paused. Sleeved singlets were the sort of thing my grandmother, Hannah, would wear layered under her pearls and clothes.

'Move on girls, briskly now. One two, one two,' a teacher fell in beside me. The wind grew stronger and those with no elastic under their chins grabbed at hats, banded in blue and gold with a motto I didn't understand, which would brand me 'dumb' if forced to admit my ignorance. Though I played scornful at the time, Nina had sewn elastic on mine.

Nina? What was she doing now? What and where? The wind whipped my eyes wet and I swallowed hard. Was I already gone from her thoughts?

The next corner streetlamp flickered on as we approached; Celia's lips lilac between her un-dimpled cheeks.

Miss Clark, chin down, tweed collar up like a brown owl, unnerved me by knowing my name. 'Natasha Ross,' her voice beat in my ears, 'Natasha Ross, I'm certain you'll settle in quickly; in no time at all.'

I had no such certainty. *What qualified her to judge?* Overwhelmed by fear, how could I live with a hundred girls! I ached to be on my own, make a bolt and run. A hundred girls, maybe more; an engulfing wave, pounding, dumping, all sense of safety drowned. Here I was at a junction in my life; no rules, no laws, emotionally chafed, ignorant of what could be asked of me for any rudimentary reason. All of a sudden, this made me mad. Boiling mad.

'Sale.'

'Get stuffed,' I said to Miss Clark.

Miss Clark misheard me. 'It's tough. Yes.' She paused, then, determined to be positive, added, 'However, it will soon pass off.'

'Piss off,' Celia breathed loud enough for me to hear, and dutifully

Miss Clark charged up the line, and if at the mercy of adults, it seemed we could band against them. 'Piss off,' Celia repeated, and we felt better as if we'd wolfed down forbidden fruit, or somebody's box of chocolates. I hoped I wouldn't be sick.

Miss Clark, like Celia, we'd discover, was from a clerical family and given to singing obscure hymns. Hymns I was unlikely to hear, but that was still to come. Five days on, the following Sunday.

## 13

There can be an awfulness to some memories. Perhaps the darkened sky wasn't so huge a bruise, and the wind a brittle cough. Arriving at the unwelcoming territory of the school through iron gates which were ceremoniously opened then clanged shut, we approached via a circular, gravelled driveway which crunched underfoot ominously. Lined on either side were flower beds, and beyond were stretches of black lawns. The architecture could best be described as Gothic.

Spooked, a stronger wind blew up and coughed louder. Leaves flew and spun. Celia slid her hand into mine. We moved towards a huge, rambling pile of them.

Nearer, we could see a high and wide door with fluted fanlight set with coloured glass. An exceptional light shone through it, like a distant fairytale. It was the point of entry each term, and at the core of the school was an old mansion in which, long ago, the Prince of Wales—the one who gave up all for Mrs. Simpson—stayed during a visit to New South Wales. His intolerant-looking portrait graced the main hall. No one actually knew where he slept, but the high-ceiling rooms converted to dormitories must have vied for the distinction. Princes, Kings, Edwards, Windsors, etc. This royalty clap-trap denoted each spartan dormitory: each had old-fashioned windows, sash cords and shutters, and their cedar sills were as wide as seats.

Duly allocated to dormitories, somehow, what with orders and bells ringing, tripping feet on staircases, instructions, and revolting food for dinner—something in a glue of white sauce then something in a muck of custard—the time came for bed. Poor Madelaine Brown—despite her label—was totally lost. Midway on a landing and causing a traffic jam, she began to cry, her head jerking in spasms till she was set on route to Windsors by an old hand. A further bell rang.

'To your dormitories and bed,' a voice pitched over the herd.

But first—before tooth-cleaning and hair-brushing and prayers by those who said them—it was necessary to undress. In this strange sleeping room with ten beds and nine strangers, I wanted to climb into bed fully clothed. The air hummed with the noise of them and was filled with the smell of them. I was never modest—not even knowing what modest meant back then—but I'd never shared a room. As these nine strangers began to bump out of everything starting from their regulation shoes up, I turned shy—shy, estranged and awkward. Alone, abandoned. Suddenly, I wanted to exchange myself for Madelaine Brown so I could cry. But I was sure any tears would convert to hysterics, and then I'd die. Already, home was distant and unreal.

What to do? After taking colossal breaths, I attempted to tent myself in anonymity. My dressing gown was red with a tartan collar, a tartan pocket and a label which read 'Dreamtime', so I hauled it over my head where it hung from my shoulders, affording privacy. Well, some, and with my heart battering my ribs, I dragged everything off. Then, as I was about to yank on a nightdress, with one jerk my 'Dreamtime' was whipped away—and naked, I was spun about to a semi-circle of jeering faces, my knobbly back to the wall. Escape was impossible. Only my eyes moved.

Quelling sobs, I'll never forget their torment, capped off by the self-styled leader, Corinne Bradley, a creature of exceptional depravity, snake-nasty, as she poked blunt fingers at parts of me. Finally, a taunt from her slit of a mouth—chilling and mean—seeped into my ears.

'You got anything we haven't got, give us a look straight away.'

## A Secret Grief

She smirked around at the others, before she began picking her nose on her awful face. A pig face with pig eyes bristling with sandy lashes, and a snout of a nose.

'Show, show, show!' with arms threshing they squealed under the probing lights of Kings dormitory. 'Show, show!' Gallops of laughter and struggling to swallow a whimper it slipped through.

Why couldn't I die? Die, I whined to myself, die. I willed it, but God, or whoever, let me down. Horror of horrors, petrified, was I cursed? Was there something on my body not on theirs? I couldn't look, and my legs clenched, implacably I stared into the distance which wasn't far in Kings. Needles punctured my skull, then the length of my skinny shape. Hadn't I heard my father state that every single one of us was a miracle of engineering! The bits of flesh covering me screamed but the screams choked in my throat. I smelled something that smelled like a skunk, while I reeked of helplessness.

Stripped bare from head to toe, now the needles were a firing-furnace red. Under the ribs which encased it, my heart would be the final bomb, with the slightest pressure, a feather, to set it off and blow the world to kingdom come. I didn't care; if all nine of them, shaven-headed and covered in ashes, begged forgiveness ... NEVER, and head on stalky neck, I stared as I burned.

Suddenly, the blur of open-mouthed faces swivelled. They could have been sideshow clowns for, oh heaven, in red and blue-striped pyjamas, hair a pale gold, Celia Sale stood framed by the cedar doorway. Bewildered, but not for long. Dropping her toothbrush, paste and mug with a splat, she dashed to the carcass that was me and wrapped her towel around me.

Next, like a good shepherd, she clucked me towards my bed and dimpled for an instant before rounding on the startled occupants of Kings. And was her language choice! Unfaltering, she told them what and exactly where to put what; on and on her floodgates opened, not repeating a single word. Hers was a riveting performance, and despite my teeth chattering like stones in a jar, I began shaking less.

Eight of them were struck dumb, but one began to snivel, then whine. Then in veneration. 'Where'd you learn all that?'

Snapping the elastic of her pyjamas, head held high, Celia said: 'Prudence.'

'Prudence who?'

Her smile was exquisite. 'My hooker sister,' she said.

That did it; they were clamouring. They wanted details of her sister's means of livelihood. Some cajoled, some pleaded; however, Celia would only tell if and when she chose.

Next, stirring the heap of my clothes with one foot, her voice challenging, she ordered: 'YOU.'

It was directed at my prime tormentor, Corinne Bradley. I was now calm enough to realise that, like the others, she was older than us. Whether by chance or design, Celia singled her out. Why hadn't I mistrusted her on sight?

'YOU,' she used her finger like she was pointing at my bag of cherries on the train. 'Get over here and quick smart.' Her lips went thin. 'Fold up Natasha Ross' things.'

My jaw dropped like a drawbridge. To my astonishment, as well as the astonishment of the dormitory, there was no need for a second directive. Shoes were placed side by side under my chair, some of my clothes folded and stacked, and some bundled into my laundry bag. My uniform and blazer were slithered onto hangers and hung on appropriate pegs.

Soon a bell rang and while the others scuttled about, cucumber-cool Celia hauled up beside me on the iron bed.

'Want to see my scar?' she asked, her tone intimate and exclusive. I nodded.

She rolled up her right pyjama leg to display a livid line on her inner calf. Solemn, she indicated each of the tiny holes in her flesh from which stitches had been removed; tiny holes like bird pecks.

There was another bell and she headed for Edwards across the corridor, leaving me awash with curiosity as to what, or who, had caused her wound. Undeniably, Celia lived in a broader society than mine.

## 14

The slow night began. 'Lights out,' then: 'No talking,' a prefect ordered, and fortress-like, the door to Kings was closed. Under it a bar of door-length gold showed that a light still shone in the corridor. Fearful, refusing to believe this might be dowsed, I flinched, not knowing what to do if the total black of night came down. Should that bar of light disappear I was convinced I'd die, but instead of heaving over, slow as a snail I sat up.

Jerking away from the huge rectangles of black which were the windows, my eyes drilled into a sort of lesser dark, needing to be assured that there were lumps in the other beds; at least next to mine. Elbows anchored to my sides; above all I knew that must not attract attention. What might they still be capable of? Afraid to go to sleep but afraid to stay awake, I ached to believe that having survived the last miserable hours, somehow, I'd manage till dawn.

Then I remembered my father telling me in a tone of elaborate reasonableness never to be afraid of the night. Night is only day with the lights switched off. What would tomorrow bring? Someone grizzled in sleep and desolate, I sniffed. Above all, I longed for the mingled whiff of Nina's '*Joy*' and Marcus' '*Craven A*' cigarettes.

Instead, the smell of camphor from stored blankets, plus strong soap from sheets, clung in the air. Creeping into distress, pillow clamped to chest, my ears were those of a fox. Straining to hear what someone whispered, which prompted giggles, a nearer lump coughed theatrically.

'Shut up,' someone hissed, which shocked me, having been taught that 'shut up' was not acceptable; more than ever, I was an outsider.

'Shut up,' from another lump, but this time it was a hoarse warning, and the room went quiet. Dark silence, they'd all sagged into sleep; all but me. What to do? Slithering down between scratchy sheets, my fingers were stiff as they sought the satin edge of my blanket. Betrayal. Would life ever come right again?

I had conflicting pictures, then fragments of a jigsaw that became part-dream on the lip of sleep. I was being shaken awake.

'Where am I?'

'Where do you think?'

Muzzy-headed, I struggled out of the narrow bed. All that seemed possible was to try to rearrange things in my head: follow to the bathroom, follow routines the others seemed to know till I was dressed, then —with much surrounding noise—hurtle down the first flight of stairs to a landing, then down another.

I was siphoned between double doors to a huge dining room, where the smell of decades of past meals filled the air. Set with tables to seat eight, where was I to sit? Then someone from behind took hold of my shoulders, propelling me towards what had to be my table, my place. Which, miraculously, it was: the napkin ring on a plate engraved with 'Natasha Ross'.

'Thank you,' I whispered, staring at my lined-up knife and spoons. '*Non*,' an irritated tone barked. '*Non*.' An irritated nod. '*Merci*.'

'What?'

'*MERCI*.'

'What?' There was a tension to everything.

So began another torture. French—rudimentary French—was spoken at breakfast. No exceptions. One of our school's two principals was French—Mademoiselle Mimi Durand, a short nugget of a woman light years from her homeland here on the other side of the world. The bottom of the world, she was frequently to infer when displeased either with it or us. I'd not set eyes on her yet.

With everyone shuffling to their place, I pulled back my chair and poised to sit down.

'NON! *Ecoutez.*'

What! Another jolt shot through me and with a gaping alarm to everything, I hunched up and fought back tears. A volume of gobbledygook was spoken by a shark of a senior at me, a stranded and undersized whale spouting a spray of despair and struggling not to whimper and cry. Circling, desperate to catch sight of Celia, rescue of a kind came my way; this girl with vocal dexterity to match the shark's, the shark having moved on.

'Listen,' said my rescuer, 'listen carefully.'

French was our breakfast language, and when we were seated, someone would bring me a list. A very easy list, she emphasised; English listed against French, which I was allowed to refer to for a week. Then I'd be expected to learn more.

'What?'

She obliged. 'Milk—*du lait*, bread—*du pain*, butter—*du beurre*, jam—*de la confiture.*'

'La what?'

'Never mind, you'll cotton on.'

'Do I sit down now?'

'*Mon Dieu, non.*' She swept hands over her mushroom-coloured hair.

'What?'

'No. We stand behind our chairs till grace is said.'

Confused again. 'Grace who?'

She was good enough to stay patient. 'Thanks for our daily bread,' and I dared not ask what that meant. 'In French of course, so just mumble your lips a bit till you get the hang of it.'

'Thank you.'

'*Non,*' she sighed. '*Non* means no. *Merci* means thank you. Got it? And you'll need *s'il vous plaît.*'

I opened my mouth but she beat me to it. '*S'il vous plaît* means please. Understand?' and if I was about to perilously attempt the French language with '*non*,' she added, 'just say: 'silver plate'.'

French! I loathed it then, but came to like it later. Much later. But later that day—having pulled through a superabundance of mysteries as if dragging through quicksand—what struck me was a grievance against my mother. Another grievance. I fumed, but fumed with an ache. Didn't she have the remotest idea what a mother should do? Nina had grown up with French, so why hadn't she taught me the breakfast words? At least milk, bread, butter, jam. Teeth clenched, together with abandonment, darkly I held my mother culpable of not only cruelty, but negligence.

This first meal of the first day brought another revelation. In all probability Mlle Mimi Durand and the English Miss Sarah Batton-Browne—our co-principals—were from a long tradition of intelligent spinsters raised on the nanny theory: you're a fortunate child, privileged; think of the starving children in India and eat everything given you on your plate. Frog legs? Toad-in-the-hole?

Many of us were told this—or a variation of it—by our parents. 'Waste not want not,' was widely subscribed to by rich and poor; the poor from necessity, the rich for a variety of reasons—frugality, restraint, Christian charity, conformity, envy, saving for a rainy day, or whatever traits fate linked in them. If ostentation seemed less in evidence or less desirable, naturally, there were plenty of exceptions to keep the pot on the boil, with lifestyles unhindered by money or taste.

My parents did not encourage waste, but they were no tyrants to the scraped plate. In fact, I was taught it was proper to leave something—a potato, a few beans—while scraping was strictly disallowed. Marcus was given to joking: 'Don't take the pattern off the plate.'

I was expected to try whatever was put before me, but Nina reasonably granted that palates were individual. But here, away from home, my palate was puzzled, and my stomach was at first indignant—then hugely offended.

The ordeal of the first French breakfast over, the hours till lunch puttered by in a blur. Allocated to a classroom, jostled into half of a scratched desk, books listed and distributed which we were set to cover in brown paper and identify with our names, yet still Celia did not appear. With an uneasiness verging on queasiness, I craned to find her, shuddering at any thought of being located in the same room, let alone near the obscene Corinne Bradley who'd poked at bits of me.

Inexplicably, being one of two chosen to fill inkwells that were sunk in holes in each desk afforded me the opportunity to confirm Celia wasn't there.

'Be careful,' we were warned, 'don't spill the ink.'

Of course we did, and a third girl was chosen to follow us with sheets of blotting paper. Pink. Close at my heels the blotting girl almost tripped me up twice, but at last, inky fingered, the job was done. Instructions, instructions, instructions, then came morning break, oddly named 'Recess', when milk and Vo Vo biscuits or Arnott's Arrowroot were set on tables lining one side of a flagged courtyard. After bumps, squeals and confusion, soon a bell rang and I was racing down the corridor towards what I hoped was the right classroom. The blotter caught me up and tried to take my hand, but I swung free of her.

Battering my shoes on the bare boards, I began to hum with suspicion. How to distinguish friend from foe? No idea; but seized by terror, could I afford prolonged doubts? Be forever shut out, doomed to eternal friendlessness with a talent for making enemies?

'Don't dawdle,' a giant of a woman directed pointedly. 'And pull up your socks.'

I muttered something and winced. Winced with a longing to be thousands of miles from here. Anywhere. On the highest mountain in the world. In Africa living with pygmies. Or smiling, a slave to fantasy, I knuckled my eyes. Divided by just the width of the aisle sat Celia Sale, dimples coming and going in her cheeks while mine flamed. 'Where've you been?' I hissed, hot and pleased.

'They put me in the wrong class.'

'Dopes,' I said.

'Bloody nongs,' she said and we exchanged grins; it felt like we'd known each other for years—or in another life.

Lunch came due. Lunch—called dinner—was the main meal of the day, with supper supplanting what was 'dinner' at home. It was lighter food which likely was unwholesome, but they weren't set to starve us. Anyone left hungry could pig out on bread and jam.

We were desperate to be at the same table but with her greater knowledge, Celia stated this could not be arranged, as she chewed her thumbnail. Not by us, heavenly intervention seemed necessary. Following inside information from her sisters, we scrubbed our hands and nails before this meal; other 'newies' did no more than flick their fingers under a tap. Forewarned we were forearmed; a blitz of unscheduled inspections could catch you out. Punishment: no pudding that day, no jelly, tinned peaches, suet roll, syrup tart or stewed rhubarb. No sloshed-on custard or cream, lumpy custard or thin-cream custard was more routine.

'I hate lumpy custard,' I volunteered, pulling a face and Celia leaned into me.

'Well what you have to do is ...' but an avalanche of girls tumbled us apart and what she was about to reveal was lost.

There were more words of gratitude for what we were about to receive—which to me was downright wrong—the procedure was to ease to one side of your plate what you disliked the most. Next, skim a glance over seven other plates, talk with your eyes, then let the trade begin. Luckily some kids, greedy or hungry enough, would eat anything. So at knee level, a conveyor belt of sorts moved under the table. Left to right, never in reverse, greasy potatoes, squares of pumpkin, whatever could be speared by a fork, anything sloppy scooped into spoons. The exchange was precarious and if caught, punishment was tough, but few baulked at the risk and you became adept.

There was an alternative, which required even greater dexterity. Pockets filled with under-boiled eggs so the whites were uncoagulated, with liver oozing blood that was mystifyingly supposed to be necessary for those of us labelled 'anaemic'. Porridge or gravy-coated-anything were the worst. No paper napkins, no tissues, only hankies. Should you be as much as a halfway-picky eater, it was necessary to scavenge sheets of paper or collect leaves to line tunic pockets as best as possible.

Once after weeks of boiled onions served daily by the current chef, we broke out in spots no matter how hard we tried—and we tried—to dispose of them. Opaque, fleshy lumps, they were larger but equally as slimy as tapioca, sago or rice pudding which came with a thick skin.

As yet a novice at disposal, I gagged on my first meal; stew with gristly meat, parsnips, turnips and swedes. I felt threadbare, abandoned. Where were the interconnected cogs and wheels; the warmth that was home?

Should they still exist, I had no means to re-enter rooms my mother filled with flowers. The scent of roses, sweet peas—whatever —seasonally spread through our house. Where a platter of fruit centred the sideboard, I helped myself. Where, on his return every night, my father rubbed his nose against mine, kissed my cheeks, and sometimes licked one of my ears. Where I smiled. Now miserable, during meals I played with a knife and fork, above all wanting to be ignored.

'What's wrong with you?'

Someone's wedge of a face hovered close and I hissed like a cat whose fur was stroked the wrong way.

'What's wrong with you?' I countered, glowering. Had I learned attack was a better defence than silence? Or the sulks?

'Nothing,' her voice was like a shrug, and she put a bit of stew in her mouth while I watched her hold it on her tongue before she started to chew like a goat.

Next, her expression was a rebuke. 'You can get it down if you have to.'

I didn't believe her, and riffled my lips in disgust. 'You can,' she persisted and panic flooded through me as the bit I had managed to get down was on its way up. 'You can,' she said again, and overtaken by a flat despair and the smell of over-ripe bananas with blackened skins, I clutched my stomach and felt it heave. If I vomited ...

Food up, down, in, out—and yet another barbaric system was still to be inflicted upon us. But it was still Wednesday of my first week, and the other barbarity was not to be revealed till next Monday came round.

Somehow Thursday and Friday sorted themselves out and somehow, with mutual support, alongside Celia I blended in. Or half blended in; Celia was either unwilling or unable to keep certain words to herself when bullied or patronised.

We only supposed that Saturday would be better; the Sweet Shop excursion, when our two-thick crocodile line of boarders were handed pocket money to squander on jaw-breakers, jelly beans, chocolate or iced coconut. Of course, Sunday held no fears for Celia, the minister's daughter, and with no premonition of what it held for me, I was blissfully unaware.

At 3p.m. Friday, lessons finished for the week—the curriculum unravelling grammar and building maths—as yet sport wasn't organised for tennis, netball and hockey, and teams were still to come, though yellow, blue, red or orange sashes to sling round the majority of our no-waist bodies had been distributed, each colour denoting 'Houses'. 'Houses' weren't dormitories; they also included day girls who enviably had houses of their own to return to each day. Lucky things, we 'newies' thought, or thought we thought.

Free until 5p.m.—even with piano, violin, dance and additional language practice—supper was at 6p.m., followed by study under either inert or snappy supervision. The day ran full circle to tooth cleaning and hair brushing: one hundred strokes if your hair grew below your ears, fifty above. Then prayers for those who said them, another bell with a hollow clang, and finally 'lights out'.

## 15

Daylight lapped round us in the school grounds and with lawns recently mown, there was a nice grassy smell. 'Nice' was a word my mother scorned. 'Nice', she'd say, if not a nothing word, in her view was a boring word. To me, biscuits could be nice, and cups of tea nice. Who cared? Not me. Right now, 'nice' was what I wanted; neither strange nor distrustful, giving me no cause to fret. There were nice and unspectacular flowers in nice, neat garden beds, trees which grew nice in the distance. Nice birds chirping in the branches, and nice sun filtered through the leaves.

Loose groups of three or four girls dotted the scene, stretching out in cliques on the grass or horsing about. 'Let's hear what she's blathering on about,' Celia said, seeing an older girl holding court, pouting, simpering and flinging her arms wide.

We edged in and plonked down on the fringe of her entranced circle.

'Where's she now, Ginny? Your mother?'

This question put to the queen apparently interested all the drones.

With a flash of her teeth and eyes, the flamboyant Ginny Jones threw her head back and tossed her marigold-red hair. 'In Cairo.' Then a stage pause. 'Cairo's in Egypt where Cleopatra lived.'

'Who's she?'

'Oh, Cleopatra. Cleo,' with the inference of an intimate or rich relative. 'Dumbo. Cleo was one of the most beautiful women who ever lived and,' after a punctuating pause, 'she never took a bath in plain old water.'

'You mean she never took a bath? Poo!' Fingers and thumbs pegged button noses in Ginny's audience, causing her to shrug dramatically.

'Cleopatra bathed in milk.'

'Jeepers,' from someone in thick glasses. 'Then maybe she smelled like Horlicks. Yummy Horlicks.'

Ginny's smile was doting. 'Queens do whatever they want. They're not like us. Besides, Cleopatra was the Queen of Egypt and almost the queen of the world.'

'How?'

'Because famous kings fell in love with her.'

'Like your mother?'

Ginny had the grace to lower her eyes, but not before somehow to me she appeared unreachably sad. 'No, not kings, but,' she held her audience in the palm of an expressive hand. 'Just a count with a castle, a Spanish matador who taught her to tango. And samba. And a few film stars.'

On request names were mentioned, and if, when I was older—by only months—these claims seemed disingenuous, my mouth dropped like a drawbridge with the rest.

'And?'

'And,' came a mystifying aside from a passing senior. 'And SHE made the upward climb on her back.'

It appeared Ginny's mother, with a party of adventurers, was riding a camel across the sands of the desert to the Great Pyramid of Cheops. The camel's saddle encrusted with semi-precious jewels—amethysts not rubies, jade not emeralds, not sapphires. Did Ginny's instincts tell her where to draw the line? A shimmer in the air, a deepening sky, anything seemed possible.

'Gee, Celia,' I was goggle-eyed, but Celia snorted before she was nudging me up and off. Scrambling to my feet, I sort of wanted to hear more. Had the light shifted? As if shadows had slipped in, left something behind, something puzzling, connected with anxiety and mothers?

Earlier, waiting for Celia to come out of the loo, I overheard something from a cubicle, the voice scratchy; the way I imagined waxwork models might talk. 'I'm never weepy when I leave home BUT I have to cry'. Then a sigh. 'Mummy expects tears. A sort of duty, like having to write to the grandparents.'

'Come on,' Celia set off at a lope, and I trotted after her. I caught her up beside the sundial where we'd been told the Latin inscription translated to: I only count the happy hours.

'Celia? Ginny's mother?' It wouldn't have surprised me to hear she was escorted on lion safaris, and encountered polar bears when drawn across vast stretches of ice by a team of huskies. Danced at balls at Buckingham Palace. Maybe partnered by the Prince of Wales.

Celia toed a foot into the grass before starting to do little kicks into it. 'Go on,' I encouraged, stopping short in my head of Ginny's mother going over Niagara Falls in a canoe, let alone a barrel.

'You won't laugh? At her? Ginny?'

'Laugh at Ginny! Why?' I scooped Celia's hand, swung it, her lips knitting in what could have been a knowing smile.

A rowdy gang rushed by. Squeals came as somebody tripped somebody up and, for what seemed an age, we stood just eyeing the ground and the hole Celia dug with her toe. A bell rang, wrinkling the air, and kept ringing. Then intent, Celia's eyes were on mine.

'Don't be naïve.' Naïve? Who taught her that word? Celia lowered her voice. 'If you don't have a mother,' she said, 'you make one up.'

'Dysfunctional' was not a word in use then.

## 16

Saturday arrived, with Sunday on its heels. We were disappointed when what was to be our first excursion to The Village and Mrs. Jenkins' Sweet Shop was cancelled with no reason given to us. Where with sixpence I might have goggled at jars of gobstoppers, stickjaw, jellybeans and humbugs. Over the years, Mrs. Jenkins' staff must have stood cheerful and patient behind their counter, though I can't even outline either of them now; I suspect they wore cardigans and small print frocks.

What supplanted that first spending spree? No one informed us but does that make matchsticks of memory? Easily collapsed while there are others that remain intact against a hurricane of what was once? Whole tracts of a life are submerged like lost treasure while other memories are burned into the skull. That first Sunday at boarding school 'was writ large' in mine.

Sunday, an official day of rest; no piano practice, etc. We were granted an extra hour's sleep, which it was reckoned we deserved in order to fortify us for morning service and the current rector's interminable sermon. A more formal dinner–lunch was the order of the day, Sunday School in the church hall. Evensong followed for hapless seniors when it was compulsory for the rest of us to write letters home.

*A Secret Grief*

THE EARLY SKY PALE, the sun rose as it should. Saturday night had rattled away in a daze, and light and air filtered through the long windows of Kings as Sunday arrived. Tangled in sheets, I tumbled out of bed when the bell rang. To date, baths were taken at night, but not on holy Sunday, and memorably on this first Sunday, midway in the queue the bath water was warmer than lukewarm. Which, naïvely perhaps, I believed boded well.

Clean underwear, blouse and pressed tunic were laid out for us and I pitied whoever polished our shoes. Neither Nugget nor Kiwi shoe cleaning gear were destined to dirty our hands. Sabbath clean, our Sunday gloves were white and virginal, whatever 'virginal' meant.

St. Barnabas within the school grounds had a greyed lychgate, honeyed sandstone, and was classically built if a bit squat, together on the site where an original house stood. Unexpectedly, the cemetery seemed ungloomy: its weathered tombstones with names and dates honed into them under a spread of alien trees. Celia had it that an old man with a hump in old clothes and trousers held up with a rope kept it tidy, and that he had done for years.

Barnabas? The name had appeal to me. So when Gus in his old musty coat turned up his toes, I named our next dog Barnabas—'Barny'—a scatty spaniel with the remarkable sense not only to growl at my grandmother, Hannah Ross, as Gus had done, but like a miracle also chew up a pair of her black gloves. Just as Gus had in his doggy life before.

However, biblical Barnabas had been named by the apostles for his good character and works of charity. Charity! Just wait. Tower, porch, stone font, flanked by aisles, transepts, a Latin cross, long, dark-wood pews, chancel, choir stalls, altar and the step-up pulpit, and the clerestory windows that lit St. Barnabas magically. Magically for me at least, who'd never entered a house of God. Soon I was to discover why.

Music hummed from the organ as we fanned right and left, shuffling into place. 'What do I do?' I beseeched Celia with her experience, who from the corner of her mouth rasped: 'Follow me.'

I did. What's more, I liked it here; the flowers spilling out of brass vases sort of reminded me of home. Candles too, for Nina invariably lit candles before dinner and later snuffed them out with a silver cone on the end of a fancy stick. Who dowsed them here? Or did they burn Sunday to Sunday in some ritual unknown to me? In a highly organised society, this seemed a world of absolute values, underpinnings to school life.

When our rector, Mr. Whitehead, dressed up in the long skirts of his ecclesiastical robes—patent-leather-like hair sleeked to his skull—grandly mounted to the command position of the pulpit and half the school shuffled and sighed, I was mesmerised. He boomed on about the rewards of Heaven if we were good, the reverse if not, and finally, wizard-like, topped it off with a miracle: fishes and loaves. Next, he mentioned the lepers' box.

Hymns culminated in an electrifying 'For All the Saints Who from Their Labours Rest', followed by the puzzle of the collection plate, prompting Celia to quietly suggest that Mr. Whitehead had the look of a man who'd skim off a bit for himself. She widened her eyes. Didn't he need to? Mrs. Whitehead in shabby brown and a hat her chooks must have pecked after the cats slept on it. Curious, I glanced towards Mrs. Whitehead, Celia choking down a giggle. 'That poor thing's vice is religion,' she let out tightly, pulling a face. Who'd she got that from?

Religion! Faith, devotion, church-going. The rhythms of the service, that first Sunday had its appeal, and if not mad about the music, I liked the sing-along. Juggling the hymn book, when acquainted with the words I felt I'd merge in. Besides the staged nature of it, in the miasma of different light and different scents—with an undertone of disinfectant—you could wander into fantasies that only God—if HE was interested—would know.

There was the blessing, then up off our knees, we began to file down the aisle in reverse, the all-stops-out organ ushering us to the porch where, hands steepled over his navel, Mr. Whitehead beamed us on our earthly way.

Earthly! Given a clue, never could I have guessed how down-to-earth it would be for me. Nor how my absent parents could orbit me into another rage. 'You're wanted in the principal's office,' a prefect said as she sidled up to Celia and I dawdling back. 'Wouldn't keep Mlle waiting if I were YOU.'

'YOU,' Celia mimicked. 'Why does she want YOU?'

ME! I began to quake. Why ME from all the look-alikes? One of many grateful to vanish in the crowd, why was I re-discovered? Made ME again?

Celia grabbed for my hand, flinging it up and down. 'YOU haven't done anything wrong.'

A posse of seniors stood in our path and, her stocking ruffs at the ankles of her lolly legs, one of them was beckoning me in a way I resented. It was a show of authority, then a shove: 'Get a move on, don't loiter.'

'We're not,' and Celia's tone seemed to rile lolly legs who must have been champing at the bit to find fault. 'Where are your gloves? You wear them from church to dorm.' Celia had stuffed hers in a pocket.

'Stuff you,' Celia flung at her back, returning to me. 'YOU haven't done anything wrong.'

No. Though self-righteous and defiant, when I reached the green baize outer barrier and passed through to where I must knock on Mlle Durand's private door, I was quaking. A splodge of light hit the polished handle, and flashed with malevolence. I tapped. No reply. Again. Again with fractionally more pressure.

'Entrez.'

## 17

Tight-corseted, Mlle Mimi Durand of the stocky body, who'd shed her church-going box jacket, was a force to be reckoned with. Seniors might sniff that Paris clothes would look dowdy on her—no elegance, no hauteur—but those seniors were a crop of sour grapes to whom chic would remain a mystery all their lives. Should Mademoiselle's steely squint come to rest on any one of them, likely she'd strip them to the bone.

Twitching a bit, and unaware I was about to experience a kindness of sorts, I toed the rug in front of her desk. Lightly accented, her voice may have been, but never having addressed me directly, it was foreign.

'*Alors*. Who do I have here? And why?' She didn't raise her head. 'Speak up child.'

'Natasha Ross.'

'Why?'

'You ...' breath stung my lips. 'You sent for me, Mlle.'

'I did?' Still, she didn't raise her eyes from what was on her desk, where, either irritated or angry, she speared papers with a stiletto-sharp pen.

I waited. Finally, in a percussive beat of sound, she expanded her own question. 'And why is it that I sent for you Natasha Ross?'

I didn't know. Nor how to answer her as nervously I watched when she laid the stiletto aside, a poking finger of one hand spreading a bundle of papers.

'Aha, aha.'

What? What was about to happen when, with forbidding eyes, she came to focus on me?

'Sit down child.'

Where? I swung about. There was one easy chair where the mud-coloured cushions could have fashioned to her shape, a sofa half-covered in books, two uprights, and a cane-seated bentwood chair just inside the door.

'Natasha,' she said with an imperious gesture and tone, commanding me to draw up a stool. Alongside her, but not too close. I began to suck up all the oxygen in the room.

'Natasha. We no longer belong to a time when formal religion is universally accepted by every young girl. With this century's more progressive views, today we recognise differences.' Then, horror of horrors, she streamed into a flood of French! Was she translating for me when she continued? 'With God the foundation of the world, none are abandoned,' momentarily to frown down to what was a letter. A letter from my parents! 'Well?'

Miserable, lost, I mustn't cry. Or sinfully go berserk and giggle. Wasn't it Sunday, the Lord's day, when behaviour should be 'exemplary' according to the pious Mr. Whitehead; who'd had his say as he hit a fist in the air then expounded on 'sin'?

There must have been a streak of compassion in Mlle Mimi Durand.

Her lips curved into a smile, which sent me reeling with relief. Then slowly and understandably—with no further French—she explained that though I attended an Anglican school, it was my parents' wish that I be free of religious instruction. No scripture, no church attendance. Of course, church fetes, lantern-slide shows or similar activities within the parish were acceptable. Under no circumstances was I to be isolated from my fellow boarders.

My tongue broke through glued lips. 'Why?'

She gazed at me, then gave a pointed sigh. She was used to being sure. 'Clear beliefs and rituals do make for a less complex life at any age, nonetheless ...'

'Yes?'

'Your parents have taken the decision that when you're older, you yourself are to decide if and when you want the luxury of a religious creed.'

Through an open window, I heard a dog bark somewhere. 'How shall I know?'

Mlle reverted to French or, maybe, just slipped up. Or maybe to mollify her own convictions, knowing I couldn't understand: '*Je ne comprends pas les parents. Jamais*,' her voice an alien landscape of consonants and vowels.

CRUSHINGLY DISAPPOINTED WHEN it sunk in that for me there'd be no more Sunday theatre ... organ music, hymn-sing-alongs, St. Barnabas' sights and smells, and crazy ideas from Mr. Whitehead, I knew it wasn't possible to mount a challenge by raising my voice and speaking up for myself. How could they do this to me? Marcus and Nina! Cruel, spiteful, selfish; topped off with something new and fitting. Un-Christian. Only hours ago, under the vaulted roof of St. Barnabas, I was willing to let God have a share in my life. Who banned Him? My parents. Ordinary mortals.

With her instinct to support me, Celia was waiting under a spread of shade in the courtyard beside the horse trough, where probably the Duke of Windsor's trusty horse had drunk, the royal hand stroking the mane of the royal mount.

'What did she want?' She looped an arm through mine.

'Tell you soon. Later,' and Celia didn't press, instead she tugged me away from Corinne Bradley and her litter of pigs, their snouts twitching, trotters clicking on stone.

With Celia's dimpling and my mouth mobile, we were getting good at talking with our eyes, perfecting a trust between us against this lot led by Corinne Bradley. Scathingly, we renamed her The Corpse; we would have been thrilled to find her laid out on a marble slab. Danced on her grave.

'Come on,' said Celia, and we secluded ourselves behind the hedge we'd come to consider our territory, a stockade of newly planted shrubs to one side. Plumped down on the grass, sprawled, then legs to our chests, chin to knees, to reveal why I was summonsed to Mlle.

Her mouth dropped before she exploded. 'You lucky devil! Why couldn't that happen to me?' though of course I knew. 'You lucky devil.'

HARDLY! For a tiny segment of the human race, spinning off the world wasn't an option. Besides, another torment lurked in the wings. Hanzi Lazar.

Hanzi Lazar was lumpy, clumsy and she smelled. Celia and I were given to holding our noses against what we called her 'wrong smell'. Three years older, hers was a pretty enough face with big melting eyes —one fractionally topped by a bush of greasy hair held back by bobby pins. Her wrong smell was a sour body smell. Ugh! When my age, she'd come from somewhere called Budapest in somewhere in Europe called Hungary, which might as well have been Broome, Brisbane or Bourke to us.

With our small knowledge and wide ignorance, we knew she was officially labelled 'Hungarian', never reasoning that labels could attach to us or ours. Our few connections didn't help: Hungarian Goulash—a red stew—and someone's Hungarian Rhapsody—very difficult to play —shed no light. With maybe cracked if not broken English, it was rumoured that Hanzi was clever. She had a brother who was cleverer, her mother's knuckles were clustered with diamonds and her father wore a funny hat. What's more, the parcels she regularly received, when unwrapped from layers of grease paper, were the most luscious cakes ever baked. And greedily, we'd watch her slice them and divide them among her chosen few.

'Sunday after bloody Sunday?' Celia was aghast.

'Yes; 9.30 a.m. to bloody midday.'

It was impossible to pretend Hanzi Lazar wasn't there, and I, Natasha Ross, was the only girl in the school to be allied with her on Sunday mornings. Marooned in someone else's destiny!

Thrown off balance and unsure, I didn't know—couldn't know—if Hanzi Lazar had witnessed and suffered things, or what threads of her family may have snapped. The idea of a history for her never entered my head. Self-absorbed and ungenerous, my Sunday exclusion was corrosive as it ate into my life every week. To be lumped with smelly Hanzi—not knowing why—fanned my dislike of her. Years later, I came to feel ashamed—for no one leaves a homeland without compelling reasons—though in some layer of my consciousness, I've never forgiven my alignment with someone who stank.

Smell? It's a mystery. Who knows how we do it? But do we ever know when we're on the receiving end? To this day. I retain an acute sense of smell.

'Want to read my poem? Want a go at my violin? Want a slice of my almond torte?'

I shrugged.

'What then?'

Uncommunicative, I gave Hanzi my coldest stare. While mute, sometimes in my head I would try not to hate her. But I did.

SUNDAY WAS NOW MY 'UNFAVOURITE' day, and each Sunday night it was compulsory to write a letter home. Home! Having been wrenched away, banished from the familiar, I felt abysmal. Misunderstood, never to know if I was missed, nor why they had decided as they did. Moody and abysmal, I'd sit at my desk spearing the school-crested paper with my pen. Time ticked on. Natasha, Natasha Ross then N. Ross—flourishing the N or R—I practised my signature, underscored with a straight line. Tempted to compose a letter from Nina to me in my head, a sort of defiance settled on the ink of the nib. It was a complex fate to be a daughter, let alone a would-be friend, to a mother I'd never reach.

The big clock kept ticking on the wall, and time crept on. The block in my head solid like concrete. I glared at the pen, dipping and re-dipping it in the black blood of the ink.

'I hate it here. Hate it. Hate everything. Hate the awful muck we're forced to eat. Hate Kings. Hate the pig set. Hate Hanzi Lazar who smells. Hate ...'

Miss Button—for the obvious reason gigglingly referred to as Miss Bottom—was in charge tonight, supervising us from her desk. 'Finish up girls,' she yodelled.

I was ignorant that having finished my hating, then addressed the envelope, it must be handed in unsealed. Tongue out, on the point of licking the envelope before fisting it down, I glanced at Celia, who, eyes bulging, was shaking her head. That left me frozen with my tongue sticking out at Miss Bottom. The room went quiet, ominously quiet, except for a belch from Corinne Bradley. Horror of horrors—while not right now being made naked by the vile Corinne Bradley—nonetheless, I was exposed.

'Put your tongue back in your mouth, that's a good girl,' said Miss Button/Bottom while behind her the big clock struck.

What! With her titters and half-concealed laughs, to me she was insane. But with my tongue swollen to the size of an elephant's trunk and unreplaceable where it belonged, I might have grown a tail, horns, cloven feet, and a stained, unhealthy colour too. I knew Celia wouldn't laugh, even as someone sniggered: 'She's barking mad. Loopy in the head.'

Curtly, Celia swung about and hissed from her unrivalled word store.

Meanwhile, my tongue converted to elastic and retracted. 'Well done,' Miss Bottom's applause was a surprise, then overlooking my performance she turned to direct at Celia: 'There's nothing like a fertile imagination to get you through life, girls.' They all giggled, and I winced.

Trying to learn to think for myself, I had to revise what to write in future letters home, as if reporting from a different planet, on a different way of life. Mouth tight, I jumbled my hair. I only knew what I knew.

But with a vocabulary unequal to Celia's, on that first Sunday of many firsts, my education was extended by another previously unknown word. Censorship.

## 18

Considered old enough to be sent away from home, wouldn't it be reasonable to think we were old enough to be in charge of our own bowels? No. Stoicism expected of us, nevertheless with regularity we were reminded that Matron and Sick Bay were available if we were ill. Headaches, stomach aches, temperatures which soared or plunged, sore throats, blue-faced with coughing, these must be reported, but any pretence was frowned upon.

Fortitude was everything, but if and when something was diagnosed, malingering was out. 'Think well' was Matron's motto; my first matron, formidable with her shelf of breasts adorned with badges of proficiency, a starched veil softening features inherited from a father with a lantern jaw. And her eyes? Rapier sharp.

'Don't try to fool her,' Celia's sisters had warned. 'She's like a bloody hawk and she'll watch you swallow the elephant pills.'

Elephant pills? Before breakfast every Monday—no exceptions—we had to stand in line, our right hand cupped supporting the left to receive lozenge-shaped pills. Two each. There seemed to be a technique to get them down; only genuine gaggers were allowed a glass of water before, open-mouthed, we were inspected. Even a hollow tooth would have been useless.

Audaciously, I found my voice. 'I don't want them,' I said with no way to embed them in my palm. 'I don't want …' I began again before my mouth was sewn up in distaste.

Matron's expression was a shade of a smile; a list was consulted to confirm that I was 'new'. 'Think well,' she said. Then, behind in the waiting line, somebody grunted, 'Think smell,' and I gagged.

'You'll get used to it.' Matron's response was practised, but indignantly, somehow I gargled them down.

Elephant pills didn't save us from overindulging fruit. Within the school grounds there was an orchard enclosed by a post-and-rail fence. We hardly noticed the rows of bare winter trees with no trace of life, or the green buds in spring, but come puffs of white or pink blossom and a certain scent, we were alerted and knew there'd be fruit. Seasonally, year by year, when plums, peaches, and apricots dragged the branches down, and before they thumped off to rot, we boarders were let loose. Blue skies above were fractured by laden boughs and hot shadows as we bit through tight skins.

Acid-sweet, the first bite curled your tongue and, juice dribbling, what filled our mouths made for luscious dreams. Maybe for the first time, we were voluptuaries, sensualists, though with little supervision, our greed often led to aching tummies and wretchedness. Your body went its own way. Diarrhoea. Prissily referred to by our mobile-lipped elocution teacher as 'an embarrassing gastric distress'.

THOUGH I FELT ABANDONED, Easter came due. Not a compulsory exodus with some boarders being too far from home, but parents willing or able to collect us could do so for the Easter break.

Marcus wrote: 'Your mother hasn't been so well, sweetie, so you and me will be off to Bathurst for the Easter Races. Motorcycle races. What do you think?

What did I think? What a crazy question. I quelled the excitement and willed the days to pass.

Bathurst was a further seventy miles west, up and over the highest point of the Great Divide of the Blue Mountains. My father said he would pack a tent into his Chrysler, which ran at a top speed of sixty miles per hour. He'd attach canvas waterbags to the front and rear bumper bars. He'd also bought a portable ice box and we were to cook on a Primus stove, and I imagined our Primus panting. He'd certainly pack a tin-opener too, he said, and the saliva ran in my mouth as I tasted the glue of condensed milk.

Nina was not coming, and if I felt an obscure disappointment, I shook it free. Though not before I remembered how, with me, Nina, always took in a giant breath whenever we rumbled across a wooden bridge in the country. Marcus rubbished our reason why; we'd have enough breath to swim if the bridge collapsed. Yet tittering, Nina played along as we swapped grins.

'You lucky devil,' Celia squealed. She was off to a nearby parish, a sort of kinship placement, with Rector Chubb having trained with Rector Sale. Easter, with Christmas, as etched on her mind as the busiest times of a churchman's year: 'No fun,' she complained, heaving sighs, while, blissfully, I buzzed.

'Guess so,' I replied, never having seen myself as a lucky devil.

'You chose your father well,' Celia said, and while we didn't discuss mothers in depth, Celia's mother sounded manageable. Unfussed and unflappable, with one foot forever hovering at the poorhouse door, to me Celia's mother—fair-haired, and blue-eyed—appeared remarkable among the old, varnished yellow furniture of the rectory and second-hand things. Blinking away from a picture of Celia's mother to my mother, wariness could press down in a maze of loving and not loving. In and out of control, wasn't it a long and precarious quest to understand a mother; mine or anyone's.

But Easter was due.

Shouting and waving his arms like a windmill, in long strides Marcus crunched over the gravel of the drive. Then a smacking kiss and he was hugging me as I hung round his neck.

Then my father dumbfounded me. 'You're getting to look more and more like your mother.'

What! My preferred image of myself was fair-haired and blue-eyed, in total contrast to the real me. Somehow, from somewhere secretive, I would be renamed Deirdre. Why this fantasy? Why Deirdre? At least her face was pointed, resembling mine.

Near bursting with excitement, and walking backwards in front of him, I watched my father's Adam's apple jerk as he laughed. We bypassed Mrs. Jenkins' Sweet Shop for Con's Milk Bar with its marble tables and spindly iron chairs. Marcus ordered vanilla milkshakes with double scoops of ice cream. When half gone, my father put on a show of disapproval when I blew bubbles through the straw.

'Is that what they teach you, while here I am labouring under the impression that you're learning ladylike ways?' Then he eyed me oddly, wagged a finger, and sure enough quoted my mother. 'Natasha. Good manners are no burden to carry through life.'

I giggled, and he snorted. 'No, seriously,' he said, becoming serious and frowning. 'Your mother is right.' Then, as if somehow grinding this through a mill of a memory that was not my memory, hands framing his glass, a tic jumped under his right eye when he said, 'Your mother is an exceptional woman, and without her, my life would be meaningless.'

Swamped by a sense that this did not concern me, my words bled into each other. 'What does that mean?'

## 19

Tree tops along the highway glinted and between the gaps there could have been an endlessness of blue distanced mountains, valleys, air and sky. Climbing up from Mount Victoria, the Chrysler hiccupped and began to smoke. 'Come on you beast,' Marcus scowled and cajoled.

Seated beside him, something impelled me to heave up and turn to inspect the Chrysler's back seat. Not just smoke, flames licked the floorboard! Small flames, but flames. My composure fleeing, fumes blew in my face: 'Daddy!' I shouted.

'Hold it, hold it. Not now.'

'But !'

'What?'

'We're on fire. FIRE.' Did he hear? 'Daddy!'

'Hold it, sweetie. Just about at the top.'

'Daddy!'

He slipped into neutral and jammed on the brake. 'Made it,' and the rhythm of his breathing strengthened. 'Made it!' he said jubilantly, 'now hop out quick smart.'

Then out himself, panting a bit, my father grabbed our tartan rug, wrenched the rear door open and smothered the flames. Next, circling the car, he was banging his foot against the front then the rear tyres in an experimental sort of way.

The world churning, it was fantastic. There was no place on earth I could have loved more that Easter. Mount Panorama wound up from the outskirts of Bathurst. Mount Panorama: the racing circuit with its razor-steep inclines, blind corners, loops of bends, and straight stretches where daredevils powered two-wheelers, terrifyingly sped from point to point. Some places and the view of the track, Marcus informed me, were blocked by the cliff face and protruding rocks.

'Scary,' I said.

'Can be, yes,' he understated, not to divulge to me that there was little margin for error. Contestants built their courage with each passing lap on a roller-coaster track which swung from left to right, up then down. Mt. Panorama's air disturbed only to settle again.

There were no restrictions, we were allowed to camp anywhere, and hand in hand we chose the site to pitch our tent next to a scented gum; up a hill to the right, but well down the mountain and its last climb before the peak. Within sight of a cluster of stalls under khaki tarpaulins; one with boiling water for tea, another with meat pies on upturned butter boxes under a tree where magpies on the scavenge loomed. There was also a stall with posters, programmes and pennants displayed from a suitcase, a drinks stall with homemade lemonade, and lamingtons laid out on an oilskin tablecloth, netted under gauze against flies.

With a kind of brilliance to the daylight, later there was another brilliance; the blink of stars on the flattened face of the night sky.

If Marcus' passion for engines wasn't infectious, his enthusiasm was. There were crescendos of noise and with the best vantage points crowded, he placed us on the high side. 'The safe side,' he explained.

When a small boy in swamping shorts scrambled down a bank and was retrieved then whacked, my father approved. Race after race roused waves of emotions; tides of cheers and then an ebb of boos if a rider broke some rule.

The excitement and cumulative noise heightened. Pennants thrashed in supporters' hands and the official flag marshals mustered at dangerous bends. Speed blistered the air when the Nortons, BSAs, AJSs, and the Harley Davidson, bunched past us. Bent near-horizontal, one bike discharging smoke like a chimney, then came a screech of brakes and an explosion.

'Nothing bad's happened,' Marcus soothed me as I buried my head against him. And nothing had.

On his suggestion, it was time for lunch. Bread rolls and cheese nipped the lining of my mouth, then, as he sat knees apart, one cheek crumpled, he gave me a wink. 'How's about we skip down and get us some lamingtons,' he turned his wrists in the air. 'Like that?'

'Yeeees,' and balancing them, I watched a nearby woman stuff cotton wool in her ears. Yum. I licked a finger and picked up bits of chocolate as well as coconut that stuck to the paper bag.

Lap after lap, menacing, thrilling, and when someone struck up a conversation with Marcus about horsepower and braking zones, a boy about my age who'd been eyeing me off with a kind of listless reproach, asked: 'Want to see me chicken me chicken pox holes?'

I did, so he exhibited one cheek and one arm. 'Gee,' I was impressed before a girl, who was his sister, offered a game of catch, so we hopped about chasing a ball. A bigger sister claimed she could read the scratches on the bark of a nearby tree, but, sceptical, I didn't think she could.

With insects turning up, that night we joined a sing-song round a fire with its smoky smell of eucalyptus leaves. A thickset man came up the hill curved over a piano accordion, followed by his gangly son, whose dome of a forehead shone in the fire light. He pulled a mouth organ from his pocket, rubbed it the length of his thigh, and put it to his lips.

'I love a squeeze box,' a girlish woman clapped, 'and a harmonica. Gee, can you do one of me favourites? *You are my Sunshine?* Know it? Gee, good-oh. My only sunshine ... make me happy when skies are grey ... da-da-dumm ... please don't take my sunshine away ...'

The man and his son obliged, and soon, a couple was up on their feet, high-stepping on a flat patch of rough grass. Then another couple, then two young girls. My father hauled himself up and bowed.

'May I have the pleasure, miss?' I giggled to him, and I didn't know how.

'Time I taught you the steps,' and ... one-two-three, one-two-three ... we were bumping into a primitive waltz of slushing notes. And I smelled the crushed grass while, spiked by moonlight, stars pencilled silver dots on the vastness of the sky.

Later, with the air like velvet, before I sank into soundlessness and sleep, I swallowed hard when Marcus murmured: 'A pity your mother's not here.'

Did he catch and hold his breath? I understood little about the fragility of love, let alone how my father's life involved love and difficulty; his accommodations to circumstance. He was the firmest thing in my life.

Most times I liked what he said—and his silences—but I didn't want Nina here now. Then as I kissed him goodnight he kissed me back, briefly spreading his fingers over my cheeks. No, I didn't want Nina here, but groggy with sleep, neither did I never want her with us.

Another day. We sauntered down to the finishing line. Event after event was greeted with shouts and a few bitter oaths. Dismounted, these champions of speed and daring converted to ordinary men. Ordinary, everyday men with commitment and guts.

'Good on ya Bluey. Ya made it Max. Whoopee Bertie, Jack, Clem.'

'Yippee.' Tossing his hat in the air and whistling in admiration, Marcus applauded the winners, and equally applauded the riders who accepted lesser trophies with a wry dignity.

Seconds shaved from records, the performance of this or that machine would prompt a parade of affection between strangers, including me when, grey-haired, grey-eyed man with a fleshy nose, impulsively swung me off my feet. He giddied me around in a circle. 'You'll not forget this day, girlie. Bugger me! Young Jonesy outpaced the pack. Slithered ahead of that Stan Hopalong by inches to take a place among the champs.' Cigarette hanging from his lips, he squinted against the smoke. 'What do you think of that?'

Bewildered, my toes skimming the ground, then Marcus caught me. I was non-plussed. 'Okay?' my father asked.

I nodded.

'That was old Jonesy getting carried away. No harm done.' And cheerful old Jonesy, who looked ready for a repeat, stopped short.

'Didn't frighten you did I, girlie?' With eyes on me, he smacked his right fist into his left palm, grinned a bit and I saw he didn't have many teeth.

'No,' Marcus answered for me, and 'no,' I spoke up, kicked my shoes in the dust and maybe meant it. I managed a bit of a smile.

## 20

As near the school gates as rules allowed, Celia's arms sawed in welcome as she hopped from foot to foot. Then bent over, she was rocking, holding her stomach tight.

'What's wrong?'

'Hunger pains.'

'What?' I was full of sympathy; because don't we all know there's a human need to eat every so many hours. 'Didn't they feed you?'

'Not much.' Her eyes spoke volumes. 'Well, not enough,' and she related the joke of all time. Rector Chubb's big sermon about an indecently well-fed society. The longest one she'd ever been forced to sit through. More awful too, she had to endure it in the front pew.

We dodged around a bush breaking out in thin, yellow flowers. 'Poor you,' I commiserated, with Celia giggling. She paid him out, the pious prick. How? She told his kids—all boys—details of Prudence, her sister, and the fluffy pink handcuffs that Prudence considered good working tools.

'You didn't?'

'I did!'

'Come on,' I said. I had our Easter leftovers. Sao biscuits, peanuts, scones, oranges and a wedge of watermelon. Plus the surplus marshmallows toasted on the communal campfire after the sizzle of meat and burned chops, and black-jacketed potatoes gritty with butter and soot. Yippee! There was more: a square fruit cake and humbugs.

'Wow!' Mouth down, soon she was gnawing peanuts from a cupped hand.

Two of the pig people from Kings became positively cordial, their boiled-lolly voices arching. Snouts raised, whiskers twitching and while I encouraged Celia to eat up, I wasn't discouraging their overtures. 'You don't mean to give them anything do you?' Celia scowled.

I did. The watermelon was going mushy, and with luck it would make them sick. Queenly, I divided it. 'Don't suppose either of you want this?' I innocently asked, my expression bland, sure that they would. Sure too that each pig would try to snaffle the largest slice, I cut it unevenly. I was young, but not a total idiot. 'Help yourselves,' I said in a mix of right and wrong and exquisite satisfaction.

Unplanned, right or wrong led me to put four humbugs aside for Hanzi Lazar. Why? A double-dyed hypocrite? She DID smell and we'd never be friends even if she didn't. Four, no, I counted out three. With grounds for a legitimate exchange three were enough, but with her tortes and strudels, I suspected she'd not deign to eat a slice of my cake, which tomorrow Celia and I would attack.

LEFT WITH LITTLE UNSTRUCTURED TIME, the rhythm of our lives was calculated by what other people—adults—decided. Some girls were able to accept their transition from home to school with apparent ease. I didn't number among them, though I suppose I adapted better than the real 'miseries'. One real and continuing 'misery' was Madelaine Brown. Maybe the end product of generational doom—or something— she was the poor labelled thing on our first departure from Central Station. Remembering the sight of her that day at least made me grateful that Marcus and Nina hadn't just parcelled me up, tagged me, and then indifferently despatched me by train.

Madelaine Brown; short, skinny, pale hair, pale skin, pale eyes which swam behind glasses, and easily given to tears, she was every bully's target. She had no natural defences, but if there was something of a mix-up when she was initially assembled, a real surprise was her bulldog chin.

If she'd failed to empathise and find at least one friend or fellow sufferer, she'd not failed to find enemies. Not that Madelaine sought them out, but any subtle interaction seemed to forever elude her. Not that Madelaine Brown had a monopoly on helplessness. Maybe a helpless air of sorts hung about smelly Hanzi Lazar too, though she had the ability to fight it, principally with strudels and tortes. Besides, Hanzi was a nosey parker, always on the prowl for scraps of information to use to her advantage.

Not so Madelaine Brown, who seemed a likely candidate for falling off the edge of the world, which, tragically, later she did. But for now, she wobbled along and, very occasionally, a thought about her like a bead threaded on a string messed in my head. No saint, and stifling exasperation and irritation, I wanted her to stand up against the taunts and injustices that came her way. She never did.

What made the bullies jab her in the ribs, trip her up, wheedle answers from her in class, copy from her books, and swaggeringly help themselves to things like her talc and her soap? However quick or bird-like she moved, all she seemed to do was turn the other cheek, which metaphorically was slapped.

'You should,' I began on the Saturday the pig people learned that for some undivulged reason, Madelaine had double pocket money. Their concern was disgusting, and after they tricked her into generosity, in all probability they'd offer her back the wrappers from her Cadbury or Nestlé bars and make a show of stuffing them in her pockets. Or buy packets of sticky cigarettes with pink tips and puff sugary smoke in her face.

'You should,' I started again, but did blank-faced Madelaine Brown pretend not to hear? 'You should,' I said a third time, before a third rebuff. So, with a huffy sigh, I changed tactics. 'Listen, Madelaine,' and held out my hand to explain that I'd keep her money for her, which should help.

Whether or not she mistook my motive, with her eyes lowered she elbowed me away. This made me mad and not about to defend myself, nastily I spat out: 'Suit yourself. No one else is going to help YOU.'

I missed her whimpered reply, turned my back, strode off and felt rotten. Yet Celia's advice was arrow-straight. 'You bloody well can't help some people.'

My senses sharpened. Madelaine Brown belonged to our tight and all-too-often treacherous world, the same as the rest of us. Celia may have been half-joking, but it wasn't funny. Ours WAS a tight and all-too-often treacherous world, with its dislocations and the natural-unnatural laws to which our parents abandoned us. Well—I ran through my head—my parents had abandoned me and with this sense of injury, I felt fully entitled to want them unhappy forever, or at least for a while.

## 21

I have no reason to tell the past as it wasn't. Yet when I visit there, do I revise facts? The truth? Is there an imagined as well as an authentic me, who assumed that how I looked, the way I saw the world and the way I was seen, was central to who I was? Who I am today? Snagged by kaleidoscopic glimpses, however sharp, these memories can be accompanied by distress. Freeze-frames of recollections which prove valueless. Inhabiting the past is strange; random memories are a slurry of the good and not so good.

My mood was troubled on the day we were instructed to write a composition in class titled 'What I would do to make someone happy'. I considered and then dismissed Madelaine Brown. Who—apart from me—did I want to make happy? My chest rose and fell. What made for 'happy' anyway? Teeth like bricks grinning between happy lips? Enough chocolates to make you sick? And why did grown-ups lie, declaring this, that or some other thing made you happy? Such as new shoes for a present when what you dearly wanted was a little cat.

What would I do to make someone happy? My first decision had to be someone. Who? Marcus? No; his life was the excitement of Nina and he was happy whenever he saw me, even as I wanted more of him.

Insistent with his: 'There are great times and wonders galore ahead for my daughter.' I believed my father was happy.

Nina?

My grandmother, Hannah Ross? My heart hardened. I couldn't imagine her dying but she'd had centuries to be happy. Besides—I pictured her face with its smile of happy malice—she had her favourite: my cousin, Marina. Marina the perfect.

Nina?

Gus? Bones and a kennel kept him happy.

Nina?

Celia? Sunk in talk, we could thrash anything out. Anyway, our connections didn't solely depend on words.

Nina?

Shrill, unfunny Miss Lamble, with her mouthful of jumbled teeth, broke into the silence where, heads down, the rest of the class scratched away. 'Natasha', she addressed me and it sounded like nails dragging over tin. 'Why are we the only little genius not at work?'

'I ...I ...' Our eyes met and chill pricked the length of my spine while my face burned.

'Get cracking.' Even her snort was shrill. 'Though I expect the result will prove more rambling than riveting.' This from the creature who on my first report card was to record: 'Natasha has a raw intelligence.'

Bollocks! (A good Celia word.)

I don't believe I ached with a need to be clever, but despising Miss Lamble, my mouth slitted to a razor line. Some teachers pretended to like us, they made a show of it; but not her, at the outset she was nasty with: 'See if your sentences can contain thoughts.' I'd fix her; drag words into pictures; my sort of composition. She'd see.

Nina! I refused to let my heart seize up. What to do to make Nina happy? What? Rein in loose fragments? Conjure away Nina's undertow of melancholy.

Free of the classroom and the vile Miss Lamble, timetables, corridors and bells, I'd transport us—my mother and me—back in time. Far back to an early summer, to life before boarding school. I was going to make Nina happy in my thoughts. Infused by warmth, a near-perfect day is about to evolve in my mind.

∼

Having dressed me, Nina pulls on a white skirt and blue blouse, and shakes out her hair. Next hats, sweaters, and all the picnic stuff are laid on the kitchen table alongside the basket of food and the fig jam left over from breakfast, which properly belongs on the shelf with its ranged canisters: Tea, Coffee, Sugar, Rice, Flour. The texture of our lives that day expands to a river bank which shelves the water, and sunlight streams in diagonally through the gums.

Marcus hefts me to his waist, carries me to the car and cranks his Chrysler to spluttering action, and, yippee, we're off.

Arrived, Marcus, his tongue thrust under lower lip, chooses the spot, then Nina spreads a tartan rug. Happy-go-lucky, Marcus dangles a line in the river, fish no more than ripples on the surface of glass. Content, Nina reads before we eat. Following what is widely accepted to be common sense, an hour will elapse before we swim in order to digest the food and avoid stomach cramps. Or worse; sink like a stone, which Marcus pooh-poohs, Nina smiles a disarming smile. My smocked play-suit is exchanged for my small swimsuit—knitted by Maggie, our family friend. Marcus pumps air into the inner tube of a tyre. Pink bonnet hugging my head, strapped into this rubber coracle, Moses-like, I'm cast onto the water squealing in shock when swirls of it splash up. Attached by a rope to my father's wrist when he and Nina stroll hand in hand along the bank, then later attached to his ankle as he floats beside me, Nina again engrossed in her book. Marcus the porpoise, sleek as he dives, resurfaces and spouts bubbles.

There is a buzz of insects in tall grass and birds call, their wings whipping the air like silk. And the world is suspended on the edge of something that has to be well-being, never to be shaken off. Happiness. 'Nina,' a voice begins ...

∼

Then another voice cuts through discordantly. 'Pens down!

In disbelief, my stomach converted to a jangle of springs. Elbows clamped to my ribs, I could have been fighting pain.

'Pens down.' Shrill, unfunny Miss Lamble peered over her pads of flesh and, forcing my head up, I stared at her mouth of jumbled teeth. 'Pens down.'

Pens down! With an injured expression, I then stared out the window. Briefly. Who'd dare disobey her? Not me.

## 22

Time passed. As it does. Rhythms of existence. But how to reconcile who I was and where? To a degree, I suppose I was reconciling with the child I was away from home, and the first term passed. Holidays due, I dreamt up a scheme that I continued to implement for years: routinely through the front door before wandering from room to room to reassure myself I was really home. Like telling a private alphabet; B unquestionably to follow A. But on that first return, what niggled was how to reshape myself as a daughter; particularly my mother's daughter. Devoted to privacy, a puzzling presence, Nina was my private jigsaw, even as it was impossible to imagine life without her. Love oddly thriving in neglect?

Something about her was always able to brighten my life, and dismay or unnerve me too, in a kind of jump-for-joy or sit-on-your-hands sort of way. 'Yes,' she'd say suddenly, then just as suddenly 'No.' If near, Marcus would wink and ruffle my hair. Where was the primal connection between my mother and me? Someone who should have been close, yet at the same time was far away. Did Nina expect too much or too little of me?

Never expecting too much or too little of me was Gus. We spent lots of time together, which suited us both. According to my green-bound series of The Children's Encyclopedia—Nos.1 to 6 with spines stamped in gold—around the world, four hundred and fifty breeds of dog were descended from the wolf. But with Gus's shortened legs, stumpy tail and ear-set, this heritage was doubtful. Not that I'd argue with The Children's Encyclopedia, which also stated as fact that 14,000 years ago man was hunting with dogs. Gus with his yaps didn't walk, but maniacally waggled across any space to reach me—we connected. With five senses and his luminous eyes, he could be trusted never to divulge secrets, blame or scold. Gus accepted me.

With one index finger circled to a thumb, an enamel dish and a bar of Sunlight soap, a favourite game was blowing bubbles. Me, eyebrows clenched and blowing the bubbles, Gus, teeth bared, up on his hind legs as he snatched at them. Familiar games, then on my first evening home, Marcus introduced a new ritual. Their jazz records a background from the room given over to bookshelves from floor to ceiling, pre-dinner he and Nina drank sherry poured from a crystal decanter; cocktails on special occasions.

About to clink their stemmed glasses, a tumbler of lemonade was handed to me. Marcus proposed that in time to come, there'd be sherry for all three of us. I'd sniffed it—disgusting—and with rolling eyes, I was convinced it must taste like pale ink. Awful.

'Alcohol is civilised. In moderation.' Sherry was alcohol and looking to the future it seemed he believed it common sense that his daughter sip it first in the safety of her home. In my head, the only thing that recommended sherry was that it came with bowls of nuts and cheese biscuits, but, smiling at Nina and raising his glass, I saw what I'd witnessed often before; my parents knitted close in a private joke.

Home and parents. Like a legend they take on a fabled role in a child's life. I remember the sun was strong on the front of the house at the end of the drive. Deep verandahs and mossy-bricked side paths. A garden with frothing climbers, vines, the trees, and muddles of flower beds. Indoors, Mavis, with her chapped hands, came to wash or iron or dust or polish or whatever was needed. Who hummed while she worked.

And MY room. For ME. Exclusively MINE. Or so I believed.

Unsuspecting that this might not be the ongoing way of my world.

My parents' lives of visitors, friends and their children were acceptable, okay. Hide and seek the favourite with us kids, then chasings which had us red-faced and sticky-haired.

'Slow down,' one father, Mr. Proctor, caught me up as I rounded a corner, thudding into his jelly belly. Regulars, they were neighbours with a daughter named Kate. His front teeth gone brown from cigarettes, Mr. Proctor had a wife whose make-up turned her cheeks mud-pink above a sallow neck. 'Slow down, we don't want you snapping an ankle, do we?'

'What?' I said with the pack on my heels, Gus in a frenzy and Kate ahead. 'Slow down, we don't want you snapping an ankle. Don't forget you're to be bundled back off to school next week.'

I hated him and his marshmallow voice. Who was he to remind me —as if I had two heads—that I didn't know where I belonged? He reinforced my sense of the impermanence of home. Mad, I wanted Gus to bite him, rip his trousers and tear through to bone, with blood to surge down his leg like treacle and fill his shoes.

Where did I belong? For sixteen days with my parents? At their breakfasts, lunches, dinners, parties, week-night radio and weekend tennis? With Nina at her piano, the door ajar, or was it half-shut? Safe in rooms, where each year my height was recorded on the broom cupboard door at the end of the hall? But didn't holiday slabs of days slide too quickly to holiday nights, when Marcus would piggy-back me to bed and tuck me in after a phantom kiss from my mother, who, with faraway eyes raised her head from a book?

Books were where she liked to be. They were all-important to her, filled with their worlds and words from which I was barred. Years later, it occurred to me that talks she and I might have had together would have been conducted with a book between. No, I didn't dwell on the future, but did suppose that with my mother nearing thirty—which meant old—maybe it wasn't compulsory to strain for a common thread.

Instead, I began to sink into the worlds that lay in books too. Reading made it easy to move out of my own skin and jump into other skins and other lives.

One bewildering world I came upon was the world of adoption. Here, in a non-traditional family tie-up was Lucy Violet. Eight years old like me, blue eyed, fair Lucy Violet who, with the cards her genes dealt her, lived among a swarthy-skinned lot. It was as clear as day that she didn't belong so, reading 'adopted', then figuring out what it meant, Lucy Violet took on another dimension.

Days eaten up, holidays flying, Kate Proctor and I were to spend the last day together. In her house, with net curtains and buttoned Chesterfields squarely set on a brown carpet, and the Proctor rooms all military neat—something monumental was revealed.

'I'm Kate with a K, but,' her voice dropped, and eyes hard on me, she stopped short, biting bits off a thumbnail with small, feral-like teeth.

'What?'

Slowly, she continued, '... but to myself, I'm Cate with a C,' Polite in her house, I waited for the rest, bracing my toes in sandals. '... after my real mother.'

'What?' I asked again, and staring at Kate I saw her mother, minus the mud-pink make-up.

'I'm adopted.'

I slitted mine and shot her a worried look. I had no answer, so I tightened my lips. Lucy Violet bore no resemblance to Mrs. Lucy Violet.

Which had to make Lucy Violet truly adopted, while I'd overheard Kate's father claim that Kate and her mother were two peas in a pod. Out of my depth, all I could do was sit, zombie-like, while, from its cage outside came the scratchy-throated shout of the Proctor's parrot who gnawed at its feathers. It was bald down one side.

'But, but you look like your ... Mrs. Proctor.'

Lolling back in a chair in her pink bedroom, with its pink dressing table and ruffled pink skirt, Kate, or Cate, had a pat, if slippery, reply. 'Everyone gets to look like someone they live with.'

Did they? That's not right? Is it? Wanting details which would add up to real evidence, didn't there have to be at least one sign to prove you were adopted?

Kate's eyes were bright, her lashes spiky. Engulfed in the world of Kate's house with all its ordinary things: beds, tables and chairs, I jumped in shock when Kate's mother—or her maybe-mother—called us for cheese sandwiches and a strawberry milkshake with strawberries picked from her strawberry patch. There were also biscuits for later, cooling on a wire rack. Lunch may have interrupted 'adoption' talk, but I was determined; I wanted something confirmed.

'Come on,' Kate ordered, her lips frothy from the milkshake and I dragged the back of my hand across mine. From the kitchen, we headed to her father's study for paper or cardboard to make little boxes for her collection of china cats. Centred on Mr. Proctor's desk, among neat letters, pencils and rubber bands, was a big notebook. Blocked in large letters, the cover declared the single word: THINK.

Adoption? Was it a word that belonged with a fanciful need?

Shouldn't Mrs. Proctor be stony and cold towards Cate; like Mrs. Lucy Violet? Who, jealous of Lucy Violet, having been daringly rescued from terrible circumstances by Mr. Lucy Violet, was brought to the thatched cottage and his swarthy-skinned tribe. Then adopted, with Mrs. Lucy Violet never keen. Mrs. Lucy Violet had a potato face and stringy hair.

With no likeness to Nina, suddenly—outrageously—the thought struck me. Mouth open, I shut it and steeled myself. 'Kate. When did they tell? That you were adopted?'

She wheeled to face me, arms folded across her chest with its little bumps. 'Nobody told,' she came back at me, refusing to be drawn on details. 'I just knew.'

What! A private bomb exploded in my mind. Adopted? To be adopted you had to be chosen. Positively wanted, and Mr. Lucy Violet must have wanted Lucy Violet despite the massive trouble that caused.

Was I adopted? Living the life of an imposter? Leaking into my head, Cate/Kate's words refused to evaporate. So, barometer-like, the question rose and fell until, holidays over, Term Two was due to begin, with thicker things for winter packed in my trunk.

Was I adopted? Hands damp, they felt boneless when I tried to ask Nina. But my lips went rigid. Instead, swallowing a sort of dread, I collected 'adopted' in my mouth like an egg for Marcus, but it settled iron hard. What prevented me from stuttering out three words? Why did I fail?

Cate said she just knew. Kate, however, was a different kettle of fish when she declared that never, never, never had she divulged her secret to anyone but me. Was this to forge—or force—a lifelong link with Cate? Or no more than this holiday association with Kate?

Either way, would it matter? What mattered was that soon I'd be in my other world. Gone from home. And MY room; a room that was MINE. Only for ME.

HOWEVER, 'in the fullness of time'—a ripe but telling cliché—I, Natasha Ross, was in for a monumental shock.

## 23

'She seems sad,' I overheard my father murmur under his breath into our telephone attached to our wall with its cream-coloured, bumpy wallpaper of acanthus leaves. My last evening and dinner was to be roast chicken and caramel pie; chicken a treat back then.

Sad? Who was he telling this to? And why? My breath tightened. Was he talking about me? If this was so, I was resentful despite my fever of love for him.

'Who was that?' I dared ask when he hung up after buzz-saw intensity among his closing words. In a perverse way, I suppose I wanted him to be talking about me whatever he said; hankering to be the centre of his world, deposing my mother.

'Wouldn't you like to know, snoopy-ears?'

Yes I would 'Yes,' I said.

'Anything else?' he joked, and made to roll up his shirt sleeves, flexing his muscles and fisting his hands.

Yes, there was. I pursed my lips, but it felt more of a pout. Adoption. Torn between semi-courage and full-on cowardice, my heart looped. The thought of adoption ballooning to the size of a melon in my head,

## A Secret Grief

but somehow I found it impossible to bring it out in the open and say it aloud.

Marcus planted his feet, raised one eyebrow, to mock-seriously repeat: 'Anything else?'

'Why must I go back to school?'

There was no compromise, no delay. 'Baby,' was all he said as he looked down at me before he pulled me close.

'Will you cry?' I sniffed out and his eyes looked hot and sharp. 'Will you?' and he nodded. 'Will my mother?'

'Your mother,' he began, and there was emphasis on 'mother' as it threatened to become an unmanageable word.

I rushed on. 'Gus will.'

'Gus will?'

'Cry.' He shook his head. 'He will, he will,' I was shouting. 'I teached him.'

'Taught,' my father corrected and might have been Nina. It wasn't fair, my parents were one against the world. Against me; Marcus, his heart roped and bound and, out of control, I pounded his chest. No one was to be trusted and struggling to pull away, he bumped me to his ribs and held me there.

'We both love you. Both, do you hear? Very much,' Marcus was saying, giving each word weight. But I didn't understand, I wouldn't. Love was one of a huge number of emotions which eluded me at eight.

He began smoothing my hair into a helmet, his tone far from forecasting anything unusual or any surprise, when he said: 'What is, and what we think ought to be, can be different. Believe me, they can,' and I felt the long purr of his sigh. 'Maybe you have to learn this early,' then a pause, 'and maybe that's not such a bad thing.' I sagged against him, limp in the air squashed between us, before Gus' claws were clicking on the floor, closer, his tongue licking my dangling hand.

'Natasha, listen carefully' my father paused. 'You are special to your mother.'

Special! Wasn't that a word that meant many things?

Years later, I read that psychological theories are rarely kind to a mother. If too involved with her child—whatever that means—she was considered smothering, devouring and overpowering. If uninvolved with her child, she was aloof, rejecting and cold. Where did this leave me? Was Nina too often occupying herself with the grief of her disappointment in herself and/or her disconnection with me, her child?

On a morning during those first holidays, when Maggie came to visit my mother for one of their regular chats, they'd settled together over coffee and an iced almond log. They made an odd pair, quaint in their differences—one ritualising trivialities, one given to retiring to her tower, brooding on the condition of being human—peacock-bright or flattened grey.

Maggie somehow always astonished me. She'd gasp at how I'd grown as if growth wasn't on my agenda, and tended to cover her gasps with little laughs or a cough. So I didn't hang about, and licking the iced slice of cake, went off on one of my snoops among my mother's things. What did I expect to discover in my parents' bedroom? Where—uninvited—I never entered day or night? Well, not when there was the chance of being caught.

Rifling through her dresses with the scent of her, pawing sleeves and skirts, I yanked one down. Slippery silk and midnight blue, I tugged everything off and pulled it over my head, letting it shiver down the length of my knobbly spine, smoothing it over my non-hips. Next, I hitched up the skirt and shuffled to one of the mirrors of their twin wardrobes. Feeling everything and nothing centred on me, I inspected myself. In my mother's dress, was I clinging to an idea of her elsewhere? Gone, unlikely to return? Yet it was me who felt fragile, non-existent and swamped in glass-like blue silk and shadows despite the sun which shone outside. Flooded by a nameless fear, I didn't want Nina gone, yet was I wicked? An evil child interfering with something I didn't begin to understand? What to do?

With courage, early the following morning I crept out of my bed. Did I hear Marcus call, sleepy-voiced, while tiptoeing, I inched the length of the hall? Silently, I managed to open the glass door of the grandfather clock which had stood there all my life. Quaking with fear, I turned the ornate key—then stopped the hands of the clock.

With the need to keep my mother safe, disabling the clock had to be a way to challenge time.

## 24

I had no choice. My life must be disassembled, reassembled, three times a year when each new term began and ended. Three times a year!

Autumn thinned into winter with the clackety, passing miles, and with my forehead pressed to the train window staring out as cold colours and contours merged, I sobbed. How many years of seasons lay ahead? But more immediately, a bag of roasted peanuts lay in my lap and my education to date taught me to guard it. The peanuts smelled good, but Celia wasn't with me. She was to arrive a day late, which meant 24 hours would feel like a month in my other place of codes and puzzles that wasn't home.

Beside me, Faith Griffith, who we liked a bit, with a watchful kind of reserve had her nose in a book. Tempted to offer her a handful, I settled for caution instead. Any nosey senior would spread the word and my bag be snatched away while my parents, given to encouraging me to share, wouldn't know the half of it. Still on the edge of offering Faith Griffith, with no warning and stiffening, fractionally she moved my way.

What?

Two of the pig people were jostling towards us along the aisle, and, on guard, I longed to be invisible.

We were in luck, they swished on, Corinne Bradley's equally awful cousin talking big with a voice like a rusty hinge: 'I'm thirteen and I've smoked hundreds of ciggies'

Faith Griffith widened her eyes to tell her book and me: 'Wish they'd choked you.'

Back in Kings, my trunk was unpacked minus the six regulation woollen singlets marked with my name below 'Virgin wool' labels, my heart skipped. Nina's may be an obstinate, confusing love, but she must care; she didn't want me with itchy armpits. I went weak-kneed.

Winter term. The rooms whistled with cold; this was supposedly healthy for growing girls. Fortitude, near to stoicism, was expected of us. We were hardly junior Scotts of the Antarctic, but battling the cold was a must, our legs bicycling icy sheets at night for wheels of warmth, and blankets pulled up over our ears. The landscape was raw with freezing air which took hours to seep away. We had no choice, we were set to toughen up, ragged coughs or not, including poor Madelaine Brown, for whom the ordinary trials of life were forbidding enough.

Not that we didn't question a staffroom where a continuous fire burned. On the afternoons when Celia and I hovered by its part-open door to sniff up escaping heat along with muffled conversations, we witnessed Miss Grenfell's arm in blue serge alongside Miss Dinell's in cable-knitted mauve and Miss Maloney's in green tweed all reaching out. Reaching out for what?

Devious, we strained to hear and heard that 'what' was a hot toddy and, again conversant with the ways of the world, Celia whooped: 'Rum and milk'. A means by which her father observed fired up the cockles of his heart. There were apparent side effects. Miss Faithfull's nose dripped in class like a stalactite. Miss Dinell's was beacon red and Miss Maloney's twitched like a whiskered cat. Additionally, their voices full of hot toast and butter, it seemed THEY had their survival tricks; probably learned as a result of what they themselves were subjected to as 'gels'.

Other words we overheard were: 'Poor little creatures. Poor dears.'

Did this mean us? Maybe; but one malcontent of a matron, who lumbered herself with an idiot husband, branded us 'privileged' and 'the suffering rich' when six seniors went down with food poisoning.

Poor little creatures! Poor dears! Those of us who learned piano and had to practise before breakfast surely qualified. Real misfortune was to be rostered first; 6am. Not good. It was dark as we fumbled into clothes, and dark as we shuffled along corridors to music rooms where you even felt the cold on your teeth. Each morning was alike but unlike, yet there was one certainty: our fingers were as bloodless as dead fish. Cold, cold, cold.

Too clumsy to attack major and minor scales, arpeggios, little studies, gavottes and minuets, a solution had been devised. Hot water. Ouch and bloody hell! Casually inflicted cruelty into which we must plunge our dead fish in order to kick-start circulation. So, our fingers bloomed purple and we nursed chilblains through June to the end of August in the name of art. And understandably, one legacy of this barbarism left numbers of us loathing Cherny and Mozart, Bartok and Liszt. Beethoven's *Für Elise* we retitled fuck Elise ... repeating it with a sort of magic. A them-against-us magic, which roused more than a casual interest in us; a sense of place in a world invaded by adults where we were powerless against their domination.

'Natasha, let the melody wander out of your hands,' Miss Frampton instructed with tedious repetition. Though memorably, later she proposed that I learn the emotion as well as the notes. But with amazing control, I choked back: 'Fuck you too Frampton' and with a devoted flourish, gave fuck Elise my best performance.

Fuck! I held it in my mouth and savoured it. I had no idea what it meant despite the dubious enlightenment of dormitory talk. I suppose even the obscene Corinne Bradley had it wrong.

And yippee, Corinne Bradley had returned with a mouthful of teeth caged in a network of wires. This not only made her more repulsive but on the receiving end of some apt names; 'Metal mush' appealed to me. Unable to shut her mouth, there was more; in addition, her forehead AND chin were pot-holed with acne. Yippee; a sort of justice was metered out after all.

'You're looking good,' I said to myself with satisfying disdain as I inspected her when leaning into the door frame, arms folded.

However, Faith Griffith—pretty when she smiled with small and perfect teeth—ventured: 'Some steel trap you've brought back this term,' defying Corrinne Bradley's steely eyes.

Our spirits soared and gradually as we observed her to be a spunk of a loner, we began to admit Faith as a friend. A friend, but as yet with limited knowledge of her. A friend-on-trial after Celia related how one of her sisters had befriended a lunatic who turned out to be an escapee from an asylum. One who appeared normal and had long ginger hair plaited over her head like a crown, and she was named June.

'What happened to her? June?' Celia didn't know, so we invented a life for her; she was happy in a garden behind a wired fence. Where—no pumpkin, spinach etc.—she grew flowers.

I suppose at a subconscious level, we realised that by facing up to the pig people, Faith was neither naïve nor spectacularly stupid. Not just intrepid, but quietly brave. How brave we came to discover because Faith was someone who'd had to learn to spit in the eye of fate. Who soon, like me, goggled at the extent of Celia's knowledge.

'Where d'you learn it?' Faith questioned, with the three of us—faces tilted to the sun, eyes closed—secluded behind the squared-off hedge of plaited leaves that we considered our territory. Where regularly we sank into talk as well as long silences. Almost out of bounds, with the 'I only count the happy hours' sundial barely in sight, we could hear the yodelling rooster and the clucking chooks who laid the eggs we faced on our plates, underdone, overdone, and occasionally just right.

'Where?' Faith asked again, while Celia sucked her teeth and smiled in a pleased way.

Celia sat up, flicking at ants. 'I listen lots.'

I thought I listened lots. 'Who to?' I asked, feeling the flat of my back against the ground and rolling over on my front.

Peering over a raised elbow, Faith was more direct. 'You mean you eavesdrop? Snoop?'

I reckoned Celia might bristle, but she giggled instead. 'Where?' 'Everywhere. Home.'

Home! Snapping my eyes into the glare, I watched a flock of birds fly over, rippling into a V.

A week later, again in our territory, unplanned we must have encouraged Faith to open up a corner of herself to us. The way Celia and I had cautiously opened up dreads and dreams for the other to see.

'My mother,' her voice breathy, 'and my father are dead.' She stopped as abruptly as she started, and on such an ordinary afternoon, were Faith's words measured by heartbeats? From a heart loaded with lead?

Mine somersaulted. Her mother! Her father! I couldn't focus; it seemed as if Faith was wobbling away along a wavering track. I couldn't follow her, and if our territory began to shrink, the sky above seemed to expand. Pulses of a breeze blew up and my cheeks felt cold in tracks where the tears ran down. I gulped. Together with Celia, it was important for us to bring her back.

At last, in a gurgle, Celia managed to ask for us both: 'Is there somebody who looks after you?'

Faith came back, lifting her eyes to me then Celia, with a question: 'Sometimes, can I talk about this if I want?'

We were nodding as if our heads might come off, the three of us together again.

Was there somebody who looked after her? Yes. There was Sarah, her mother's sister and Sarah's new husband, Neal, who loved her too. Her aunt and guardian-by-law, Sarah, undeterred, wanted to see things made better for Faith, to guide her as well as cherish her. Awful things couldn't be changed and couldn't be understood but never was Faith to believe that she had done something wrong herself. SHE HAD NOT.

Sarah had explained that children could blame themselves for a tragedy. Wrongly. And when the going got hard, as Sarah said everyone must expect at times, Faith was not to give in. Sarah knew that the future was do-able and bright. With Neal, she wanted Faith's life to be right; as right as they could make it. Like many grown-ups. Sarah had long-range plans.

Additionally there was Faith's Great Aunt Billie; a great aunt and her old-as-Methuselah husband, Rudolph Marshall. Who, with a sense of entitlement, liked to be called Great Rudi due to his age.

'Faith?'

Faith answered our unspoken questions. She was four when her parents died. Staying with Sarah for an extended weekend for four nights and three days, her parents were guests at a country wedding on the tablelands. On the return trip, near to home, a mist came down: dense, unseasonable and lethal. The accident happened at a level crossing. She'd helped her mother wrap up the wedding present—a crystal wine jug—in layers of tissue paper before putting it in a silver box.

GREAT AUNT BILLIE: her sparse hair was dyed mahogany-brown. Swept back from her face where her skin was corrugated by age, she was stern-looking only till she beamed with pleasure at the sight of Faith. Given to short laughs, she'd extend her liver-spotted hands.

Great Rudi, blandly handsome still, kept no plans on hold though he looked old enough to die. His answer to a question—any question—came in so many strung-out sentences that we'd lose the thread.

Built by convicts, 'Clifton', their rambling stone house, was huge and from its crenelated watch tower, the grey-green-blue distances were too vast to take in all at once. What we did take in was that, long ago, any convict desperate enough to make a run for freedom, if seen from the watch tower but not brought back, stood a slim chance of survival.

Smoke could be spotted from the tower warning that fire might roar up from below, advance on the house and, like binoculars, Celia held hands to her eyes. Set in its grounds, beyond flower beds then a kitchen garden with vegetables and strawberries in netted beds, a sea of grass waved before the tracks petered out into bracken and crops of rocks, plunging into valleys, sheer-sided gorges, waterfalls and hidden creeks.

Further up the mountains from our school, Clifton had its own siding and private platform built to accommodate visiting dignitaries and State officials when the railway was pushed up and through to the Great Western Plains. There was the main entrance, the tradesmen's entrance, servants' rooms, a harness room, a sewing room, bathrooms with the baths on brass claws, and mouth-wateringly the kitchen had the smell of baking cakes and shelved pantries to store Vacola jars of bottled fruit. There was also a garden room, a music room, and there was even a room where a telescope was rigged up to probe the night sky.

What Celia and I found scary about 'Clifton' didn't frighten Faith, who, after we guzzled lemonade, led us on a tour. With the windows hung with layers of curtains—velvet, or something stiff, then net—the house seemed dark, as if the lights were only on outside. Pleased to be asked to lunch, but not to sleep, we liked Aunt Billie—Mrs. Marshall—while her cook guessed what we liked to eat. There was even a girl to offer 'seconds' when Aunt Billie tinkled a china bell.

Once, memorably, with me not keen on marmalade pudding, Mrs. Marshall had raspberries brought in and put in my place. The huge table was set with silver, sugar casters, and crystal sauce bottles dressed in crochet, with drawstrings round the glass necks!

Invited during term time, this could be followed by a drought lasting months when, apart from a skeleton staff, the house was closed. Aunt Billie and Great Rudi crossed the world to travel 'home'. 'Home' was England; the map of the world still quite pink.

Encouraged to poke about, wandering beyond the house was thick with warnings. Repeated warnings. About sheds, outbuildings, yards with white-washed posts where loops of clothes and sheets hung from lines, and a dairy with a tethered cow.

But Great Rudi, with caterpillar veins on the back of his hands, would gesticulate, and Aunt Billie, if present, would turn her head to look keenly at him. 'Not out of sight,' he'd state, which didn't make much sense because we could be out of sight in the main rooms with their china doorknobs, let alone deeper in the house with its smells of old carpet, ancient dust and other lives. 'Now, any questions?'

Lips sucked in, we learned to swallow them back; questions would start Great Rudi off and verbally running as if he was dosed with castor oil. Or elephant pills. 'Not out of sight,' he'd repeat, his rheumy eyes wandering over our heads to a grove of saplings and shadowy trees, then a ridge rumpling away to the edge of a gorge. 'Not out of sight.'

Where did we head? Out of sight of course. First through the grove of saplings, we pushed through ferns, then bracken under low boughs, snivelling at insects which flew up our noses and into our hair.

'Go back?' Not yet, we grinned, the paths narrowing, and snags scratching above our socks.

'Ouch,' Faith hitched up her skirt, a thread of blood seeping down one thigh. Licking a finger, she drew it the length of the scratch, covering it with spit while I dug in a pocket, passing her a hanky. 'Ouch,' she said again, 'it stings.' Then: 'Gee,' she raised her eyes, with me between them, and Celia biting a mouthful of hair.

A grassy patch opened up. We halted, stock-still among bush noises of hums, clacks. Sort of scared, I coughed, then Celia let out a cry.

'It's a grave,' her voice went hoarse. We saw a mossy headstone, and there was an urn centred on the raised-pebble rectangle under which a coffin must lie. Grass spread out to form a square that was cornered with four iron posts looped by a heavy chain.

'Whose?' I whispered, afraid the air was thickening and turning to Faith for the answer. She heaved up her shoulders, blinked and shook her head.

Closer, and up on our toes, we peered. Toppling forwards, Celia grabbed at the chain and steadied herself before wiping her rusty hands hard down her skirt. 'Will we?' she moistened her lips and hesitated. 'Will we scrape a bit of the moss off the stone with a stick?'

We didn't dare. Instead, we hopped over the chain excitedly, leaned close and, squinting, managed to make out weathered letters and words which told us: 'Here Lies William Rudolphus Marshall'. The date was undecipherable, but not William Rudolphus' age. Four years old!

Above, a bird squawked harshly as if its throat was dry like mine. I shuddered; out of nowhere to think of a small skull six feet deep among subterranean cobwebs, spiders and worms. My scalp pricked and was tingling, and my skin went cold.

Faith, who often said something surprising, surprised us with something that shouldn't have been surprising. Something we would have deduced soon enough. 'This must be Aunt Billie's and Great Rudi's little boy.'

'Did you know they had one?' I asked. 'A little boy?'

Had all the love they offered him been too much for him to bear? A little boy, who'd be a grown man today. An old man! Not as ancient as Great Rudi, but likely with thin hair. Bald. With a rubbery face, and a waterfall of chins?

Faith didn't know. But what about the shelves of photographs in silver frames in numerous Clifton rooms? Among ornaments, mementoes galore, ostrich feathers in vases, trophies for this and that, and stuffed birds in glass cases; nothing of their small boy? Frowning with the effort to remember, Faith was sure she'd never heard of him. No mention of a boy who died.

Four years old ... half our age and ceasing to live. Death was not something Celia or I were able to grasp. We huddled closer and a whip bird called. Ooh! Was he—William Rudolphus Marshal—here and now about to slip free of his grave?

'But,' Celia began.

'No,' and suddenly angry Faith slammed her mouth shut, hunching into herself for long moments, before clumsily she took each of our hands and the three of us settled down. 'He ...' and she pointed her nose at the grave—a clearly tended grave not choked by long grass and weeds. 'He would have been family.'

Family? Was 'family' a wedge in time? Where, between loss and gain, everyone knew their place, and needed to know? Where everyone came before someone else and someone else always followed?

## 25

With a childhood broken in two, approaching my tenth birthday I lost four months of school at the age of nine. Invalided at home. Boarders; not just individuals, we were a species, then, with no warning, I individualised myself.

Assembling boringly the same way each day, with additional standing when there were guests to address us, I began to feel odd. Not much at first but then the sounds filtering down from the stage, lectern, and even the piano—where by rotation seniors thumped out the school song—began to buzz together. Then hammers tapped my head and I'd lose balance, sway and faint.

This began in summer, so at first it was put down to the heat. Duly I was seated by an open door. Matron put on a cuddly disguise until the fourth episode when, brutally dismissive, in her nice-nasty voice she said: 'Natasha Ross, you're seeking attention.'

'But, but,' How to tell that I felt tottery, lop-sided and odd? Was I a fascinating case of some rare disease? Incurable was a notion that swept into my head along with rising waves of panic.

'This must stop, it's all in your mind,' she spat out while I continued to want to spit out the Monday elephant pills.

Some of our class resented me and 'my act', as Matron labelled it, but the majority cheered me on; a welcome diversion and Amelia Hanlon, a bookmaker's daughter, started taking bets on whether I'd faint or not each day. Losers paid out in licorice or sherbert bags after the Saturday crocodile to The Village, and it wasn't long before helmet-haired Amelia was keen to elevate me to a second-best friend.

'Here she goes,' someone would pipe up. 'Here goes Natasha,' and the prefect of the day, licking a thumb to turn the pages of the morning's announcements, would cock an ear and stop midway.

If separated from Celia or Faith, there'd be someone else to haul me up, set me on my feet and steer me out. Fast becoming a celebrity, initially an unwilling celebrity, I began to bask in the limelight.

Soon apparent that I was not buckling over with heat, in turn Mlle Durand and Miss Batton-Browne called me to their private quarters. Kind and concerned, they came to the decision that I was to proceed to Sick Bay with its white walls, mosquito nets and carbolic smell.

'I don't want to, don't want to,' I said with fierce tears which Mlle wiped away, explaining that it was only cautionary. Cautionary? What was cautionary? Was it mumps or toothache, paralysis of the legs, or worse?

Dr. Brown who was called in had a doubting face, loose lips and, adept at monologue, he pronounced me fit, with his bit of a smile never reflected in his eyes. After further episodes, my parents were informed, and a second opinion was sought. Dr. Saxby was not only gentle with his questions but concentrated when he examined me. Instructed to produce a dribble—a urine specimen—in a glass phial. He ordered a repeat the next day.

Escorted to the station and an early train, I was directed to a reserved window seat where I sat opposite a framed photograph of the Three Katoomba Sisters, with a railway carafe of water bracketed in brass capped by a cup.

'Natasha you are not to speak to strangers,' was the final instruction, which meant I didn't speak a word to the other occupants of the glassed-in carriage with an empty corridor running alongside. When a woman in a rhubarb- feathered hat asked my name I felt stupid, glimmered a smile, and pointedly looked blank.

'Cat got your tongue?' teased a man maybe known to her because, good-naturedly, they exchanged a laugh when I stuck out my tongue to prove no cat had got it. Feeling very stupid, I gave the smile I gave to strangers, and shifted back in my seat. I wanted to pull out the pull-out table that separated us, but with nothing to put on it except my hands, they'd probably conclude I was an idiot.

Soon enough: 'Valley 'eights, Valley 'eights' was being shouted from the platform in reverse. A whistle shrieked like a call of distress, and rocking from side to side I was speeding down the mountains, alone in a train. No Celia, no familiar teachers or friends. Not even a pig person escaped from the sty. Scudding clouds above, blurs of trees, a river, more trees, and open land rushed by. Swamped by desolation and loneliness when we thundered into a tunnel without even a shaving of light, any courage I had evaporated and fled. How to hold in my panic? I knew I must. So: 'It's all right darling, yes it's all right,' my distant mother assured me in my head.

And it was. We escaped the tunnel with its clogged smell and slowed through a tent of mist, then gathered speed. Somewhere the rhubarb-feathered woman stepped down and off, to be replaced by a rust-haired girl who looked me over, then slumped into sleep.

Paddocks, smaller paddocks and houses appeared, then squashed-up suburbs, before the view became outer-city goods yards with centipedes of stationary trains. Central Station drew near. Nina too, and Marcus to meet us at the specialist's rooms in Macquarie Street.

I was diagnosed with nephritis—inflammation of the kidneys. The total and prolonged treatment? Bed rest.

Never having watched myself like a fly on the wall of my own life, startled, I saw myself grow. My feet, then my ankles started to stick out from my pyjama legs. Then skinny calves, as if I was being extruded by a lengthening machine. Not that it hurt; not like the awful machines in dank, medieval torture chambers in the many books I gobbled up in four months. As well as grizzling, I frequently went into the grumps. I refused to eat, then demanded to eat, howled with rage, was broody, bumptious, and kicked or pounded my bed. I lay with my back to the door of my room, my legs pulled up. I flung things on the floor, at the ceiling, and out the window to be told, threatened and cajoled not to tire myself. I was indulged by family and visitors like never before.

Ordered complete bed rest, I wanted to get up, only to be told 'NO'. I begged, but was not allowed. Angry, I was convinced they were treating me like some person who wasn't me.

So, one morning I lifted the blankets and sheets. I found the floor with my toes, but my legs had forgotten how to prop me up, or how to cross my room to the door, which prompted another squall of tears.

I surely must have tired Nina, who, waxed with exhaustion and eyes ringed with shadows, disguised her anxieties despite her '*Joy*', which to me was scented with both lovely and unlovely memories.

Curiously, it was my mother who suggested I start a diary which, with a solemn promise—crossing her heart—she promised no one else was to read unless I gave permission. I was confused. Was I to invent a world from what the real world failed to provide? With chunks of words?

I frowned. Humped on the side of the bed with my legs dangling down, I jumbled my hair. 'What am I to say? To write?'

'Whatever comes into your head. Think of your diary as a friend.' The corners of her mouth edged up and Nina held me with her eyes. 'A friend in whom you can confide. Tell anything at all.'

'But nothing's happening now.'

Bewildered, I looked from my mother to what this room of mine held. My things in my room were familiar enough. My desk with the shelf that levered down, my cuckoo clock, the jar where baby teeth had been left for the tooth fairy years ago. A big, tattered teddy and his miniature, the sunshade sent from my uncle when his ship docked in Japan, and my lucky horseshoe with its luck that could run out if it fell or got turned upside down.

Vulnerable, I turned querulous, and felt justified as I moaned. Everything could have coalesced to: 'Nothing's happening now.'

Nina eyed me in silence for a moment or two, glanced out the window, and then back to me as her face softened to a smile.

'You're wrong; something's happening to all of us, all the time.' She paused, circled the ring she wore on her little finger. 'We're thinking. Or imagining. Ordinary thoughts, secret ones too. Big and small.'

Suddenly, I felt puny and afraid. Did my mother see the past as well as the future in me? Was my horseshoe the right way up for the last time? Was a diary going to be evidence of me to be left behind?

'Natasha?'

'Am I going to die?' Some kind of shadow passed over her face and her eyes filled with dismay. I screwed mine tighter. 'Am I?'

'No,' she took my chin in her hand, raised it and I think—feeling desperate for it to be true—that what my mother smiled at me was her love.

Day after day trundled on and pushed into nights, where flopping back in the chintz bedside chair, legs spread, heels to the floor, Marcus played at being cheerful. Yet, given to compressing his nostrils and puffing out his cheeks, he could let the air explode, occasionally being tripped up by circumstances to admit: 'I'm whacked,' before he'd rally. 'Well, just a bit.'

'Dispirited?' I overheard someone ask him. Dis-spirited? A gone-wrong wizard, a witch?

Among a stream of visitors, there was my Aunt Annya when she was off duty and free. Nina's older sister by two years, with her odd but captivating smile—odd only in that it spread over her face slowly—as she concentrated on my recovery. She was mad about the theatre and actors, and champing at the bit to take me out to matinees at the Australia Hotel marble foyer with its palm court orchestra. She swayed in her sleek silks and high heels, fingers clawing her hair like a half-mad scientist. Attaching a cigarette to a long ivory holder, she refrained from lighting up in my room, but elbow to crossed knee, her left wrist folded into her waist. Then into a pose: 'Tooooo elegant,' she'd rake her hair back from her forehead, then croon at me wearing the new pyjamas she'd bought, along with more books.

During earlier holidays, Annya had taken me to the theatre twice. First to 'Maid of the Mountains'. 'Highly appropriate,' she trilled, with her being my maid FROM the mountains, adding with a wink: 'I'm the aunt to expand your horizons, little love.' Next was another musical, 'Lilac Time'.

Annya was a charm of an arm-piece, Marcus' friends would still declare. Alike but unalike, but it was unmistakable that Annya was Nina's sister, though her voice often took on a dusky drawl, burnt butterscotch. Tall and independent, who can tell but the extra bit of mothering she might have experienced—some incalculable touch or attention—may have moved something in her that jammed in Nina, shuttered away though perhaps something already frail. Undeniably, chance plays a big role in life, and nothing is ever really over, as I would come to discover for myself.

Visitors. Of course, there was my grandmother, Hannah, in one or other of her ugly hats skewered to her head by a vicious hatpin, Their Majesties to accompany her containing treacle tarts, lamingtons and cherry cakes. 'Why not bring Marina?' once my mother asked as Hannah pulled off the black skin of her gloves, 'Natasha would enjoy seeing someone her own age.'

'What?'

'Why not bring Marina, Natasha would ...' and I heard the starch in my mother's voice.

'What?'

'Natasha is not infectious.' she pronounced to her mother-in-law, whose expression conveyed serious doubts. 'Nephritis is not catching like measles,' and I suppose I smiled a kind of smile. Then as if somebody else was thinking in my head I heard a voice—mine. 'Why do you love Marina and not love me?'

'What!'

If she'd been a real dragon, there'd have been smoke coming from her nostrils, and fire. My mother scooped up my hand, squeezed it.

'You love her a hundred times more than me,' I said reproachfully. Then, no stickler for numbers, readjusted to 'a thousand times more,' unassailably primed by the certainty that my grandmother would not drag me along our hall and lock me in the bathroom again. Did I experience a certain thrill? Enough to stick my head up and over the parapet, adding: 'Is it because she's pretty. And fat like you?'

'What!'

The voluble Hannah Ross was monosyllabic. So conversationally and rationally, I went on. 'Only 'cos she eats too much cake.'

'What!' iron-jawed Hannah Ross repeated yet again. My grandmother's eyes were fire-filled, and I plastered myself to Nina, whose eyes shone. She then gently disengaged herself, and threw me an unreadable smile as she straightened my sheets before taking decisive steps to the door. She cast a backward glance at Hannah, whose shelf of breasts heaved thunderously. A long diamond brooch might have been lightning about to strike, but quietly exultant, now my mother was ready to quell the storm, against a mother-in-law overstuffed like her one of her horsehair couches.

'Tea, I think I'll ask Mavis to put the kettle on.'

'What?'

'Tea, a cup of tea. Then Mavis can come in here with Natasha, Chinese Checkers, Monopoly, whatever they want to play.' My mother was breathing audibly through her nose. 'I am looking forward to your cherry cake. And hearing more about the person you mentioned who brushes her dog's teeth.'

'What?' yet again, and huffily my grandmother began to arrange herself to move.

'Natasha?' Was Nina expecting me to apologise, though there seemed no reason why I should? 'Natasha?'

'Yes?'

'Cherry cake or ice cream for you?'

## 26

Mavis had worked for my mother for years. She was lovely, with a broad backside. Part of our domestic canvas, each day when she arrived, she changed into her clean but washed-out 'house frock' as she called it; faded flowers and prints, her lips painted up to shine, her hair under a net like Gwennie's mother.

Mavis was never furious, never snappy. In the garden when I was small, we'd search for holes with earthworms and chase butterflies. And it was with Mavis that I planted my elbows on the kitchen table when we ate lunch. Nina—though not in Mavis's hearing—corrected this.

On weekends when visitors frequently arrived, Mavis was capably there. Among them, the Jagodas. Long-standing family friends. Victor Jagados and Lily, with their tribe of five, their surname made from the unpronounceable Polish when their father immigrated from Europe, unreservedly adopting Australian nationality. Lily was one of my mother's two flatmates in Elizabeth Bay prior to her wedding.

Living seventy miles south in a spread-out and chaotic house with its sleep-out large enough for ten beds, dry cow dung or green coils were lit to smoulder under the beds to keep the mosquitoes down. Every summer we had memorable holidays with them; the lagoon, which channelled into the sea, lapped close to the verandah steps at high tide.

Their two older girls—Jennya and Belinda—book-ended their two bony boys—Trevor and Alex—who laughed louder and longer than anyone else I knew. Then came their youngest, Sony, both of us born in May 1928. Sun-tanned and sea-bleached, the children included and absorbed me as soon as we arrived, my father's fist on the horn as we came through their gate. We played whatever they played: bailing and riding in the rowboat, poking into rocks, splashing about, or racing off to the curved sand of the beach, freckled with adults and kids. There was a sole shop nearby on a slab of concrete that sold milk, bread, sausages, citronella and calamine, as well as homemade ginger-beer ice blocks.

Aunt Lily, as I called her, was blonde with gorgeous features. Like my mother, she loved books. She clearly loved my mother too; finding the time to read and make enormous meals, if never a bed. Meals where you elbowed in to help yourself with an elastic arm or you'd miss out, with the boys eating huge amounts but in need of a refill by the hour, so I was introduced to bread and dripping. There were good basic meals as well as popular favourites such as the green prawns, which were boiled up pink in a huge tin can, plus the flathead my father and Uncle Victor caught, gutted, then tossed on an open fire, along with black-jacketed potatoes taken from the embers. They were sooo good with butter and salt. Our job was to collect driftwood to keep the fire glowing.

Aunt Lily, who was raised as strictly as my mother, was intended for a very different life. Engaged to someone called Sebastian, somehow she met Uncle Victor from Poland when her wedding plans were at fever pitch. Sorry for the trouble she caused, nonetheless she jilted Sebastian, and romantically eloped with Victor. Despite dire warnings, she never lived to regret it, quite the contrary. Love overlaying common sense, with no domestic experience, she muddled through. Perhaps that was why, years later, thoughts of Lily prompted Nina to offer me a rare piece of maternal advice, which took root. 'Housework IS there forever.' The intimation: if you've no one else to wash or clean, don't fret. Just do as much as your standards—or hygiene—demand.

What was important to Lily and Victor was the education of their brood; Lily for them to learn as she learned, Victor to ensure both his sons and daughters had the education he missed in his homeland. So far, Jennya was a scholarship girl, with Belinda, Alex and Trevor likely to follow. And Sony, of course.

'Think, my children. Warm your minds,' Uncle Victor would encourage his brood, his 'berries' as he called them. I was to learn that the Jagoda surname translates to 'berry' in English. Given to overlooking the need for new shoes, recently he'd ordered Everyman's Encyclopaedia in twelve volumes.

'Natasha,' he addressed me one evening, 'you know that Albert Einstein, born in Wurttemberg, had the sense to go to Switzerland and cleverly, he became a naturalised Swiss citizen. Smart as well as the mathematics,' he tapped his head. 'You know that?'

I nodded, though of course did not know; nonetheless, to be rewarded with a hug.

What I did come to wonder was whether Aunt Lily ever yearned for a space exclusively her own. Somewhere like what Marcus termed my mother's 'capsule' to escape the world. With her five lively and loving children, I calculated that Lily's capsule would need to be elastic-sided; stretchable to accommodate a capacity crowd. But Lily was affectionate and seemingly there for us all. To me, she was an angel walking on air through her noisy, sand-gritty house where the cobwebs knitting the corners could have been lace. House proud? Yes, but in the sense that she was proud of her houseful of kids.

As much as I adored being there when we left again, I suppose I liked to open a door, close it behind me, and to be alone. But not with my mother, consumed by her inner isolation. So, maybe I was my mother's daughter? In part, this had to be true.

I was deeply touched when the Jagodos—welcome as ever—phoned to say they were planning to come to Sydney to see me and my nephritis. At Marcus' suggestion, it should be a chance to introduce Jennya, Belinda, Alex, Trevor and Sony to some of Sydney's sights: Taronga Zoo, the Harbour Bridge, the Botanic Gardens, and the Manly Ferry.

'I want to get up and go, too,' I appealed to my father, expecting to be understood, fruitlessly. This sent me into a tantrum. Then, to my surprise, Nina acknowledged my right to be angry.

'No,' Marcus was firm

Nina fell silent, while sullen, I broke from Marcus and curved away. I didn't understand what was happening to me, and grumpily I fixed my eyes on my pasty-white feet. Why, snail-like, did they carry nephritis on my back? And so often able to read my mind, why did my father only read what he wanted to read for me?

MONTHS CAME AND WENT. My imagination ran wild in those six months when it seemed nephritis was eating up the years of my life. But time progressed, and I progressed. I recovered, and was five inches taller.

Celia wrote faithfully while I was away and there'd been lots of other mail; letters from Mlle and Miss Batten-Brown, affectionately known as Sweetie, or B-Brownie when she was out of favour. Even a card from the vile and unfunny Miss Lamble with her pathetic attempt at humour addressed to 'Neffie Natasha', which she circled kidney-shape.

With parcels of words, Celia kept me up to date: tennis and netball matches home and away, a decent cook who—'rot his guts'—left after three weeks, boringly awful lantern slides by missionaries from Tonga held in the Methodist Hall, a midnight feast when Hanzi Lazar, who was given to making trouble where she could, canvassed for new friends. Matron had acquired a whiter-than-white front tooth which flashed against the yellowed grey of her others, and someone had given St. Barnabas' Mr. Whitehead a dog whose eyes bulged from its skull. At The Village fete and sports day, frumpy Mrs. Whitehead—chained to Mr. Whitehead, till death they do part, and who regularly judged the bottled fruits and jams—was outclassed by a visiting bishop's wife. A daygirl won the egg and spoon race, Kings won the team rounders, someone's ankle snapped in the three-legged and, slithery with sweat, the firemen won the tug of war against the combined grocers/butchers/bus drivers. And surprise, surprise, she'd come to like Fuck Elise, but was stuck on her second Chopin Etude, and mortified that there were dozens more. I almost heard the sigh Celia had written in, and her omitted 'bloodies, blasts', and worse.

The greatest of friends, Celia related the everyday humdrum as well as the news. One of her sisters—not Prudence—was to marry someone called Alphonzo with a 'z', and her mother, by nature tactful, found this preferable to Ananias. Celia's father was quick-smart with the rebuke that Ananias derived from Grace of the Lord. Not bad from the Reverend Sale, who with Christian pride bore the moniker: Matthew Mark Luke John Sale. And, Celia wrote, it was rumoured that riding lessons were to be introduced next year. Could I picture Miss Bottom at the trot?

More graphically, what I did see was so much where I wasn't, with Faith regularly drawing pictures. The deep rock pool where we were taken to swim with its insects, creepy crawlies, the occasional snake. The green water curtained on three sides by bush, foliage and strips of orange bark like outsized rind peeling from the trunks of the angophoras which rose behind. Soggy mud like yellow bread at its edge. Somehow, Faith was able to capture the heat and blood-freezing cold we felt when we jumped in too.

There for me to see was Celia with palms up, trying to decide whether to swallow dust or chalk to scratch her throat and ensure she'd squawk when forced to audition for the choir; our singing teacher Miss Frampton forever punching the air in time and cleaning her ear with a key to hear our major and minor scale. What's more, very gratifyingly, Faith drew Corinne Bradley with her face puce, mouth stuffed and unable to spit out her equally revolting cousin's birthday cake, its greasy candles having been found in her bed. There too was our science teacher with her face green and her hair not rats' tails, but rats, and our nauseous prefects glued to a telescope on the lookout for any trivial offence, ready to pounce.

So, bonds strong if miles apart, by way of Celia's and Faith's talents, I was kept up to date with lots of what was going on in my absence that for me seemed to be going on forever. My favourite picture on paper and in my head? Celia and Faith side by side reflected in a heavily framed mirror, with Celia's eyes stretched to golf balls, and Faith nudging Celia in the ribs. Distanced as we were, they focused straight at me, with both scribbling in outsize letters: 'Wish you were here' with kisses and hugs.

## 27

After being an addled exile, returning to my second habitat wasn't easy. Far from it. Baffled, two of me wrestling in a ten-year-old skin, there had to be a word for this. But if there was, it didn't exist for me.

Having been the centre of attention at home, once again a boarder I could have been pleated with a frill of hysteria. Hung in a void, with no immediate context, and no recently familiar things. As a fainter, my days of glory had passed. That was no bad thing; but Celia and I self-diagnosed and agreed that when our lungs went tight and we became breathless, it was a home-sickness thing.

'You, Natasha Ross, are just a nobody like before,' a pig person sauntered by, tossing her slops at me. 'A n.o.b.o.d.y.'

Stupid as it was, I had to resist rushing to a mirror to check my reflection, which would be a three-year older face than my face when first sent away to school. The pig person's accompanying piglets gave off squeals like small trotters on the run, and I smirked. I resembled them in no way, yet still had to contend with their jibes.

Everything changes but nothing changes. *Plus ça change*: French at breakfast, piano practice at awful hours, lousy food, the pink-corset torture device for round-shoulders, bells, bells and bells. A new day girl

## A Secret Grief

named Deirdre Ireland with a birthmark on one cheek like a map of New Zealand put paid to my longing to be a blue-eyed blonde blissfully named Deirdre. What's more, Hanzi Lazar, while no sweet-smelling bed of roses, smelled less like a drain.

Now I was taller than both Celia and Faith. Behind OUR hedge we chewed over elementary biology. Weren't we taught that our bodies were remarkable machines and Faith, for no reason she could explain, yearned to grow and measure six feet tall.

'My legs are lanky. Planky. Too long,' I moaned, before Celia was reassuring, as reliable as ever with knowledge of the world. I'd be thankful one day, she advised. 'Why?' She draped an arm round my shoulder. Did I want thick-as-a-log thighs? Saucepan-lid-kneecaps? Bulging-bottle calves? 'Nooo.'

'Nooo,' I was to say to Mlle the following day.

Having sent for me, she sat ensconced before a tray set with a blue china cup and saucer, and a plate-matching sugar bowl and jug. A glass of milk stood alongside the teapot, and I was full of nerves. Elf-sized cakes—*petit fours*—were arranged in a circle on a silver dish, and another held black-covered squares. Something called 'caviar' was rumoured to be Mlle's indulgence and should this be it, caviar could have been a spread of compacted fleas.

'This is for you.' Head at a tilt, Mlle passed me the milk and as I listened with a slack smile, she said: 'Natasha we are extremely glad you are recovered. That you are once more well. We wish you to continue so.'

'*Merci Mlle.*' Astonished, I had the presence to reply before I gulped down the milk. When offered a petit four; '*Merci Mlle,*' I said again, but was worried. How to refuse the caviar?

'Less than your best has always kept you near the top of your class. You are not a child with a peppercorn brain; always among the first five.'

'Not in maths,' someone who had to be me blurted out.

A pointed sigh. 'Quite so.' She frowned into her cup. A plan had been devised. Once a week, unaccompanied, I was to take the train at 3.00 p.m. several stations further up the mountains to Woodford. At 4 p.m., to arrive punctually at The Boys' Academy, formerly The Academy for Young Gentlemen. Here, Mr. McMannus, not only the principal but a mathematician of note, had agreed to coach me and ensure that I was on the 5.30 p.m. train back. Crocodile-less—just me—returning, she said, with little time to spare before the evening meal.

'Noooo.'

Deliberately, Mlle placed her cup on her saucer; I heard it clink. She smiled at me, then sighed like a bagpipe. 'Are you thinking that you will be nervous alone?' That in winter it will be dark? That ...'

Though pummelled into us that we must not interrupt, I interrupted. 'No.'

'What then?' Lips drawn apart, her smile widened even as her teeth seemed too small for her mouth.

'I hate arithmetic and algebra and geometry and trigi-something ...' I was spluttery, tense.

Mlle, who was supposed to understand our personalities and our anxieties, interrupted me. 'As yet, you do little geometry. While trigonometry is still to come.'

'I'll hate it. I will, I know I will.'

'Natasha. Let us separate the facts from the distortions.' What! Was this some sort of new French? 'Here ...' and she was offering me a second *petit four*; white and sugary, capped by a frosted nut. 'Please take another while,' and reluctantly I took it, fingering it, 'while I explain the matter to you.'

Mathematics was my weakest subject, and after an absence of four months, additional work was called for at a high level. Generously, Mr. McMannus had agreed. I was, she said, capable of extending myself in everything else.

Mlle stood in her stout shoes, walked me to the door and glowering, helpless, with no ploy to prevent yet another disruption in my life, the additional mathematics was scheduled to happen. Tuesday of next week the ordeal was to begin as an unnerving weekly event.

The next Tuesday at 3 p.m., the sun was masked by clouds. A half-hearted drizzle started, the train jarred into life and I swallowed back tears. At Woodford, I left the train. Steam hissed, huffed, and lurched away, the guard in his van lifting a hand in a wave, while the cluster of passengers drifted out of sight. Expecting to be claimed, I stood unclaimed, chewing the fingers of one glove, an exercise book to my ribs, pencils and a rubber in a pocket. The light was threatening and pale. What now? I felt empty. A built-up outrage surfaced and swarmed over me, and poisonous as a snake, I hated my parents. Hated them. They'd done this. Stranded me. They were far away, while I was marooned at Woodford for no other reason than to just add up, subtract and divide!

'You called Ross?' He was about my height, and wore a motto-ed cap over a face with erupting skin. I must have nodded because he led off, throwing a hand over my shoulder: 'Come on.'

Mr. McMannus was ancient, with an academic stiffness attached to his bones. Dressed in a worn suit, a high-starched collar cut into his neck. His face? Cherub-like, amiable, with a wispy beard which once might have been torpedo-shaped, while a bit of hair wandered over his head. What's more his eyes were kind and twinkled as he arched forwards, taking my hand between both of his.

'I daresay,' he enunciated, 'it shouldn't take long to get you on track.' Mathematically, he meant, and zombie-like, I nodded. 'However, first up, it's my place to persuade you that you can learn.' Ushering me into his study, jumbled with books which were shelved to the ceiling and piled on the floor, with papers everywhere else, he cleared two chairs and went on. 'Not to struggle against learning with what you've convinced yourself you don't want to—or cannot—learn.'

How did he know? Astonishingly, he made the hour fly, a marble clock chiming on a cluttered mantelpiece. Reluctantly, it began to seep into my head that soon I'd like Mr. McMannus, and his sisters, one of whom he said would walk me back to the station for the 5.30 p.m. train.

'Yes dear, of course,' possibly the younger Miss McMannus told him with no unwillingness as she carefully hung my coat on a hook in the hall. 'Though not before the child's eaten after the work you'll put her through.'

'Splendid,' and gripping his left lapel with his left hand, he touched the other to his temple in a sort of salute.

So, each Tuesday when I finished, they sat me down between them, not that they ate. I had a sandwich of either ham, fish paste or egg and watercress, a plate of shortbread dusted with icing sugar that one of them baked, and seasonally an apple, cherries or grapes.

Rain was slanting down that first Tuesday, and walking close under Miss McMannus' umbrella, I smelled the comfort of her: mothballs from the cardigan she'd pulled on, plus a drift of a scent between lavender and lemons—and my widening world. Unaware that come winter, each week would include fright and the dark.

Figures in the landscape after my first lesson, on reaching the station where the stationmaster had planted perennials in an old iron bath on clawed feet, one of the Miss McMannus sisters—it took time for me to distinguish which one—took my hand. She held it protectively while the 5.30 p.m. squealed into the platform and juddered to a stop.

'Thank you,' I said and expected her to leave. No. She waited to watch me find a seat and settle, with the train ready to gather speed before she waved me off. Then, looking deeper into myself, I didn't find the same need to cry I'd felt when, earlier on the 3 p.m. train, I was racked by unshed tears.

## 28

You imagine the past as well as remember it. The highs, lows, the ghosts that leached to your mind.

My world was expanding and things began to appear more manageable for Celia, Faith, me, and the rest in our intersecting lives in our miniature. A skewered sense of belonging? Not entirely, but you get used to it in a way and I was beginning to work out, if not fully understand, what was important, and what was not. Cottoning on that my life was not to be overlooked, like some.

In classrooms, Madelaine Brown sat halfway in the middle. Then farther back then farther, as if fading out of sight. Then hey presto, Justine Straffe appeared like a puff of magic and Madelaine had a friend. Pert-nosed and string-thin, she was a girl who chewed as she talked. She talked a lot; mouthy but nice, and I was delirious with a second-hand revenge when certain scraps of her talk began to circulate.

At some big charity event, Justine Straffe's father—who owned a paper mill —found it necessary to publicly snub Corinne Bradley's father, a man on the money-and-connection trail. Oblivious to what went on beyond the confines of the school gates, a report appeared in a newspaper, with hints of financial charges to be laid, which a vigilant day girl brought to show us. Celia summarised that day girls carried in whiffs from the jungle; in the main, they were our sole conduit to the outside world. They went beyond the cloistered locale in which we existed. Questionably a privileged life?

But that year come July, the outside natural world—for a day and a night—was set to be more than a landscape to me. It would be centre stage.

Out of class, there were the routines of sport and leaping about under the supervision of one of two games' mistresses; Miss Ramsay who kept colour prints of dog—man's best friend—on her locker in the gym, and the nuggetty Miss Bryce, with legs like loaves of bread, who was generally considered more fun.

They were responsible for introducing the paper chase to the boarders' sporting syllabus. Never intended to include day girls—who might have known the terrain—these took place twice a term on a Saturday, planned not to clash with inter-school tennis, hockey or netball, home or away. The darling of several of us geared to tend the flame, Miss Bryce wasn't much older than the seniors, but even given her bounce and energy, she didn't appeal to me. Nor, as Celia, Faith and I agreed, her regular scent of perfumed sweat.

In February and July, whipped by heat or cold, our paper chases led well beyond the school grounds; a watertight reason was necessary to be excused. Up and down gullies tracked for bush walkers and bird watchers keen to commune with nature, our tracks were marked out by Miss Bryce and her current student pets—a mass of shifting muscles set to scatter shredded paper from their cotton pouches. Apart from the fuss of synchronising their wrist watches, they could have been bare-legged girl kangaroos in gym slips. They set off with a half-hour lead, while eager for freedom—running wild—we chaffed at the bit, before upon hearing three shrills from the starter's whistle, we were off.

With birds above—which I willed to be wild geese—dry shells of sound under our thudding sandshoes, scents of the earth and the bush, boulders like small castles weathered and honeycombed, hairy trees and tough-barked eucalypts scarred by broken limbs, we dappled the narrow tracks. Something that could have been timelessness enveloped us as, not possible to run two abreast, we hurtled on, jumped, scrambled and slipped after scraps of paper—not maybe dissimilar to the peas scattered to keep Hansel and Gretel safe. Not that we worried; we were unconcerned we'd lose our way.

Panting for breath or clutching a stitch, at intervals we'd slow, straggle, gulp in air or splash our mouths with water from a trickle between rocks. Then push on to glimpse knobs of grape-blue ranges and peaks. Skeining in and out of sight, dramatic gorges would fall away and plunge from the path to be hidden again, with valleys hollowed by purple shadows depending on the sun.

This Saturday in July, the sun was pale. And though we were cold— our noses, hands, knees and thighs marbled or mottled pinky puce— with sweaters knotted at our waists and yelping, we were bursting to go.

Gravely, a senior mistress with doughty, old wires of whiskers on her chin gave out instructions which routinely concluded: 'Keep up, girls. No loitering. Remember if anyone's forced to stop, the two directly behind her MUST stop. WAIT. Then ...' she'd volley like a cannon; 'put your backs into it. Catch up.' Whispered around that she was once a former madam in a select brothel, her much-used: 'Put your backs into it,' the giveaway; the odious pig people referred to her as 'antique bum'.

Both Celia and Faith had been clever enough to be excused this day; which made it gloomy for me. 'No loitering, catch up,' I barely listened, I must have heard it a hundred times before.

With faces as hot as red discs, noses beginning to run, and air puffing from open mouths—even the blatherers voiceless with effort —we pushed on. Swerving to avoid stumps, clumps of low bushes, rocks hung with creepers, ferns and wild flowers that I tried not to trample, I felt somehow I could have been folded in isolation. Feet melting, invading this world of interlacing branches above roots tentacled by earth, a satin-sounding bird called and soon I became conscious the light had gone from bright to less bright. We were ribbed in grey.

With no warning, the track wound away, plunged and curved out of sight.

Midway back in the pack, a lump of a figure was ahead of me. 'I gotta stop, gotta stop,' Eunice Caswell said, jerking her pigtails, half-turning and threatening to sink down, then limping on a few steps and stumbling against a tree, blocking my way.

As the rest of the pack swerved, avoiding me then her, they puffed on and passed us, a jolting train, with wheels of legs spinning and windows of eyes staring, a prefect throwing back: 'Catch up quick.'

The last person that was to stay with Eunice with me? NO! Janet Bradley, cousin of the disgusting Corinne, chugged to a stop. Obeying rules, the rest were almost out of sight. Gone, and left in the air was their spurting breath. Then silence. Cold air on my bare legs.

'What's wrong? What?' I scowled at Eunice, who came from clay pan country with sheep and dry plains.

'Got blisters.' She heaved breathily. 'And a stone in my shoe.'

'Show,' I demanded.

Janet Bradley's head and stomach lurched forward, twitching a bit, while wobbly-legged Eunice yanked off her shoe, then sock, to reveal a satisfying bubble on a red heel.

'See,' she said wistfully, and I had to nod.

The sun had faded and was now blurred silver in the uncertain light. Nearby water purled over a rock. There was a further sound, fainter; a break and tide of rhythm which must have been the bush. A net of white mist began to surround us, with trees growing alike; the same size and same colour. I didn't want to believe they would soon merge with the track.

'Shove your shoe on.' I was shrill.

'But it hurts.'

'Shove it on you baby,' I said. Running my tongue along my lips, I tasted salt.

I was surprised to see Janet Bradley fumble at her pocket and produce a wadded hanky to pad Eunice's heel.

'Hurry up, I said. I wanted to sense the rest of the pack waiting ahead on the track. I wouldn't dare think otherwise. 'Put on your sweaters,' I ordered next and clumsily we unthickened our waists and dragged damp wool over our hair. I wasn't waiting, and started to run in anger along the track in anger, with Janet close and Nancy limping behind.

'Wait for me,' she was calling, but we didn't slow. Not yet.

THE TRACK FORKED. I tripped and went down, my hands digging the gravelly earth, hauling myself up to see a smirk on Janet Bradley's flattened face, Eunice still camouflaged by mist. WHAT was that? Crouching behind her? What WERE they? How many? To pull us limb from limb. Or worse. Pulse thudding, and wanting to burrow into a sheltering place, Janet Bradley brought me back with an edge to her nasty voice. 'If you hadn't fallen over! And you're scared.'

Tight with humiliation, I pinched back tears, but Eunice scared me more. Her fingers knotted together and twisting her hand round and round. 'Which way?' she asked.

'Which way?' then came from Janet Bradley, and I wanted to plug my ears.

They can't depend on me! I willed them not to as my eyes shifted from them to the two tracks. All about there was breathing; mine, theirs and the mountains, the sticks and stones. In spurts of fear, I rammed my knuckles into my teeth; the earth smelt damper and stronger. Shivering, I sank down on a flat rock, reached for a twig, snapped it, with the snap rousing me to sounds we should make.

'Shout,' I said, startling them, 'shout.' So we shouted and shouted, waited and waited, hearing no answering call. Janet kept it up well after Eunice and I realised it was useless. 'Stop, stop,' I had to shout at her, with her eyes bulging like a toad, cheeks striated by dirt, and hair matted to her head. An egg-shaped head.

Showing initiative, and snivelling as she set off, Eunice hobbled a few feet along one fork, then the other. Paper lay strewn on both. Strewn or wind-blown? Our dilemma became real; awfulness smothering hope. Overhead branches were disappearing fast.

'Which way?' again she asked me. Having an unchallenged command that I'd not sought and didn't want, a choice had to be made so I made it, hating them. 'Top track, dummies; you should know the same as me.' But when we shuffled along the top track, the coded trail gave out.

Seared by dread that I'd chosen wrong, I ordered: 'Stay where you are,' and shot back to the fork to follow it the other way. It had no more paper than the first! I calculated that they must have hugged the high side, with the lower fork leading down. Thoughts of deep, deeper and deepest, yowled in my head, and when you got deepest, you could drown in dirt, in layers of leaves, mulch and muck that had formed for a million years. At least.

Back with Eunice and Janet on the higher track, something nagged in my head, and I twirled about with my nose striking Janet's chin. She let out a mouse roar, with Eunice whimpering: 'Oooh...'

'Shut up!' I hurled at them, beating my shoulders for warmth. 'We're going back.'

Their squashy brains prompted them to yell: 'Why?'

'To leave a sign,' but I refused to think for whom. Or when. And idiot Eunice started on a story she'd read about how the lost boy and girl ... 'Shut up!' exploded from me again.

At the fork, we gathered rocks to make a pile, with Eunice informing us it was a 'cairn' and how the lost boy's nose cracked off when he blew it. Frostbite.

'Get on with it,' I said, and bending down, their heads banged. Twice we were forced to rebuild our cairn, having started with small stones and rocks which kept toppling over until we shunted bigger rocks into place. ' There has to be something to be put visibly in place ...'

'What?' they gawped.

'Something to tell it's us, so turn out your pockets.' Mine provided an elastic band and a ball of silver paper, Eunice's a hair ribbon, sixpence and two pennies, and Janet's a flattened scone, a crumpled hanky, and a fluff-coated toffee stick. She was scraping off the fluff, having it halfway to her poking tongue. What a skunk! Swooping forwards with one swipe, I grabbed the tacky thing.

'It's mine, it's mine,' she bawled.

'Not with three of us and nothing else,' I said. Then with commend-

## A Secret Grief

able foresight, Eunice grabbed the squashed scone, dividing it three ways, with Janet muzzling hers to her mouth as if one of us might snatch it back.

Feet tingling with cold; we had to move on. But not before something to identify us was left behind, topping the cairn. But what? They didn't know, and I didn't know, stupid Janet peered back as if some rescuing horse and carriage would come clattering up the track, her hanky ready to wave. Hanky!

'Is it name-tagged?'

'Yes,' and despite Janet's cranky fuss, we pinioned it in place like a turret flag to signal our rescuers. It must.

'Come on,' I said. Licking my dry lips, I set off. Indian file, we blundered along the track of this unknown escarpment, with Eunice's intermittent whining whipping the surrounding air with: 'Wait for me.'

Twisted trees hung with a gauze of mist. Existing shapes dimmed. The light pearled to grey. The track was nobbled by roots and stones. On wobbling legs, our feet made a particular sound, and I was tired. After more shaky steps, I halted. Shivers shuddered through me. Slithering to a stop, Janet pulled up at my heels, Eunice, neck stretched out like a tortoise, bringing up the rear.

Shivering now, forehead corrugated, I wanted to be bundled up, safe and secure. Not face the truth. No confetti-ed trail. No girls. We'd missed them. We were missing from them. LOST. Fear fluttered between us like a captive bird. We were right to be afraid.

'I'm cold. And hungry,' Janet was blubbering, her nose running again. 'I want my toffee. It's mine.'

I saw red. Celia would not have whimpered. Nor Faith. They would have agreed that any food must be shared. We'd lick in turns, I decided, when Janet made a grab at my soggy hair. That did it. There was no need to pussy foot around as thoughts of Celia came to my aid. Hadn't she extended an apple of learning and hadn't I bitten, chewed and digested it? Breath leaked out from their open mouths as I scalded the air with a few of Celia's well-chosen words.

Eunice awed. 'You'll go to hell,' said Janet whose face was an ugly scowl. And worn-looking, the way she'd look one day.

Gratified, I said it all again. Slowly, and having jolted them, a sixth sense urged me not to lose the advantage. 'Get moving. Follow me.'

Janet was bleating and poking her gym tunic between her legs. She'd wet her pants. Yuk.

'We should stay here. Or go back.'

'Back to what, arsehole? Back to where?'

'Oooh,' from Eunice, who was turning into a great oooh-er. 'The pile of stones.'

'We wouldn't have needed to build it if we were just going to stand there, fuckwit.'

'Oooh ... '

The mist was thickening. Pulpy. We had to search for shelter; an overhanging rock, or better, a cave. 'We'll lick the toffee. In a cave,' I said.

We stumbled on, our feet tangling in hidden traps. I tripped again, grabbing at a branch of fallen tree as I went down, then a stump rose of its own accord like a huge cheese grater as it scraped my knee. I cried out, and Janet's face wore a greasy smile as Eunice hauled me up with pinpoints of blood popping through my skin.

'Lick it,' Eunice advised, so bending over, gingerly I did, before with a dangerous stab of confidence, I found myself in charge again. 'Where's this cave?' she asked.

Hands hard down, I coiled up onto my feet, straightening in the cold, the backs of my knees sweaty. 'Come on.' I was shaken. Petrified. I felt stuck together with putty, but somehow I lurched forward to a trot and they were close behind.

Sure to stumble if we moved fast, they couldn't see my face crumble. The way ahead shortened. With light gone, we'd butt into white pillows of thickened mist. And cold. Clawing cold. Burrowing through, we risked hitting our heads or tripping should the track take an unexpected bend. Or worse. I bit my wrist. Blundering over a cliff. Bottomless. So, arms outstretched, touching swirls of mist, I slowed.

Too dangerous to be paralysed by fright now, when my arms ached I let them drop and dropped pace to stop.

'Why are you stopped?'

With my eyes straining, breath quickening, and not knowing what to expect—an animal, a ghost of an animal, awful hulks of shapes—I had no answer. When I whipped round; Eunice was jelly-eyed, beyond her Janet was distorting and wavering as if I was seeing her through water. There was no going back; back was dizzy, shadowed, blocked out!

Eunice grabbed my waist, and Janet grabbed hers. Shuffling, grunting and forced to inch on, when I ordered them to flatten into rocks, they did. Mist curdled layer into layer, clotted denser than before. We might have been snails with no protective shells. Panic screamed to rush from my mouth.

Stomach contracting, somehow I had to suppress the screams. 'Where are we going?' The question was muffled and faint.

'On.' I sneezed. 'To a cave.'

'You know a cave?'

I had to know a cave. Dry as a desert, piping hot. What did they want?

'Yes,' I said, rigid and unsure. Any more and I'd go out of control.

And we found one. Speckled dark with a fetid smell of underbrush, mould and animal droppings. Layered in fear. With rain seeping through the mist, worming our way in and crouching inside, we didn't get dry but we didn't get wetter. It was cold. Edging back, horror pulled me taut enough to snap, touched by something sticky-fine—cobwebs. Vainly, I wrestled against screams.

Even so, we were glad to have arrived. With hunger loose in our stomachs like empty bags, licking the toffee turn by turn—no biting— took up a lot of time. When it was gone, gone too were the clumps of bushes and shaggy branches. Then gone were the shapes of their faces. And mine gone to them. With my fingers up to my eyes, I squinted. I could barely make out my dirt-caked nails in the final smear of light.

In a shaky falsetto and cold, cold, cold, I tried to start up *Ten Green Bottles*, but Janet and Eunice puttered away miserably on the ninth. Then a thin wind came whirling up and night humped down. It was black. Janet was the first to cry. Then Eunice and me.

We'd given up saying how much we liked chocolate cake and bacon with floppy eggs, and toast with butter and jam. Janet wanted strawberry, and Eunice wanted apricot spread on a wedge as solid as a step. Mouth-watering, my choice was cherry. Next, we wanted a fire with juddering flames, warmth or—second choice—a radiator, glowing with three bars.

Rugs too. We wanted to be husked in heat. When language and wishes divided us, Eunice and Janet cried for their mothers. Me too.

The earth thrummed under me and soon, lost in gushes of wind, the world turned in circles. A trick! Hungry and afraid, an awful pain gripped my tummy and with my head pressed tight to my knees, I rocked to and fro.

That was when I began to tell myself a story in my head. But it mixed itself up, talking words I didn't know—choked gobbets of words. Cold, cold, icy raw. I was far away. Floating. A red balloon tied to my wrist by a length of string, tearful I was torn between a giant wish to release it and let it go, and the pain of losing it. Yearning, wanting it both ways ... to stay and go. To tell someone who wouldn't have had the need for this explained to them.

Blasts of air drafting in were strong. Strong enough to carry me off. Where? I was too cowered to think. Then, shivering to the marrow of my bones, with no warning—everything changed. Detached, free and free-floating, my arms and legs were numb and weightless.

Next, the stale air was driven away, and I breathed slowly, easily. I began to smell something good, and pressed my nose into it. I reached another place. I was merged to another body; the body of a bird. My feathers rifled, and when I chose to chirp, it would be bell-like, with cascades of notes. No hurry, no hurry.

Then I lost time.

## 29

Three schoolgirls lost in the mountains. Imagine that today! Police, trained rescue squads, sniffer dogs, abseiling Army troops, numerous volunteers, medicos standing by, helicopters, television newsmen, front page headlines and trauma counsellors.

I didn't know where I was. Somewhere with a low-voiced conversation in a place where the air no longer hummed with fear. Warm, warm enough to melt my bones. Lovely. And a fragrance. Something that was not the smell of rancid vegetation, soil and crushed insects, not dank. With a mammoth effort, I pushed the lids up over my eyes. I lay in a spartan room with tightly tucked-in sheets and a white blanket. I could have been toothpaste in a tube.

'*Mon dieu!* God be praised. Thank God!'

I swallowed, gulped voraciously, and gulped again, as if shells crusted my throat. 'Is it really you?'

Mlle Durand and Sweetie insisted that yes, it really was. Mlle, with pouched nests under her eyes, clasped and unclasped her hands, while Sweetie, with her high-bridged nose and skin that usually glowed was pale, excessively pale. Her gaze was steadfast on me.

Where was I? Dizzy with relief, the answer came when a nurse arrived to murmur over a chart hooked to the end of the bed, followed by a doctor with a stethoscope hooked to a white-coated chest. Mlle? Sweetie? How had they arrived here at the hospital? Sweetie owned a bicycle with netted wheels and wire basket on the handlebars, but it was not likely she'd doubled Mlle. Who was actually directing a smile of great sweetness my way?

Eunice? Janet? They suffered shock and exposure; me, I suffered hypothermia.

'Hypothermia, a condition in which a person falls asleep because the body is totally chilled.' A tic pulled at one side of Mlle's mouth. 'You drifted into sleep.'

Sweetie took up the story, with her placid authority: 'Like a bat, a bear or a dormouse. Who store up food and sleep through winter. They hibernate; bury themselves under snow in countries where it snows. Or in a hollow tree or ... '

'A cave?' I said, frightened enough to cry out before they both leaned over me. One to pat my shoulder, the other my cheek, and I began to cry, because what I smelled was the scent of '*Joy*.'

DISCHARGED AND RETURNED TO SCHOOL, Celia was hopping up and down when I arrived. Faith was Faith alongside her with an unopened tin of McIntosh Toffees from Aunt Billie.

They were unopened in my honour; at first opportunity, we prised off the high-hatted soldier and crinolined-lady lid. Linked arm in arm as we moved from geography class to the science lab, slithering as we did on any waxed bit of floor, I stopped dead in my tracks when Faith declared: 'Lucky that awful Janet Bradley was with you.'

I was speechless, with Celia sucking in her cheeks as she urged me on, the bell continuing to ring. A battery could have started up in my chest, while my feet pushed through treacle 'What do you mean?'

What? 'Janet Bradley?' But we reached the door and the opportunity was gone, Faith whispering: 'Tell you at lunch,' and the Bunsen burners hissed.

I felt a growing unease. Fumbling under the table, I had no luck passing on poisonous green peas, but more luck with a coconut slice.

Released at last, I had to remind them. Were they sparing my feelings, trying to shield me? Yes, both of them said grudgingly. Not grudgingly against me, but grudgingly in the belief that Janet Bradley had not only behaved well, but bravely.

'What do you mean?'

'She decided you had to build the cairn, made her hanky the flag,' Celia said.

'Chose which fork to take in the track,' Faith chimed in. 'Found the cave ...'

I darted my wounded eyes at them. How could they? Compelled by my silence, Celia went on. 'Shared her scone. Next her toffee, cause she didn't want you to be hungry. Or starve.'

That did it. A dreadful sense of injustice began a slow burn, before heat slammed down and I was roaring. 'That rotten ...'

Faith was impressed by my delivery, and Celia impressed that she was an apt teacher, throwing in another adjective, our solidarity of foul language restored.

Then with bitter dignity and tears rising, 'Not fair,' I said. Recounting the true facts, I had their loyalties. Their support was all I needed. We knew life could be warty and a bitch, and that Janet Bradley, doubtless awed by her own cleverness, was a bloody, double-dyed funk.

The decision was taken to talk to Eunice, not for corroboration—they didn't doubt me—but to figure out the best way to bring Janet Bradley down. Eunice was willing, and armed with our joint man-coming-through-the-door-with-a-revolver approach, we four-cornered Janet with her gang. She was preening and suet-faced with a greasy smile spread over her face. But not for long. Soon she was rhubarb-red. And as sour.

'Aren't you the walking-news programme,' she sneered. Hardly lacerating wit, but it hurt before riled by a few home truths, what followed was a glutinous mash of words from her.

'You're a baboon,' an interested onlooker observed with salty disdain, while someone else barked in caution: 'Beware, she bites.' Others fell about clutching their ribs. While stamping her feet, slavering Janet Bradley tripped herself up with accusations and lies transparent to any imbecile; lying as native as breathing to the Bradleys. Suddenly, Celia, Faith and I held our ribs, spewing out laughter.

    Vindicated, I enjoyed it. And didn't. Life was fair, sometimes wasn't. Had I taken a cognitive leap?

## 30

Day on, day on, day on, whether galloping at a breakneck speed or grindingly slow. With the demarcations of each day set to follow the framework of living that day, another year sped by.

Memory may be inaccurate, but it IS our memory. You imagine the past as well as remember it; though this can mean taking a trowel to it and scraping off layers of detritus, as well as conflicted loyalties. What's more, there can be a problem remembering lies, even lies told for tact.

Such as telling Madelaine Brown—a girl for whom there seemed to be no safe place—that one fine day there'd be a prince for her, and with her charms bowling him over, she'd be the chosen above all-comers for sure.

'Will there be one for you too?' she asked, her voice dreamy. Perhaps she was searching to find herself reflected in a pair of princely eyes.

I was doubtful, Faith was hopeful, and Celia wanted one—but a moody prince. Justine announced that a prince of industry would be more in her line. Feminism was years ahead, but we were achievers too.

'And,' Madelaine said less tentatively, 'I want a room with a white carpet,' and, after an intake of breath, 'and a white piano to play.'

Madelaine Brown, hopeless at piano, had had to give up; she couldn't play.

'A white baby grand,' I suggested, not wanting her to see any pity I felt for her. She nodded vigorously.

Mirror, mirror on the wall, we prepared and acted and giggled through the set texts of plays, musicals, our forms of pantomimes, dramas, and term performances, interspersed by holidays: three times a year following each of the three terms.

Holidays! Always a highlight, eventful despite certain lows like when Nina could wander away with headaches. Brutally callous, I resented them; any sympathy distanced, speculating if maybe her brain had sprung a leak. Or the times when I felt I was a secret to my mother, not her daughter. When her silences and her withdrawals barred me from her, and I felt stranded in the dark, where all there was to do was wait and fret.

On my father's desk, there was a recent photograph of my mother; beautiful, gracious, loving.

Does the camera lie? How is life shaped by what is missing?

One day—still to come—there would be an astonishing deceit that still lurked, biding its time. Was every family a place for secrets?

Nearer to hand, not a deceit but a huge unhappiness loomed. One of life's mean tricks. There was a shifting light of shade and sun as Celia, Faith and I met up again to take refuge behind our hedge.

With Faith running late, I sensed Celia must have been searching me out as I approached her. When I reached her, her face fell like a stone. Why were there no hints, no premonitions, let alone shadows of dread? One of her sisters may have been giving out a clue when last month, she wrote to Celia 'that living with Pa Sale was like 7 down, 2 across.'

Now Pa Sale, The Rev. Matthew Mark Luke John Sale—with his own imperatives in the world—had despatched a special message to his youngest daughter.

'What's happened? What's wrong?' my voice cracked to a shout. There was no shout in return; her lips were drawn and closed off. 'Celia?' A scutter of birds flew overhead. Still nothing. 'What?'

Fingers twitching, she opened an envelope, extracted the letter and dropped the envelope before she was smoothing out a page against her hip. 'Listen,' Faith joined us, and Celia's voice shifted key as she started to read.

With the family of eight reduced to three, the Reverend, Mrs. Reverend and Celia were to leave not only New South Wales, but Australia. For Africa!

'No,' stubbornly I contradicted. 'No.' This couldn't be true. I wanted to smile at her, negate this, but only managed to gulp out: 'NO.' Repeat 'NO.' Apparently it was a Sale family thing to talk about dreams, but it had never occurred to Celia that this meant anything beyond sleep-and-dreams.

Methods of betrayal vary. So much for her father and his Christian living, the love and fellowship clap-trap. In a single page to his youngest by six years— five sisters having flown the coop—her father had turned the remaining Sale household into a treacherous swamp. Or a desert. He wrote that his dream was to convert, then minister to heathens in darkest Africa—Tanganyika to be exact—a dream he had fostered over years. He'd declined the first choice offered him up from Lagos, then the capital of Nigeria with its legend of being the white woman's grave.

'But you're just a child!' I said, and Celia, undaunted Celia, my fantastic friend as well as a high sophisticate in my eyes, burst into floods of tears.

Floods! Crocodiles, rhinoceros, lions, rogue elephants, quicksands, hippopotami, stampeding wildebeest, hyenas, and the tsetse fly swarmed into my head. Savagely, I wanted to set my face against the terrifying place that Africa could be and let her father leave for somewhere else. Anywhere else, and leave Celia behind. With us. Arms limp, hands open-palmed at her side, Celia passed the letter to Faith, then me. With huge restraint, I resisted jumping on it and grinding it with my heel.

Now it was Faith who swore. 'That god-damned ...' then she choked up. For wasn't it Celia who was god-damned? By her own father, doubly wicked considering his back-to-front-collar, the myth of loving kindness. A random event had made an orphan of Faith. Her father was dead. He would not, could not, inflict such hurt, while my father, Marcus, would never ...

Suddenly alienated, I felt foreign. More foreign than on that first Sunday, years back, when I was barred from church. In what could have been another life when I was almost eight, hadn't Mlle presented me with the suggestion that I had been given permission, one day, to choose a religion? Or not?

Her accented English played over in my head: 'We no longer belong to a time when formal religion is universally accepted by every young girl. With God the foundation of the world, none of us is abandoned.'

Furthermore, it was my parents' wish that I be free of religion, and free to choose my own doctrinal path. I'd hated them for this, but wham! It struck me that as wrong as they were with the Sunday broodiness this imposed on me—and Hanzi Lazar's parents—there was more involved. Rightly or wrongly, they were allowing me to try to think for myself. As for the Sales! Having relinquished Celia to work out survival tactics and live a separate life like the rest of us, why claim her now? Why take her away? To Africa and the perils there!

A well of affection running between the three of us, we couldn't keep our emotions tidy. Furious at such an injustice, Faith and I were shaken while Celia licked at the tears that ran from her cheeks to her lips. This was unacceptable. Celia the hurricane had been reduced to a puff of wind. The Rev. Matthew Mark Luke John Sale had a great deal to answer for. Who was he to reckon he could gladden pagan lives? Hating him, I swore that I wanted her father damned. I didn't understand the concept, but Faith was noisy with hell and brimstone.

'Hell,' I ground my teeth, with 'hell' being a name for the worst that came your way, which her father deserved. 'Let him rot in hell and stinking misery,' rushed out uncensored. Why did Celia have a father stupid enough to think he was good enough to jump the queue to heaven?

'Could be a mistake. Or a damn cock-up?' Faith spat out between clenched teeth.

Clang, clang. A bell rang on and on. Staying, we pushed our luck with the rules, doggedly dragging ourselves up and savagely kicking out

## A Secret Grief

on our way to the classroom where, raging, I wanted to paint the walls with disgusting words.

'Come along you three.' Her sentences precise but never cold, Sweetie was about to take a class in poetry and waved us to our desks, we shuffled in and sat down before her. Sweetie always wore lovely pastel clothes under dull cardigans the colour of mud. She discouraged self-centredness, pointedly encouraging curiosity.

'Keats, Shelley, we don't possess the lives of the past. Yet what we'll read today tells us that in every age, we need our poets.' Sweetie gathered up her shoulders, straightened, then frowned at Amelia who was following two flies crawling up a window; Amelia Hanlon likely calculating the odds.

'Amelia, your attention please.' to continue. 'For only in words can we express what seems most human in us. Our thoughts and feelings about life as it goes on.' Her hands folded over a page. 'Here poets are the masters; loving the lastingness of things. With insights that take the leap to include both the future and the past.'

Sweetie nodded round. 'Keats, like Shelley, turned from personal grief to the outer world. Because aroused in their minds were images of beauty which led to a truth. That beauty and joy never end; they are eternal.'

'But don't they have dead thoughts too?' Unaware I'd opened my mouth, my cheeks flamed red.

'Yes, Natasha, melancholy dominates many of the poems: Keat's Ode to a Nightingale, Shelley's Ode to the West Wind.' She paused. 'Turmoil in earth, sky, ocean, the images of nature,can reflect human strife.'

'But?'

'But frequently with the suggestion of renewal.'

Chin drooping, Celia raised her head, then her hand. 'What's renewal?'

'Hope. And why not.' Unspoken, Sweetie seemed to be imparting to us that yes, she knew we were eleven years of age, before bending again to Percy Bysshe Shelley: 'If Winter comes, can Spring be far behind?'

## 31

The stars at night looked as sharp as barbed wire, and the days were too real; they flashed by in bouts of anger, blame and distress. Our thoughts and feelings were invaded by our helplessness. Stumped, acceptance was tough.

Parting loomed, then the ache of absence. Maybe the world held too many people bleating about the unfairness of life, but losing Celia was unfair. However unwilling, there was no choice but to try to see her future while desperately wanting it otherwise. Powerless to change things, often we sat just looking at nothing. Malignantly. Dog days, when we were forced to recognise she was not going to be with us next term. Pleading, let alone bargaining, was futile.

Yes, we'd write every week and try to provide a circle of sorts around her. Thick letters, with pages tied with bits of string. Or wool; there were no staples or paper clips back then. Hadn't we already found out how many stamps were needed for letters to Tanzania, Africa?

With no choice, first we'd have to scribble off to our parents, then start on the important things to her. The new things in our lives: like procuring a razor to shave under our arms if and when the fluff appeared, falling madly for Mr. Darcy or Heathcliff though I had reservations, when our breasts would develop—or not —and cup size, how big was enough? The shapes of our noses and chins, with everyone hostage to their genes. What one day we'd name a baby boy or girl. Who we currently hated and adored.

Life is infused with threats and regrets, and we sought ways to dull their blows. Would Celia's father with his back-to-front collar change the world for a better place, knee-deep in his preparations to worsen ours? Of course, we didn't take in our own selfishness.

'Does your mother want to go?'

Sadly, Celia shook her head, stared at the ground, and heaved sighs. It seemed her mother went in for inter-denominational love which Celia explained, but her sisters worried that, contrary to any front she maintained, she suffered anxiety wherever she was. A shabby manse with shabby things, or a thatch-roofed hut with a dirt floor to call home. All Faith and I could do was stare abjectly at our feet.

'Try to think of it as a great adventure for Celia,' Marcus coaxed in reply when I wrote of Celia's fate. 'Friendship involves protection; don't be too dejected because this won't help her, or you, or Faith'. Still tempted to argue, we tried to work at a better approach. I gave her my marbled fountain pen which I treasured, and even if she didn't say she'd treasure it, I knew she would. But she did say yes, she'd treasure it till her dying day. She'd use it to sign her last will and testament.

We kept exploring possibilities, and also set out to practise wide-kneed squats, because in photographs we found of Africa there appeared to be a real shortage of chairs. Additionally, grinning like keyboards, we used anything on hand for drums. Weren't messages drummed from village to village in Africa? Happy, sad and warning messages, a primitive telegraph in a place with few telephones. Of course, there was no chance of a rehearsal, but it was likely she'd help her mother cook in the jungle over an open fire in a great, bath-sized pot. So, emotional and strained but not maimed, Celia grimaced and reverted to herself again. Someone who'd live fearlessly wherever she must be.

'Besides, one day,' we'd say. One day, one day, garbled in my head.

I was ready to kill the pig people and their litter, led by the pustular Corinne Bradley, when, with sickening sweetness, one of them was revolting enough to mention cannibals. Smacking their loathsome lips, knife-quick Faith said: 'Any cannibal crazy enough to as much as taste you would spit you out, wash out his mouth, and run a mile. PRONTO.'

Too soon, parting dawned. The sun appeared briefly in a patch of sky, disappearing, then reappearing. Softened by the party Mlle and Sweetie arranged for her, there were piles of this and that in the way of gifts; little symbols of farewell. Something else I was able to give her—sent by Nina—was a leather riding crop. With all the animals in Africa, Celia might have a pony to ride.

Courtesy of Great Rudi, Faith presented her with a pith helmet and a fly veil, and jointly from our pocket money, we bought her a diary with lock and key.

'I want you to write something on the first page,' Celia requested, voice low, tilting her chin. And as I watched her falter, struggling hard I couldn't keep even a sort of a smile going. None of us could.

'*Roses are red, violets are blue, honey is sweet and I love you. Goodbye,*' Faith wrote, complete with a drawing of roses, violets and a honey pot.

I chewed my pen. Choking up, words felt empty. Panicky, I didn't want to write anything to finalise the parting and drive it deep, then deeper with certainty. With tears scalding my eyes, I wondered if I snatched up the diary and ran, would Celia run after me? Yes, and we'd run away to—we exchanged a long glance—where?

'Write something. Please.'

Still I baulked. Verbally sterile and resistant, I tugged at a hank of my hair. Then, holy cow! Percy Bysshe Shelley poked me in the ribs, eerily transposing inexact words into my head, and I felt the grain of the paper under my pen. '*Winter comes but Spring always comes after it each year.*'

Our hair tousled, eyes streaming, and our bodies crumpled as we clung; we were parted. Celia walked to a waiting taxi with the door held open, then it closed. Driven to her future. Away.

## 32

Someone put a note in Hanzi Lazar's locker. The handwriting was disguised by slanting the words, then blotching the ink. The writer could have used two pens. Or was this composed by a pair—or more—of enemies?

'My grandfather says you are Europe's riff-raff. Not wanted here with us.'

Hanzi might be nasty at times but this was cruel. It left me feeling distressed for her, with something of the sense that things happen elsewhere to other people. To wonder if Hanzi stuffed down hurt and anger along with all the food she stuffed in her mouth.

Hanzi, I supposed, had an uncertain identity. Maybe she was from a turbulent family, but why be labelled Europe's riff-raff? Whatever that meant.

Mlle Durand must have known. It infuriated her. 'Whoever is responsible will be punished.' With her features gravely composed, she paused to deepen her voice before the assembled school. 'Severely punished. The culprit—or should it prove more than one—is at risk of being expelled.' Her eyes raked us row by row.

A collective intake of breath might have been the sea sucking back from the shore. Next, she dismissed the babies, everyone under nine, with the rest of us to remain seated. Addressed at length, it was not possible to see the shadows, only feel them, when Mlle spoke of the bitter memories that survivors of the First World War must live with. Supposedly 'the war to end all wars', but opposing politics, outlooks, hatreds, racial injustices and indignities beyond belief, an ugliness persisted in many parts of Europe. Europe was no more than a far-off place of different peoples in coloured countries in an atlas to us. Yet, Mlle went on, the struggle of good to overcome evil in men's hearts and minds now appeared to be eclipsed by the dread of further battles and strife.

There were moans of distress, but someone giggled. Suspended in awe or disbelief, numbers of us lowered our eyes, but mostly we were vexed as we listened, while behind her the big clock with its Roman numerals ticked.

Mlle pinched her eyebrows together as if she was suffering real pain, then returned to deliver her final point: 'Here in our tiny corner of the world, we must consider others. Others than ourselves. Responsibly adapt to the idea that beyond our circle of family and friends everyone —*tout le monde*—is human like yourself.' Mlle, hands extended, circled the assembly to peer at each of us before she smiled her deliberate smile. '*C'est tout.*'

But that wasn't all as we shuffled to our feet. What followed must have sent someone pale and blank. Sweaty. 'I expect to see the girl,' she paused, 'or girls, responsible for Hanzi Lazar's distress at my study door within the hour,' indicating that day girls were not exonerated. With no traps of questions to catch whoever was guilty, someone must own up.

Day girls—our messengers from the outer world with their sources of news— had begun to bring in snippets of a different world: keep the flag flying, fascist leaders coming to power, growing tensions, the Great War, Hitler youth, a man called Chamberlain, leftist ideals, pacifists and defence. It seemed that in the lead-up to World War II, and the years that followed, their parents listened to news broadcasts, though not us. The wireless was a sacred ritual for the families who owned one.

June Coney, nice enough and good looking but for one squinty-eye, said her family huddled round it in their lounge room. And, oh boy, was her father cranky if she, or her brothers Joey or Brian talked during the news or the broadcasts from overseas. Also enjoying each instalment of Dad & Dave, Mrs. Coney was addicted to the Sunday night Luxe-Radio-Playhouse.

Normally not much of a talker, June recognised a captive audience. Chamberlain, no she wasn't clear who he was, 'but my Dad says that with his trips back and forth ...'

'Back and forth from where?'

June shrugged. 'Dad says he's too much of a gentleman to deal with that bastard.' June's colour rose pleasurably: 'That bastard, Hitler.'

Bastard! Celia, where are you? Tangled by lianas in an African jungle? Astride an elephant or at least riding a sure-footed pony?

I missed her. But if the world dropped into pieces, or blew up, Faith and I wanted to believe that it would not stop our letters crossing oceans.

Our days and our routines swept on, not overly bothered by the tides of history. With one exception. Mlle and Sweetie could have hung out a sign: *No Further Vacancies*, as more and more city parents enrolled their daughters, concerned that when—not if—war broke out, though thousands of miles from hostilities, their daughters would be safer out of cities. Inland from coastal towns.

Two more beds were installed in Kings, which didn't bother me. We weren't really squashed, and I liked Jocelyn with her overlapping teeth and Ruth, who just ignored the jibes from the pig people. They piqued and soon lost interest in anyone that they didn't rattle or reduce to tears. So, watchful and excited for what came next, I was ready to defend her should she need it.

A final insult to Ruth, who soon we saw was clever as well as warm and untidy: 'You and your big brain ...' and Ruth came back in the sweetest tone with: 'How come? The skull is non-expandable. It's just a matter of how you use what you've got.'

I was sure that the smell in the air changed at this; the nearest pig person giving off a hot stink in a mess of legs and arms, their sniggers were only honks before they sank into talk. Sullen talk.

Survival is tricky. Especially in an atmosphere of rules for anyone newly away from home. Maybe eager to shake off her background—though mystifyingly, Jocelyn was given to alluding what went on in her parents' bedroom—in a wider world she seemed content here rather than her home which, from what she told, sounded like a dull place. With no interests beyond his work, her father was a dentist, while her mother's diversion appeared to be crochet and Bible classes. Jocelyn's Bible actually wore a crocheted jacket! It was off-white; which she informed us was ecru.

## 33

War! What was war?

It was Sunday at 9p.m. on September 3, 1939. In Kings, were we still talking, fuming over injustices or arguing, peacefully humming to ourselves or whispering threats? Secrets? Maybe yawning or asleep, while others read under the blankets with a torch. Read what? *Wind in the Willows*, *Georgette Heyer*, *Gone with the Wind*? Were there seniors excitedly discussing newly acquired needle-tip bras? Juniors clasping battered teddy bears to their little chests?

Beyond King's open windows—whatever the season—were there stars crisp as chips in our Southern skies? Or clouds thick with menace and portent?

With a world crisis surpassing trivial or stark domestic crises, momentous words must be absorbed. 'Fellow Australians, it is my melancholy duty to inform you officially that, in consequence of the persistence by Germany in her invasion of Poland, Great Britain has declared war on her, and that, as a result, Australia is also at war.' declared Prime Minister Robert G. Menzies.

There was more. 'No harder task can fall to the lot of a democratic leader than to make such an announcement. Great Britain and France, with the co-operation of the British Dominions, have struggled to avoid this tragedy ... But, in the result, their efforts have failed, and we are therefore, as a great family of nations, involved in a struggle which we must at all costs win, and which we believe in our hearts we will win.'

On Monday morning, our lights were switched on earlier than usual, and some may have been left burning all night. Breakfast was a mishmash of French whispers. Neither Mlle nor Sweetie were present, and that day our assembly was early. Day girls scurried in pulling faces, but few words were exchanged.

Unusually, 'God Save the King' was struck up as soon as we were seated, which had us immediately on our feet again, all for Britain and King and Empire; the whole bit, the entire staff soberly dressed in browns, dark blues, greys and weed-greens, no bright jackets, let alone scarves; our peacock, Miss Karl, toned down to a sparrow, even the colour-mad Miss Florine—invariably a vivid sack of something—had scraped the palette clean.

Next, heads bowed and, ritually as well as domestically out of place, there was the patent-leather haired Rev. Whitehead accompanied by the down-trodden Mrs. Whitehead with what we giggled and labelled as their brood of blackheads, scrubbed up for this moment in history.

Menzies further declared: 'The lion has roared, the cubs are with you.'

The cubs? Canada, New Zealand, South Africa and us; Britain's war was to be as keenly felt as Australia's war. Weren't we part of The Empire spread pink on the globe? It was not unfashionable to be patriotic then... the Nazis were unspeakably evil.

War! What was war? To us it was like wrestling smoke. How were we to understand? Frightened, yet excited, with no idea of what the immediate future held, we were innocents in terms of cruelties, raw courage and violent deaths. On hearing that trenches were being dug in some school yards and air raid practice drills introduced, from our perspective I suppose the hazy nature of war quickly changed from thrilling to a sort of gravity.

Madelaine Brown amazed us when, smiling away any awkwardness, she guessed that growling like thunder, bombs and explosions blew buildings to smithereens.

# A Secret Grief

'Smithereens?'

'Broken bits of everything.'

Helmet-haired Amelia, eyes glittering, began to list the bits: 'Walls of bricks, steel girders, plaster, pipes, glass...' then, in character, reckoning the cost. 'Thousands of millions of pounds.'

'But people?' was my contribution, with no real grasp of the nature of war. 'Smashed up and dead,' spurted a soft-lipped mouth.

'Like my mother and father,' quietly from Faith, which sent me grabbing for her hand, holding it as if I'd never let go, tinny sounds scratching in my head.

Celia and I had sadly agreed that Faith had 'lucked out' with her parents, and I just wished Celia was with us still.

BRITAIN, alluded to as our mother country, many young men clamouring to join up as one family of the British Empire hadn't even started to shave. They knew next to nothing about girls, and nothing about war. If there was a connection between unemployment and early enlistment, economic circumstances rather than political commitment built up by three decades of need and The Depression were motivating enlistments, we were ignorant of it. Unlike the dole, a job in the Army provided five shillings plus three meals a day.

'My brothers are in it for fun. For adventure with a capital A! Their school mates too. Simple as that,' said Eunice Caswell, relating how her twin brothers were volunteering for the Light Horse; eighteen-year-olds who belonged in the flat, claypan country where the sky met the earth in a straight line. Faith and I envied them. Tall on high steppers, we pictured them prancing into battle, with bridle, bit and stirrups jingling, and saddle leather polished to match their horses' rumps. That was until someone acquired a copy of Pix magazine and began showing it around. Its cheap paper was full of a stark episode in Germany: Kristallnacht. Page one: grainy black and white pages of Jews being beaten, herded together, and taken away. Page two: Hitler screaming at seemingly endless columns of troops or Hitler Youth.

What? Where? Mystified, we found ourselves in alien thickets, determined to be extricated and stay apart.

A prefect had a letter telling her that her father had hurtled along to the Victoria Army Barracks in Sydney to join up because the king was in danger. Our heads together, Faith and I discussed what would be done to keep the Crown Jewels safe from the Germans. Especially the coronation crown, the orb and the sceptre with which we were familiar due to the widely distributed picture of George VI wearing them with fancy velvet duds and ermine cape.

'Yes', Betty Blunt, whose mother had apparently wanted to call her Margaret Rose, pursed her lips to inform us, 'my dad was at Victoria Barracks before they opened the gates.'

'Oh.'

If the King called, Betty was adamant, you joined up and went. Puzzled, we supposed that if she was proud of him, we should be proud for her. Her letter also revealed it was her father's duty to go to war to protect her and her mother and big sister.

But privately, some of us believed that her mother and her dad's girls should take precedence over the king. Didn't King George have castles and moats to shelter behind, while they only had a house with a picket fence? Even so, in a flurry of patriotism, her sister was sending off to Melbourne for a dress printed with miniature red, white and blue flags. She was planning to wear it to please her father, but mainly a boyfriend who, again for king and country, was as keen as mustard to march up the gangway of a troopship bent on fighting the enemy.

With the tradition of the Anzacs and the perceived invincibility of our soldiers, young men were not joining up with a belief that they'd be wounded, captured or killed. But, loud and clear, didn't history lessons and books show that peace was far from the natural order of the world?

With snatches of voices and the tock-tock sound of balls on racquets, Faith and I lolled into what had become our special territory with the sky greying, our hands and knees chilly, and our skirts tucked between our thighs. With the 'I only count the happy hours' fountain in sight, and before the dark seeped down, steadfast, we continued to be linked with Celia here. All of a sudden, as if prompted by Celia, Faith shouted: 'Bloody hell. Why do we have to have a bloody hell war?'

'Dunno,' was my brilliant reply. Yet here we were safe. Why? And drawing on our few rules, we dug deep to remember small school branches of The League of Nations. What had they taught? Speaking many languages, twenty states had grown to sixty states worldwide; tied up into legal charters with promises and buckets of goodwill. Why? To prevent war!

'Bloody hell,' we screamed... loud enough for Celia to join in, but all that we achieved was to fire a few sparrows into flight, set off the gardener's chained dog to bark, and possibly stopped the hens laying in the chook house. A wind sighed. Tins attached to a scarecrow rattled over the vegetable patch. Bloody hell!

## 34

If near to a million Australians were to serve in the branches of the armed services - 993,000 the accurate figure - Marcus was not numbered among them.

No candidate for a white feather, though likely a pacifist at heart, he chafed under the restriction of 'Protected Industry', making several attempts to circumnavigate it and enlist. He wanted to join the Air Force on active service, but anchored by his qualifications in aerodynamics, there was no release for my father from De Haviland's aircraft factory. With a wry expression, Marcus was given to quoting Samuel Johnson: 'Every man thinks meanly of himself for not having been a soldier.'

'What's this?' I quizzed when I arrived home for holidays—my parents having debated the safety or not of returning when end-of-term came due. Hadn't there been city schools evacuated? The threat of invasion, evacuations and internments had reshaped the family decisions of separated husbands, wives, parents and siblings, but Nina stood firm. 'Yes,' my holidays were to be spent at home with them.

Having carried my trunk to my room, Marcus massaged his arms. 'This' was a gas producer mounted on the back of the smaller car he'd exchanged for his 'gas guzzler' following the introduction of petrol rationing.

## A Secret Grief

My mother's face was expressive, and Marcus amused as he indicated its shortcomings. 'Grubby,' he grinned. 'No; filthy as far as operating the engine goes,' followed by technical details which meant nothing to me. It produced roughly 75% of petrol power so it provided a way of covering distances as well as saving petrol for the national need.

Rubber was also a wartime need. Elastic was scarce, and corsets and roll-ons were fast disappearing from shops. 'Bulge for Britain' was a new slogan along with 'Dig for Victory' and 'Give till it hurts' to encourage fundraising, that sort of thing.

There were more changes at home. Behind the garage, my father had designed and built an air raid shelter. Stocked for emergencies with tinned fruit, condensed milk, peach jam and camp pie—which Nina stated to be more disgusting than tinned tongue – additionally there was a medicine chest of sorts in a hatbox, as well as essential tools. At ground level stood a pile of sand.

'What's that for? To build sandcastles?'

'To put out incendiary bombs.'

'Incen ... ?'

'Bombs that start a fire.' Marcus picked up a bucket, scooped sand, and let it fly.

Air raid shelters might symbolise the threat of invasion, but soon it emerged that poorly roofed shelters filled after rain. They converted to paddle pools and homes for tadpoles and frogs, and were ideal for mosquitoes to breed.

During a tortuous visit to my grandmother, I overheard that she'd employed someone to dig a slit trench. Its purpose? To be filled with 'treasured possessions'— silver, china and embroidered linen. Intriguing too was Hannah Ross' withdrawal of funds from her bank, which she'd had stitched into three sets of corsets.

Supposed to be self-reliant and entertaining myself, my ears flapped with the promise of an outing to the pictures, later tagged the movies or the cinema, and for some reason being elected to accompany my grandmother couldn't have been the worst of chores. An usherette with a torch guided us to pre-booked dress circle seats for Walt Disney's *Fantasia*. It was preceded by Cinesound News, with patrons unaware that the news was censored. Dutifully, we rose to our feet for 'God Save The King'. Then the ever-bulky Hannah Ross sat inordinately straight testing the comfort—or not—of her moneyed corsets, after instructing me not to squirm.

'She,' my mother sniggered the next day as she related this to an open-mouthed Maggie over one of their coffee sessions. 'She swore the seamstress to secrecy, and gave her two pounds to keep her quiet.'

'Bribed her? Mrs. Ross?' Maggie squealed as she bent double with hands clasped to her head and her newly rippled permanent wave that was greatly admired by Nina. 'Two pounds!'

'Maggie,' Nina hooted. 'Imagine! Buttons on HER knickers fit to burst,' she said with fingers clutching her waist and knees locked together.

Later, when I was older, I came to suspect that through Nina, Maggie lived some part of my father's life vicariously. 'Serve that old dragon right,' she said, her voice high, 'serve her right.'

My mother couldn't let it go. Duty-bound by marriage, she acknowledged her mother-in-law's birthday annually, but the divide between them ran deep.

'I've just the book for HER this year,' Nina nudged Maggie. 'Published by the Red Cross last month.'

'Titled?

'Guess.'

'How to Rid Yourself of Vermin?

'No.'

'Certain Relatives Make for World War III?'

'No.'

'Tell, tell.'

Nina's smile was exquisite. 'A recipe book,' followed by a significant pause. '*Dishes Tasty Tho' Austere.*'

~

EVERYONE HAD to either fight or work to help the war effort, and as an experienced driver having completed a course in car mechanics, Maggie became part of a civilian transport pool.

At school, our windows were pasted over with a crisscross of brown paper strips to prevent shattering the glass, while at home the black-out curtains made for spookiness. But with the onus on households to prevent chinks of light showing through, it created a cosiness and a bonus of intimacy with my mother, who at night knitted balaclavas for the Comfort Funds for soldiers. She taught me to cast stitches on long bone needles for a scarf, then painstakingly wrestle a row of plain wool by turning and twisting it for a row of purl.

Marcus went to weekly VDC meetings—Voluntary Defence Corps nationally set up to invent refinements for weaponry or anything useful. With him away from home regularly, Nina could be moody. Not that she wasn't forgiven. But was her attitude unwarranted? Despite Nina's opposition, regular weekends took Marcus off on bivouacs, where, testing theories and new ideas, someone often injured themselves. Sometimes seriously.

'Not me,' claimed my father, 'I am not about making improvements to grenades. I'm not one of the mad-keen dynamiters.' Unwilling to disclose how his expertise was put to work, he was emphatic that he was just a small cog in the wheel.

It was Nina—the conundrum that was my mother—that I worried about.

Someone who, mouth aslant with a weary smile, was a martyr to headaches and moods, her twitching foot the giveaway. Yet someone beautiful, often strong and resolved, who'd go to ground bent on solitude. Or at her extreme, entertain enthusiastically, rocking with laughter—something she was very good at—as if she was in love with the world. As a child, I was trying to accept her and her life, but was I expected to accept what I didn't understand? Break through the denial that Nina denied me proper love? 'Home' was where the hurt was, but equally a warm skin with me inside.

What happens when you walk into your own memory with its bewilderment of fragments? Who knows what we weave into our early experiences as undercurrents? My parents' relationship was—and has remained— a mystery to me.

## 35

Manpower during the war included womanpower. Mothers with babies and toddlers were exempted, with others pitching in to do what must be done. Hours were long in munition factories, jam factories and pickle factories, or wherever their skills dictated they go.

Voluntary efforts underpinned the war effort, and Nina chose to involve herself as a volunteer—fundraising, serving meals at a canteen which fed troops in transit, and preparing Red Cross food parcels. At a welfare centre, my mother took on the heart-rending task of helping callow young men write home and later—with the Japanese advance a reality—she learned to type letters for relatives of Japanese prisoners of war.

Nightly trips home through browned-out streets could be daunting. Managing homes and families in the role of housekeeper, shopper, plus coping with rationing, also a challenge.

'Is Nina overdoing it?' bluntly Maggie asked my father, a man she'd long since observed never failed to light up whenever Nina appeared. He was still in love with his wife all these years.

'Maybe,' he replied. Then choosing his words carefully: 'but I for one welcome the distractions. What's more, she's doing something compassionate with the letters she helps them write,' his expression bright. If Marcus felt remotely defeated, it did not show. 'Don't we all need hooks to hang on to today?'

What hooks did I need to hang on to? Did my father's hair have bits of grey? Did his smile have a sadness to it from time to time? No, he was there as usual, meshing fatherhood with love. It was my mother I found unreachable. Bit by bit, her lack of affection squeezed me out and mixed me up. Who to tell? Scraps of language rasped in my throat and lodged there. Small incidents hurtm such as when Maggie arrived to be scooped into a hug by a Nina I didn't know. She didn't spontaneously hug me; she offered just the briefest touches instead.

This seemed to be the order of things. If my spirits sank, I suppose I loved her as she must love her sister, Annya. Her brother too; Michael whom I'd rarely seen and barely knew. Then, out of the blue, via Nina, there was a request from Michael to me. Older now, would I write to him? Letters to a far-off uncle from time to time?

Two recent photographs of Annya and Michael stood framed in our sitting room. Both were in uniform. Annya was a beautiful Women's Auxiliary Air Force (WAAF) officer, who, when enlisting, had written how frightful she looked in a beret.

It was impossible for her to look dreadful, but when she was issued with jeans, Faith and I giggled like mad. Men's jeans, more a boiler suit so outsized that when she rolled up the legs, the crutch dangled between her knees.

Michael—Nina's brother, my uncle and the midshipman who as a boy only twelve had joined the Navy—continued to sail the seven seas. Glossy, handsome and defiant, he bore a likeness to Nina as he stared from his frame at me. If his mother failed him by dying, and his father by a cold personality and rich neglect, then, by needs of his own, Michael had to learn to look after himself. He had no choice.

TIME FLEW, as it does. Forever split between home and away, I returned to school. War stories ran rife there. In the main though, it was peripheral to us, imposing no crisis in most of our school lives.

Faith met a boy from Queensland, north of Townsville, who was certain that any plane flying overhead was 'Jap'. He could tell by the sound of the engines and urged his father to shoot them down. One night, barred from the local pictures with *The Hunchback of Notre Dame* showing in a haze of cigarette smoke, he sprawled on the back steps of his house. Search lights probed the sky and suddenly it lit up like a Christmas tree—he was shadowed by the vast silhouette of a bomber. One of ours, but he believed he was the target as its landing lights scanned for landmarks. He told Faith he wet his pants. Who wouldn't? Despatched south from Australia's front line to relatives, soon the rest of his family was ordered south as well.

'My brothers,' boasted girls who had them, 'swap amazing things.' Some kids were lucky enough to have bits of military stuff; badges, buttons and stripes. One had an Arab dagger from the Middle East! And if school-age brothers felt deprived when no enemy aircraft flew over them, their teachers were mightily relieved. Ginger Meggs, the comic hero—face punctuated with freckles—was shamelessly used for propaganda. Ginger and his gang exposing Japanese Zero aircraft, black marketeers, etc., who, no exceptions, met their just deserts.

Amelia Hanlon's family shelter had to be expanded. Her parental authority strong, but her young brother's will stronger. He dug in his heels, refusing to budge from his bed during air raid practices and alarms. He reckoned the war to be a personal affront and without his Raleigh pushbike beside him, he would rather die than leave it unguarded during a raid. We were impressed.

Moreover, the enemy was an object of loathing at his school with 'Houses' renamed Churchill, Roosevelt, etc. But Amelia was mighty peeved because her mother was too angry with the world to listen to her. Her doll's house had to remain in her room, so to placate her, her bookmaker father initiated bets against an attack. 'Unfair, unfair,' we sympathised, and those with brothers pulled the longest faces.

Acned Corinne Bradley—whose spots weren't improving—came out with a crazy tale about tracks on a sand dune near her grandparents' house on a northern beach. Tracks left by a Gestapo general on a German-made bicycle put ashore from a submarine!

'Aw, pull the other leg. A general pedalling a bike! He'd goose-step, you idiot,' a realist intervened, and to her fury, the realist was supported by one of her gang.

'Go pop your pimples,' was suggested to a round of applause.

We were expected to contribute to the war effort at school. Principally by wasting not, wanting not. Paper was in short supply so we wrote shorter exercises, shorter compositions, and saved the brown paper bags that came our way. But for what?

Seniors—given first-aid classes then allowed to practice on us—dreamed of lipsticks, with Starlite from Woolworths considered a luxury, while dresses for their dances and end-of-year formals were trimmed with mosquito net; no coupons required.

Adults complained of another ration shortage—grog. But, yippee, rice and sago being in short supply was a real blessing for us at boarding school, sparing us the usual mush topped by grated nutmeg. Ugh!

Then real excitement loomed. We were to be treated to the spectacle of hundreds of young soldiers in khaki uniforms and slouch hats. Because OUR Army generals—mystifyingly referred to as 'Top Brass'—hit upon a plan to toughen the raw recruits. Fitted out in full uniform, they were to march up and over the mountains in Army boots to test and improve their stamina. Training to endure!

Patriotism high, with this great cross-section of military force, who could overrun Australia? The local community buzzed. Helpers were marshalled to meet foreseeable needs or emergencies, billets were organised for officers, and camp sites for 'enlisted' men, who, when we actually laid eyes on them, were just big boys dressed up to play soldiers and Army games. With their backs as straight as they could manage, striding abreast with rifles slung, the packs on their backs must have weighed a ton, with Army-issue tin plates, mugs and other things dangling as extras.

Were they tough and courageous? We hoped they were. Giggling, we also hoped they carried a photo, a lucky charm or special letter folded small.

Next, true blue and loyal to King and country, posters began to appear directing that 'Careless Talk Costs Lives'. One well-circulated poster declared that 'Hitler Has Ears'; proof that Hitler was a figure to despise—depicted with elephant ears and his bit of a moustache.

Shielded from the atrocities and unaware that freedom and democracy were threatened and nations were at risk, we were ignorant of the anxieties adults feared. 'Business as usual' was another war slogan—it meant little to us other than school and routine, our day-to-day lives. But day-to-day life took on a thrill when the troops began to arrive. Our closed world was widening, if minimally.

Seduced by patriotic zeal and called upon 'to join up', bellowed to stand 'to attention' or 'at ease', this apparently was more exciting for them than the lives they had lived. People cheered, flags were waved, and girls and women of all ages ran out, kissed them, and hung on their arms, which doubtless was new to most of them. Led by brass bands playing jerky tunes: 'Tipperary', 'Colonel Bogey', and 'The British Grenadiers', the latter the signature tune of the ABC to introduce the evening news. Later, after Singapore fell, it was switched to an abridged version of 'Advance Australia Fair'.

The soldier march disrupted our full week of school life. Informed that 'our boys' missed home comforts, the community went into overdrive. Churches held meetings and dances, and they provided meals—ham salads, shepherd pies, jelly and cream—while hot and flushed over their ovens, the local ladies baked roasts, scones, and lamingtons, as well as queen and meringue-topped puddings, plus Anzac biscuits galore.

Sports were organised where practical. Concerts and divertissements went into full swing. Some offerings in church halls included lantern shows, during which I twitched as if there were ants in my blood, an affliction that beset me all my life when excruciatingly bored. The slides from visiting missionaries were dull and yawningly flat for us, and must have hit the pits for these hundreds of young men, while, far but near, I was convinced I heard Celia groan.

Then came the request. We were invited to put on an evening concert for the troops, to be preceded by two tableaux. Number one, British to the core, was to follow the bush legend: 'The Man From Snowy River'. There were frantic rehearsals, and there was Eunice in jodhpurs astride a cardboard horse. Painted chestnut, piebald and roan in art class, a clutch of riding bushmen followed on similar mounts. To each side of the stage, a chorus lineup—with sheaves of gum leaves like giant posies held at navel level—alternated stanza by stanza by stanza. Miss Clarke at the piano faithfully produced the pounding hooves.

Tableaux number two opened to a full-throated 'There'll Always Be an England' from our combined choirs, augmented by a sing-along audience. Centre-stage was Faith. Believe it or not, Faith transformed into Lord Nelson of Trafalgar when dressed in white satin breeches, a jacket, and with a frilly cravat high on her throat. And then there was me dressed like a ragged Moll Flanders who—on cue—had to hand Nelson the telescope after his exhortation: 'England expects this day that every man will do his duty.'

So, what did I do? Dropped it, with the telescope rolling as far as the blinding footlights, making for a real mess of a retrieval. My mob cap tangled with the buckled shoes of Nelson's second in command.

'Pick it up, pick it up,' was hissed, and aflame with shame, the blood in my head pounded. But I'd unintentionally provided relief as hoots of laughter, whistles, and boots thumped the floor.

'Good on ya,' hit the ceiling, resounding through the rafters. I wanted to die.

In retrospect—much later—worse was inflicted on the audience. A ten-year-old songbird recruited from the day girls—pretty, blonde and plank-chested— warbled 'We'll Gather Lilacs in the Spring'. Then, horror of horrors, she was followed by three tap-dancing, paper-creped daffodils rendering in three-part harmony 'Birds do it, bees do it, even educated fleas do it ... let's fall in love!' They were staged against a screen of waratahs, faithfully traced through tissue paper then coloured fire-engine red.

Embarrassed-cum-amused by us as silly but good-natured kids, they greeted us with more hoots and whistles while what must have been intended as the 'serious' act of the night was lined up. Seniors in cardboard mortar boards and black gowns rendered Shakespearean soliloquies in elocuted tones. The audience shuffled shoulders and feet, coughed like sick kookaburras, and smothered guffaws. They were enduring. Well, sort-of-enduring, till they were released and supper was served: fish paste and egg sandwiches, thick-sliced if scrimpily buttered date and raisin bread, and honey rolls.

Naturally, the dances were more popular. It was whispered that Mrs. Reverend Whitehead was overheard to grump, 'Where there's dancing, there's sinning.'

Her view made little impression, but as food for thought in the dormitories, it was chewed over, squealed over and generally misunderstood. Dipping to the Pride of Erin or a progressive barn dance, a partner could be shy, cheeky or born with two left feet. Who could tell, Prince Charming just might loop around, briefly present everything a girl desired before he was swinging off on his enchanted way to current tunes as well as old favourites like 'She's my lady love, Lily of Laguna'.

June Cooney, our nice enough day girl of the squinty eye, had some intriguing snippets for us to discuss. Endlessly. Mrs. Cooney—big and good-looking with no squint—was a hospitable mother who, with a surfeit of energy, invited young soldiers to meals. June was leading an exciting life, and according to her, most of them ate like horses, and some like pigs, though her non-judgmental mother declared them all 'lovely boys'.

However, launched on what we were sure was their great adventure, some were teary-eyed, homesick, and, comforting as best she could, gossip was rife that she selflessly met every challenge. Called to duty, Mrs. Cooney knew they'd change and mature. But how much?

## 36

'We're interning enemy aliens,' the rumour buzzed.

'We' was our Australian National Security Regulators. 'Enemy aliens' were European enemy aliens born in Europe. Non-British and put at its crudest by who else but Corinne Bradley as she charmlessly mouthed: 'People who talk funny and can't speak English proper.'

'Properly,' Faith countered, and I loved her more than ever.

At the official level, enemy aliens meant Germans, then Italians, but there were to be many injustices—lightning raids on homes, businesses and even schools; people locked up or sent to camps with barbed-wire fences. Members of a family could be separated, and it was grisly for anyone loyal who loved their new country.

This set me thinking of my uncle-by-adoption, Uncle Victor Jagoda, and my Aunt Lily and their family of five. Thankfully, they were far from any state of war. And all was well, Uncle Victor was a Pole. Poland was an ally, and he worked in the fishery industry, an essential industry. Aunt Lily was learning to drive a truck, maybe as huge as the Army trucks that formed the vanguard to the long march as the soldiers made their preparations to leave us. Flags waving, there was a flurry among the locals—and us—when at the end of the week the recruits began wending out of sight.

June Cooney brought us news. Before the Army moved on, an officer knocked at their door—she didn't divulge whether back or front—and requested her mother by name. He presented her with boxed gifts of Rheingold and Porphyry Pearl which we were left to conclude were for services well done, with never as much as a hint of her lacquered hair out of place.

All too soon and reluctantly, we were returned to our routine, which included letter writing come Sunday night.

'Dear Michael,' I addressed my mother's brother, which triggered a sense of being on equal terms with the stylish naval officer framed at home. There was a lot to tell, and I filled three pages, doubling up and using the back of each sheet. Then pen to chin, I took a break to watch a moth bump against the light, feeling the breeze from the open window. It was no chore; I'd come to like writing from my interior world. Conversations with absent people had their appeal, especially Celia, who never felt altogether absent from me. Despite distance and time changes, I imagined her against jungle drums and alien tribal gods, with the moon shining down on tiny meerkats by their burrows on the savannah. Or on gawky, ladder-necked giraffes.

But back to Michael, and his salty world with its smell of the sea. Nautical. While fathoms below, creatures of the deep were doing what I guessed creatures of the deep were primed to do.

'Finish up girls.' A pause. 'Finish up Natasha,' and I drew a sleek ship, a sleek giraffe, and a full moon above both.

With daylight saving our days lengthened, but I had no idea how long and harrowing a fast-approaching day would soon be for me. How could I? It was a day when I was scared witless of how it might end.

Geography in progress, there was a tap at the door from a messenger of little significance, Madelaine Brown. I was called from my desk by Miss Alston, who, pointer in hand, was directing us to Alaska and Eskimos. Not yet widely renamed Inuits—in their tongue 'Inuit' signifying 'Man'—we learned that Eskimo was said to be a name of reproach applied to them by the Algonquin Indians. Interesting.

Miss Alston whirred. 'Their economy is based on fish, sea mammals and land animals,' she said, the tick of her voice strengthening. 'Nominally Christian but their earlier beliefs attributed a living soul to inanimate objects and natural phenomena. Cheerful and friendly people,' she turned to acknowledge the waiting Madelaine, whose expression was bashful and hesitant. 'What is it, dear?'

Was there a mystery to danger and survival? The fairness, the unfairness, the lottery of life?

'Natasha. Mlle wants you in her office. Immediately.'

There was no sinister undertone, but I was baffled. Baffled; not yet alarmed.

'What's she want?' I hissed to Madelaine who haired off down the corridor as we left the Eskimos.

'*Entrez*,' came back quick as a flash after I tapped Mlle's door. On entering, two policemen rose from where, awkwardly, they sat. They loomed over me like twin volcanoes—one pale-eyed, the other dark.

'Natasha,' Mlle named me, her smile gentle enough before she turned to them. 'This is Natasha Ross.'

'How do you do,' I answered as trained, swallowing down what had to be alarm, just short of fear.

Suddenly through the open window came the sound of clapping; applause from a group of seniors outside engaged in ... I didn't know. Then abruptly, it stopped. The light in her room was mixed and gloomy in corners. Mlle indicated I was to move closer until her scent was apparent. Closer, and my body loosened. A bit.

'Natasha,' one volcano erupted, 'careless talk costs lives.'

Scared, I smiled anyway, but how was I to trust myself and my perceptions of things?

'What?' I asked before 'I beg your pardon?'

'Careless talk costs lives,' he repeated, and helplessly, I turned to Mlle who intervened.

'Is it necessary that you take the child to your police station?'

'Afraid so, m'am, err madam.'

And horror of horrors, I heard myself squeak 'Mlle Durand ...' which thankfully he ignored.

'Natasha Ross will be confronted by the evidence.'

'Is this necessary?' she asked with an involuntary shake of her head. Then, lips pressed in disapproval, she exhaled a long sigh at his nod. 'Of course, I shall accompany her.'

'As you wish,' and the second policeman extended a hand with hairy knuckles that weighed down my shoulder. I hated his hand on me. Surly and with my face suffused by heat, I was guided to the door.

'Come along,' he wheezed, and I was directed to a van—a paddy wagon, Faith recounted later. My eyes filled, and our surroundings were a blur. Memory at whatever distance can be startling, with bias and denial built into it.

With a narrow verandah under a bull-nosed iron roof, the police station was constructed of stone, its doors thick-varnished timber planks. Built in colonial days, had convicts been shackled to these walls? Were their cells the cells where I was to be locked away? Flogged? Frightened, I shook.

If wildly I imagined a diet of stale bread and water, at least I was spared that. Offered a glass of milk on arrival from an ice chest set under a row of hat pegs, I refused, but was persuaded to drink it by Mlle. She said it was essential that I keep up my energy as she was taken to wait elsewhere, leaving me in a room furnished with a desk, two upright chairs and a bench. A murmuring, bakelite AWA radio squatted on a shelf. I registered a ghostly reflection of myself on the surface of a small window. I didn't like it and slammed my eyes shut. I wanted to keep them shut to close off from this room, but I couldn't.

Next, a solemn-faced sergeant flicked the radio silent before he proceeded to take my name and age, noting them in a thick book before he set about fingerprinting me. 'This won't hurt,' he said before adding with a wink, 'we'll make a criminal of you yet.'

'What?' I said with increasing panic.

'Top priority winning the war, girlie,' he replied before running his tongue around the inside of his mouth. Dismally, it dawned on me that policemen only spoke to prisoners in code.

Soon the original interrogators reappeared and loomed over me: 'Come this way, young lady,' then rumbling under his breath and dowsing what might have been a smile, I was moved yet again. On one wall, there was something familiar; a map of the world, much of it British-Empire pink. Then I saw the posters. The war posters: blocked letters shouting: 'Dig For Victory', and staring down was Adolf Hitler with his giant ears and black-toothbrush moustache.

'Sit down, Natasha Ross,' one said, so I sat. The rungs of the chair hard against the flesh of my calves, I clung to the seat on either side of my thighs with tight fingers, which might as well have been clinging to a raft swept out to sea.

Insisting she rejoin me, a purposeful Mlle now stood well-anchored on both feet as she faced my tormentor. '*Mon Dieu qu'est que* ... Question the child on the matter under concern, but in a civilised manner if you please.'

He stuttered out a laugh followed by: 'If you will allow me m'am ... Mlle Durand.'

The fiercer of the volcanoes entered, extending something at me. A letter. My letter to Michael! Holding the pages fan-like, he proceeded to poke them under my nose. 'Is this your handwriting?'

Nettled by this silly question, I wanted to shout: who else would be writing to my uncle? But an accidental criminal, cowered by what seemed to be the molten lava of his eyes, I could only nod and bite my lip.

'*C'est impossible!*' Mlle reached over, gripped my hand and kneaded it, emitting a hoarse little moan.

'Troop movements are of the greatest secrecy, my girl. If divulged to the enemy, they can cause ...' but a sharp gesture from Mlle and he left the sentence hanging. Ominously. Flecks of spit were at the corners of his mouth. 'Are you not aware of the need for security?' and his hairy knuckles stabbed Hitler on the wall. 'Well?'

Adult anger is terrifying to a child. Did I look up at him, my face expressionless and blank? My brain struggling to remember something? Then, simmering to the top, what occurred to me was that for all the notice I'd taken—Hitler with his ears flapping to fuel his evil plans —I might never have seen it. Muddled and emotional, what I wanted— and badly—was not to be here. I wanted Marcus, Nina scented, if not by

'Joy' but a second favourite, 'Je Reviens', and to be home with its comforts, confusions and Gus.

'Natasha,' Mlle spoke my name. The next best place had to be school and its confusion.

He hadn't finished. If he doubted I was the enemy set on destroying Australia, did he see me as a master spy ready to torpedo the King's Navy or attack Michael's ship at sea? His pointing finger skewered me in the chair.

'Speak up, speak up,' he demanded, but my tongue clogged and failed me.

AT LAST, it was over. Outside, a blue sky had turned stormy—stormy, like the man in charge when Mlle, tired but not bullied or made to play penitent like me, suggested that a more balanced approach to a schoolgirl's letter should have prevailed. Yes, yes, she inferred that she understood he was doing his job, and with discretion, she gave his job the higher calling—duty.

'My patriotic duty,' was his pompous reply.

Patriotic duty! Her restraint fled. A torrent of French poured his way which was not doused when, *sotto voce*, rude as well as ignorant, an underling came up with: '*Inky-pinky parlez-vous ...*'

Mlle Durant paused, drew a breath, and shrugged. Then, collecting herself, she returned to the English language with dignity. 'This is scandalous,' she said.

'What!'

'Summon THE taxi.' There was only one in operation due to the shortage of petrol, but instead the paddy wagon appeared.

The paddy wagon! Her elitism resolute, Mlle was adamant she wanted the taxi. This involved a fifteen-minute wait during which the second, less-volatile volcano with his pale eyes, appeared. Was it from the goodness of his heart that this man offered Mlle the fare? Proud, frustrated and indignant, Mlle turned an alarming shade of red.

Opening his wallet only to be slapped by a further torrent of French, he slapped it shut.

Gloved hand to her brow, Mlle expressed the hope that any future matter which may arise between her establishment and the local constabulary could be conducted with more concern for the sensitivities of her young ladies. She had growing girls in her protection, far from home. With a delicate quiver of disdain, then, as if forcing herself to smile, she thanked him minimally for his gesture of offering the fare.

'*Il a une peau epaisse.*' Met by my blank expression, Mlle translated: 'He has a thick skin,' and her eyes on mine were warm.

Then, with no warning, a tap on my shoulder frightened me half to death. My school gloves had been left on the fingerprinting desk.

Finally over, and freed for hours from classroom lessons, it could never be said that I learned nothing that day.

## 37

Faith pinched me at the waist. I pinched her back and, forced to stare at something, we stared at each other's foreheads to stop from screaming. Screaming with pleasure.

Babs, the glorious Babs, Barbara Moody was approaching and we were wreathed in smiles. Hierarchies are a part of school life, and with few exceptions, seniors sat at the top of our tree. Babs, the Head Girl, gilded the highest branch: seventeen on her last birthday, almost hatched, soon to fly away and blaze her trail in life. Final exams within months—the Leaving Certificate—followed by the formalities of speech day, the rituals of farewell, then along with her peers, Babs would be leaving us, going off to the big world from which the rest of us must remain locked away, a minor gulag, not that there weren't certain powers to be negotiated behind the walls.

How we'd miss Babs: her diction perfect when, pipingly, she read notices at assembly. Democratic at House meetings, gazelle-like but forever victorious on the tennis court; desolate, we felt weighed down if we dwelt on the fact that soon she'd be gone.

With an ever-attendant group, her best friend was Ginny Jones with the marigold-red hair, whose 'pretend' mother and her flamboyant travels were restricted, of course, since the war broke out.

Babs, forever dimpling a smile at her own reflection, must have acquired every skill by osmosis. We marvelled at her talents, her aplomb as well as her prettiness: her chiselled nose, her downy skin. Despite her unattainability, just once we would have liked to pat the fine hair on her cheeks and her arms. But there were no strategies to do this, let alone the means to see ourselves reflected in her kitten eyes.

'Hello, you two,' she said, glancing up from the mirror of a compact she always seemed to have in hand.

*Hello, you two!* 'Hello,' I tried to reply brilliantly but failed. Comparing notes with Faith, we were gripped by the fizzing excitement of a crush. All we could do was simper and giggle stupidly.

'Share the joke.' Babs paused for divine seconds, beaming like the sun.

Then, as if the air between us was bewitched, she wiggled her fingers in farewell, pouted to make a kissing sound with her lips, fluffed her golden hair and waltzed on. She was due to be collected for an outing with her brother, who endearingly called her Bunty. What a pair! He'd be in RAAF uniform, his hair closely cropped under the cap, and here she was in a drop-waisted dress that was blue. Heavenly blue. Everything to do with Babs Moody could have been heavenly blue. Why didn't we have a camera to snap a picture, a keepsake, then another with her brother? If only their retreating blue backs!

Suspended—caught between child and adolescent—we existed in a separate age. Prepared to believe all and nothing, what caused girls like Faith and me to develop this joint crush on Barbara Moody? Inter-school debating could well have put it up for argument; hot words through the smoke of the sheepish self-consciousness we felt. Doubt-less less important than 'Populate or Perish?' or 'Modern Women Belong in the Home?', but 'Why are Crushes Experienced by Adolescent Girls?' could be a subject to shed light on our little psyches, our backgrounds, and our parents, to help us through.

Nina was no perfect mother, but she was the only one I had. If I'd ached to stroke the fine soft hair of her arms, or been held sufficiently close to see myself reflected in her eyes, I had no memory of it. Only a yearning for her response and warmth. Even when close, my mother was absent with little connection. She gave off a sense of separateness and perhaps that was why I formulated a policy. Never ask. With the codicil: don't lose hope.

More and more Nina read, with reading being a solitary and private act of immersion in other lives. Her head was full of their sentences, actions, and dreams, which must have made me feel that I was swimming uphill for her attention and struggling to get back to shore and into her life.

Now, in whispers, Faith and I concocted a phantom conversation between the Moody gods.

'Bunty,' deep-voiced I asked, chin to chest. 'Who were those two young girls you waved to when I strode up the drive?'

'Bobbie,' Faith answered—we'd chosen Robert for Babs' brother—and naturally, Faith had made it affectionate. 'Those girls are endearing young pets ...' Faith/Babs paused. 'Little sweethearts.' Clever Faith because 'sweethearts' was a territory we were keen to explore. Unknown territory.

Biologically, we weren't entirely ignorant, but the nuances of attraction and lovemaking and actual sex were another country, alien.

'Sooo?' I/Bobbie appealed.

Empathetic, Faith took up the research. 'Bobbie, how many girls have you kissed this week?'

There was no hesitation from Bab's big brother, outfitted in Air Force blue and set to cut a swathe through any mob of females. Nonchalant in the role, I smoothed back my hair with one hand and plucked my chin with the other. 'Bunty, let me think. This week? Ten. Yep, ten at least.'

'Oooh,' said Babs/Faith. 'Did you, did you, undo their blouses, pull up their skirts?'

'Only those I gave a box of chocolates to. Cadbury Roses.'

'Oooh,' Faith sucked a cut on her finger. 'Oooh ...'

Bobbie/me cleared my throat with a cough. 'Oh yes; as well as the lass with the spray of frangipani pinned on the shoulder of her party dress at the canteen dance.'

'Did you kiss them with your mouth open or closed?'

I/Bobbie hesitated, enigmatic as I lifted my clean-shaven chin. 'That depended, Bunty.'

'On what?'

'You'd hardly want to kiss them hard if they had buck teeth.' He/me gave this further thought. 'Or at all if they had bands,' I clarified. 'Bands like rat traps on their awful teeth.'

'Mmmmm,' and with great satisfaction, Faith and I pictured Corinne Bradley, who no man alive, let alone Babs' brother, would want to kiss, should she be the last female alive on earth, with the rest of her gang consigned to a leaky ship and towed out to sea. Sunk.

## 38

Mlle was frequently heard to state: 'I don't see my girls with limited prospects.'

Yet it was the real Babs Moody and Ginny Jones with the marigold-red hair who were to add to our education with facts not to be found in any of our texts. Would Mlle have been amused, shocked, or warily alarmed? Surely not uninformed.

On the periphery of circles of seniors, on the sidelines of tennis, netball and hockey matches, or at night brushing our hair before bed, like Hitler's vile little ears open to troop movements and sea manoeuvres, our ears flapped.

Related with many a theatrical shudder as well as highlighted by expressive index fingers, there were amazing reports and among them were the following list:

1. While our soldiers stereotypically may be preoccupied with swearing, gambling and drinking, the newly arrived Americans in Australia were obsessed with sex. A common request: 'Want to stop and have a tickle up?' Every stroke of their hands went further under a skirt. They'd be off to fight

in the war in a week or a month and soon could be losing arms or legs or dead, so...
2. Americans showered girls with presents: chocolates, flowers, nylons, clothes and money.
3. They fed you drugs. Spanish fly, then raped you.
4. Prostitutes—for whom a 'charity root' could pave the gangway to embarkation—were able to look after themselves, but nice girls who swarmed around like flies got into trouble.
5. Yanks had a passion for immature girls. Some as young as twelve!

And so it went on. Open-mouthed, we listened; we understood here and there, not totally mystified in our innocence/ignorance.

From someone we thought was shy, Mary Moore, re-named Meeky Mouse, we were informed that vice squads roamed parks and the back seats of cinemas to pick up tarts and nymphos under twenty-one. Girls on active service!

A bishop's daughter revealed a mother's cousin who didn't give a damn what happened to her kids while she ran around with enlisted men on their final leave.

From Ginny, who one day would develop a knack for losing husbands then age to a woman who invented her life by watching old movies, we picked up that we should be patriotic—go out with our own boys who didn't give you anything except a fuck.

From a Walt Disney fan seeing *Bambi* for the umpteenth time; when little lost Bambi called that she wanted her mother, a voice boomed from the back stalls: 'She's out with a bloody Yank.'

Yanks, it was said, all came from towns with sex arcades, and shocked, titillated or just unenlightened by what we heard, it was the adored Babs who astounded us and shook us to our roots.

On a balmy evening out-of-bounds, specks of insects tumbled about. Nearby were a few banana trees, and Faith and I volunteered to sneak in, pick and hand over any bedraggled leaves for certain seniors who rolled them, set them smouldering, and then tried to smoke them. They experimented with lettuce leaves from the kitchen garden as well. Our reward? Permission to stretch out among them—elbows to chins— and experience a sense of inclusion even though we were forbidden to interrupt, let alone talk. Not that we had anything to contribute.

Someone coughed and Babs jabbed her in the ribs. Pinned to the moment, all ears, we waited. We were sure that our Babs Moody would have something worthwhile to relate. She did.

'You got the VD cough?'

There were bursts of curiosity, gusts of snorts, snickers, giggles and the revelation that VD was venereal disease. Acquired during sexual intercourse! Constantly taught to be fastidious with language, Babs, who won prizes for English, could have taken out another prize with her explanation.

'Go on, go on,' she was urged, but she shook her head. Her smile, if angelic, was veiled. Queenly, Babs inclined her head, raised a slender hand, nominating Ginny to follow if she dared. But Ginny—now rumoured to have nipples sharp enough to poke in your eye— had nothing to add on the cough or venereal disease. All she had was information, but riveting information on how to dance beyond the progressive barn dance, the Pride of Erin, and the waltz.

'Well,' Ginny began, and I remembered when Celia and I listened and heard that Ginny's mother, Mrs. Jones, was taught to tango by the greatest Spanish matador and waltzed with the Prince of Wales, as well as cheek-to-cheek with film stars.

Now Ginny was updating to jitterbugging and cutting-a-rug. 'You're grabbed around the waist, everyone screams and they swing you between their legs.'

'Between their legs!' we screamed.

My hands curled at my sides. Was Babs outclassed? No. The air was warm and musty, the sky a wash of pinks, and, hands primly interlaced, she waited till the noise levelled off. 'Our soldiers have buttoned flies,' she said, hauteur in her tone. 'The Yanks, Americans,' she might have been translating for our benefit. 'They have zips.'

Ginny managed a silly, forced smile.

'In their pants?' Meeky Mouse's gasp was audible 'Gee! You'd want to look? She paused and the pause was electric, her voice a dare. 'But you wouldn't, would you?'

'I would,' Babs Moody was sure. Babs Moody, one day to grow fat and lazy; soft and underused.

## 39

There must be countless strategies for deceit. For countless reasons. Inhabiting the past can be strange, where you must make your own relationship with your parents. It's clotted with complications for me. And hurt. Though I wouldn't know for an unbelievable twenty more years.

Banished to school, great changes were made. I was replaced by another child. A term-time girl-child who lived my life for two years with Nina and Marcus. She inhabited my room, and slept in my bed.

For as long as I could remember, my father—the person I trusted above all in my world—had told me: 'Trust yourself.' He was later to add: 'No one can make you feel inferior unless you consent.'

So how, when, where or why did I trust—or not trust—myself?

I don't know, but I felt that you need a brain riddled with holes to lose your memory altogether—holes through which it leaks out. But aren't there different versions of reality?

Years later, the revelation that opened my eyes was bitingly true. No feat of imagination, it forced me face-to-face with too many imponderables and hurt surfaced.

Why?

Sony Allasando, née Sony Jagoda, who married young, was in touch on a brief return from her home in New York. Both Nina's and Lily's lives were spent by then, over; and if there's a jaggedness to death, that's another thing. For another time. Death the shadow that sits behind us all.

Sony, alluded to as my 'twin', both born in May 1928. As children, we were close. We'd drifted apart to erratic exchanges of Christmas cards, vague invitations to meet up in London, Paris, Argentina, where her husband's family lived, her own family of sisters and brothers here and there, dispersed. Sony—no blood ties—my unrelated 'twin' of whom with affection, I remembered this and that. Toughened skin on the soles of her feet, skinny as a tadpole, breath smelling of licorice; that she gabbled like a goose—a lovable goose—long hands with dirty fingernails, her mother's smile, the flea population of the coast who took up residence in her dog. Good recollections. Sony's generosity: pennies for humbugs, things. How imitating her brothers, she'd spit into the palms of her hands to shout: 'Righty ho'. Above all, her breathy mile-a-minute voice, a Sony who never lied, told tales or whined.

Who could have guessed how we were locked together in the oddest of unions? A stinging union, the depth of which I wouldn't —couldn't— reveal to Sony, her head on a five-star Australian pillow for only six hours before she was off again, pillowed in cloud.

Morning coffee in the foyer of Sony's extravagant hotel, sliding feet on parquet, flowers in massive urns, the scent of luxury as strong as the smell of hamburgers trapped in a take-away joint.

'You know your mother rescued me.' Seated opposite Sony, the skinny tadpole with tough soles, was a dazzling woman in silk, Florentine sandals on pampered feet.

'What?'

'From the country bumpkin I was.' She pushed her wrists together for emphasis. 'Gave me what I missed out on at home.'

'But...'

'Natasha, don't mistake me,' no wistful tone, 'home was a happy place for me, but like any family, we fought. About everything.'

'Nina?' A quivering smile.

'Nina taught me so much. About books, theatre, and music. She took me to concerts in the Town Hall.'

And now, with the fingers of one hand holding my lips together—tottering—I was struggling to compose myself, mould this to reality, a corporeality that had to be mine.

'Yes. She introduced me to French, with little readers,' Sony's lips curved softly: '*Noe et Les Animaux, La Queue du Chat.*'

In the warmth of the foyer, I sat frozen. This picture of Sony's was no emotionally-near-glacial Nina with her silences, which too often were the silences of my childhood. Struggling to juggle the meaning of what Sony was relating was unthinkable. My experience of Nina was particular to me. This was insane, inane. A send-up. Crazy. Sony had to be hallucinating, and I felt my body thinning, stretching. Should I try to reason, defend, or attack? Living in the past and here the present had grown treacherous. Stupefied, somehow I was trying to watch myself think.

'When?'

'When?' Sony was repeating. Then leaning towards me, caringly, she was peeling my fingers away from my throat, taking them in hers. 'For the two years I lived with them. In term time. With you away at school.'

Nina, someone else's mother while I was away at school! Away at school! All that meant. That wide and treacherous world. Thorny with difference where your little life must be reassessed, revalued. Where, unable to process justice, or injustice, you needed strong bars to hold to support you, know who you were. Where stars picked in a lonely sky at night. While Sony—there wasn't enough air—everything shifting from unreal to too real. My mother, Nina, someone else's mother! Why?

Our story was re-jigged. Aunt Lily and Uncle Victor sought a better schooling for their last child than local education provided, with teachers in short supply. But why risk city dangers in war time? The possibility of invasion in their town with the steel works seemed threatening, with the possibility of alien soldiers secreted ashore on unsettled sites along the coast. It was decided that if the worst came to pass, children would be as well protected in the city.

Invasions, attacking aircraft and bombs ... it was Sony's bomb that exploded in my head. She was oblivious that she'd robbed me of something denied me in childhood. By her, but not by her! Here and now in the plush hotel with its pampered guests, I found it impossible to feel other than vulnerable. Smiling, her mouth moist with concern, she was talking, but I wasn't listening. What did this mean to Sony in transit? What to me? A couple passed us, the man to chortle; and move on by ornate lamps towards a baby grand piano.

'Natasha?'

I had to make a connection though could not concentrate; but fuzzy, absorbed that Sony had not become my surrogate until the age of twelve. She returned to her family during the term holidays, and she was permanently returned at fourteen. When we were both fourteen!

'Natasha?'

With an uncertain hand to my older heart, I felt it ticking. Still alive, and Sony was asking: 'You didn't know?'

You didn't know? Lost between fear and scorn, was it bewilderment or a smothering secret I felt distorting my face?

'Natasha?'

What was that smell? Whiffs of bitterness, and I was gasping for air?

'I ... I ...' my cup and the coffee pot collided, with coffee oozing over the low table, spreading down my legs to my shoes, but thankfully, not on Sony's elegant sandals and feet.

A waiter hurried to where we sat, concerned as he handed me a white napkin, mopped at the table with another, and bore off the debris. While soon Sony must be off and away. A reluctant Sony, sad and unwilling to leave me precariously strung midway between disbelief and distress. Which I could not deny. If we gave ourselves days or weeks, we could talk, but it would be talk, talk, talk about things that were over and gone forever.

'It's so long ago,' I said, even as minutes were shredded by seconds and I kissed her cheek. I suppose we clung as we had when, aggrieved, we parted as children. Now aware that the past never wholly recedes, indelibly traces a part on our heart, my worldly Sony, *sotto voce* was telling me: 'Many a parent can propel a son or daughter towards psychiatry.'

Then drawing back, but with her fingers still touching the tips of mine, Sony said: 'Remember the sandcastles we used to make?' And I nodded to see those castellated battlements we constructed from our upturned buckets of sand.

'Yes.'

'And how the next day we'd rush to the beach,' and Sony sighed, sad, as we'd sighed then. 'To find them washed away by the tide.'

ANGER SEEPED in and out of me. Why the mystery? I hated that word: mysteries only happen when, lips sealed, people withhold things. Secrets. And over unbridgeable distances, questions festered in my head.

Why was I never told?

Was I blunderingly inept never to uncover a clue?

Scrupulous, were Marcus and Nina determined never to leave one? If not, why not? Wasn't it human to slip up?

Was my lingering presence erased by Sony's? Was I non-existent when away at school?

Did my mother jettison part of her undemonstrative life when she took Sony in?

With all the shades of meaning to the word 'parent', if I set about trying to reassemble mine like a jigsaw, what—if anything—would it reveal? Would the pieces click into place? Genuinely unable to understand, I think the everyday questions tore at me more.

Did Gus creep into Sony in my room?

Did she sit for meals at our table in my established place?

Did she spread her books and papers where mine were cleared away?

Did she lie in bed listening to my house and my world, winding down at night, and stirring with daylight?

Did she hear my father cough as he lit his first cigarette of the day?

Did I lurk in my room when she was there? Hidden in cupboards, drawers or my books? Additionally, her favourite toys—a teddy to remind herself she was safe, maybe a Polish doll in a peasant dress?

Then at thirteen, was it a mess of a room with her posters of movie stars? Her clothes on the floor? That sort of thing?

Did Sony smell what I smelled? Every house has its own smell.

Did my grandmother find her a charming child?

Did my mother show her affection?

Did my father kiss her good night?

On and on, fantasy and possible facts; thrashing out my arguments, nervy thoughts. To little avail. No visible snatches, not a glimpse from this hidden past. Yet even as I turn to look back at each staging post, driven forward I must accept what I didn't understand.

So, a lingering grievance, which at certain hours can still darken me today.

## 40

There's a twisted sense of humour to time. It flies, it drags, but inexorably, it marches on. On tip-toe or noisy boots. On regulation school shoes.

Faith and I exchanged glances. Amelia Hanlon and Justine Straffe, Madelaine Brown too. What June Cooney was saying was hard to take in; day girls experiencing life in different ways. They were women of the world; touched by a more eventful day to day than we lived in our cloistered boarding existence at twelve, back when 'twelve' labelled you still a child. A child whom a contemporary twelve-year-old would consider impossibly deprived. Add to that repressed, let alone unspeakably daggy; no Jag, no Esprit, let alone—believe me—no jeans! Nor Nikes, Reebok or Adidas; 'runners' were no more than persons who ran, and pumas large feline quadrupeds also recorded as cougars.

Not that we were considered ourselves altogether divorced from sophisticates. We judged June Cooney to be one. For didn't June Cooney, with her little Australian terrier, Delilah, prove a formidable team? Delilah was taken on daily 'walkies' alongside the Grammar School with its snickering boys, lounging boys, over enthusiastic boys, mocking boys, dribbling boys, and sheepish boys watching this girl and her dog progress. Nubile, pert-breasted June was a leader in the development stakes; her squinty eye no more a disadvantage than specks on a butterfly.

June Cooney's mother must have given her a head-start, what with her sociability and hospitality during the Army march. With her stiff-lacquered hair and make-up, Mrs. Cooney was an ardent cook: lamingtons, tarts and melting moments regularly on offer to June's friends. Yet her mother ran a tight ship and each afternoon her daughter had to change out of her uniform to ensure it was kept 'spick and span'.

Obediently, June replaced it with a swing skirt and knitted top that was one of many her grandmother provided; her old fingers forever click-clicking in the belief that knitting held arthritis at bay. Silk and cotton knits for summer, and wool for the winter months. But didn't her grandmother appreciate that 'little June' bloomed to 'big June'? Or was June's mother, overly keen on the 'spick and span' forever washing her jumpers and shrinking them in the name of cleanliness?

'And he said to me ...'

Excited, we hung on for the revelation, hoping 'he' would be named, followed by a word picture to rival Errol Flynn or Tyrone Power.

'Yes?'

'John Smythe.' John Smythe! Was there a more ordinary name than 'John'? But at least 'Smythe' had to be an improvement on 'Smith'. A slight improvement.

Amelia whispered to Faith who whispered to me, 'Can't judge a book by its cover,' in the next breath to let us know that Amelia wasn't giving odds.

'He's as tall as me,' June said, and then held back for a few seconds for effect. 'Red hair', then pensive again for seconds, 'between red and fair.'

'You mean ginger?' at which June's breasts swelled in a deep sigh, her blonde head swinging between yes and no.

'Got pimples?'

'A few.'

'Where? Forehead or chin?'

'Oh, just a few.'

Next it emerged that John Smythe also had few words. The strong silent type. Or was it few of the right words?

'Like a great ape?' As unkind as this was, we were edging towards a truth of sorts.

DELILAH SAT FAITHFULLY at June's feet on the verge between the path and linked wire fence which looped round the Grammar school oval; younger and lesser boys kicking a ball and rutting the grass with their football boots.

It was autumn and the afternoon was beginning to close down with a chilly edge to it. Loose lips in a flap of a smile, captivated by our June, John Smythe was unaware he risked boring her with an account of the latest outgoings for his stamp collection. A 6-cent George V from Ceylon, a 2d Coronation from Fiji. Last month, he'd swapped a 3 anna from India for a 35 krone from Norway.

What was June waiting to hear? How pretty she was? Prettier than any rival for his attention, apart from film stars? Though hadn't there been murmurs of her likeness to Deanna Durbin, minus the singing?

'I'm cold,' June shivered, bending to scoop up Delilah and settle her under one arm. 'I should be going home.'

'Aw, gee,' said John Smythe, 'don't go yet'. June relented at this implied compliment and cuddled Delilah to her side. Sophisticate that she was, she had related to us lesser beings that it made her shiver, just letting her mind wander to how she would feel if John Smythe cuddled her.

But having delayed her, boofish John Smythe plunged into his stamp collection again, proud to boast that he'd been voted in as leader of the Philately Club.

'I gotta go,' June Cooney decided.

I<small>F SHE WASN</small>'<small>T</small> interested in his stamps and collection which now ran to three albums, I was.

'Does John Smythe have a half-penny Great Britain Silver Jubilee?'

I was immediately interrupted. The pressing questions boiled down to: 'What happened next?'

'Want to know? Really want to know?' She was playing her audience like a trooper, her downcast eyes glinting when she raised them. Fisting her palms, she opened with: 'Weeellll …'

'Tell, tell, tell …' We stood circling her like a clutch of brainless geese.

Two passing seniors stopped abruptly. They listened briefly, then moved on, with one throwing over a superior shoulder. 'Sounds neanderthal to me.'

The other bent double to crow: 'No stiff competition for THAT title round here.'

'Tell, tell …' was again the plea, and June Cooney's expression a cross between pleased and smug.

'Weeelll, I said that I was cold. Again. And besides, it was getting late; soon it would be dinner time.'

'And he said?' We anticipated John Smythe's voice, even with his sparsity of words, vibrating like a tuning fork. We also imagined the gathering night sounds and vicariously smelled the food cooking in her mother's kitchen. Maybe a roast, browned potatoes, and gravy without lumps the size of golf balls.

'And he came closer,' June knew how to create suspense, she was masterly.

Madelaine confided later that she had to press her feet down hard so that her knees wouldn't shake.

'And …'

June Cooney, who soon enough would become a heavy woman, went coy. Of course, we begged. Would, could, John Smythe mumble out: 'I like you!' in his awkward way?

'He came closer, grabbed at me …'

'Oooh!'

'At my hand,' she had the honesty to amend. 'Then …'

'Go on, go on.'

'He said, "You don't feel cold to me," June squeaked out. John Smythe, having at last stepped up close, had grabbed Delilah's paw!

Languishing against a tree, Amelia pulled up straight and mimicked John Smythe cruelly, slowly, which didn't seem fair.

'Seems he doesn't know where to put his hands,' came from a girl most of us considered thick.

Then, swallowing giggles, someone was quizzing June in a sort of a bark: 'So you and Delilah must be look-alikes?'

June yapped back: 'Course not, course not.'

While hooting and clutching our ribs, we all fell about, which didn't seem fair either.

## 41

I read my letter again, then once more. Miraculously, my Aunt Annya had escaped serious injury in a plane crash. Stationed at an Air Force base in Queensland, the pilot and pilot-in-training were less fortunate. Immediate fears of a back injury to my aunt were not confirmed. Coming down on woolly red earth with jagged mountains ahead was considered lucky, the rescue speedy despite the fact that the DC3 was off course, though not impossibly far.

There'd been time spent in hospital, with no details given to me even as I imagined Annya swathed in a silk kimono and touching her narrow feet to a hospital floor in scarlet mules. I refused to let into my head the hurt person Annya might have become, but hadn't. The week after next, she was to spend four days with Nina and Marcus. Nina was intermittently plagued by migraines, and some days not seeming to fully possess her life. Yet wasn't my mother equipped with an inner life all her own?

With my face the colour of paper, Faith said I read the words with dread but scurried back to safety; Annya's and mine, something inside me balancing her pain to my lesser pain. Then sniffing her lovely scent, I saw Annya with her aptitude for happiness, fully attached to the world.

## A Secret Grief

Annya, like Nina with a flair to what she wore, indulged me even if her visits were brief. She indulged me more by talking to me, listening to me, and engaging with what I said. Or was it that the less intense Annya lived a larger life, with my aunt more at ease with me than my mother.

Ordinary days at school were spent doing ordinary things, and the following week came a second letter. Then more news: Michael's ship had arrived in port. Home from sea, and moored near Garden Island after dodging into Sydney Harbour through nets that were destined not to stop a Japanese submarine.

'Michael's back,' I read. It meant my uncle, his sisters and my father would all be reunited under the same roof, our roof. Without me! And my giant question was WHY? My heart was sinking, with no mention of permission being requested by my parents for a special weekend. Absence from school demanded strict and essential details which must include details for return both to and from home!

Home was somewhere with its universal pull where I re-established myself during holidays three times a year: I touched doors, sash-cord windows, furniture and bricks around the fireplace. Home absorbed my parents and the lives they lived there—Nina with her sense of entitlement, and Marcus' enduring love. If it drifted up from my subconscious that I was less important to my parents than I wanted to be, I tamped this down. But did they think of me as a nuisance? Worse, did they even think of me? With Annya and Michael being with them, was I just an oversight? Far off from darkest Africa, fruitily Celia's voice came loud and clear: 'A damn cock-up.'

The blue sky turned bilious, rain fell and my world turned meaningless. Why hadn't Mlle or Sweetie informed me? If not Miss Boskie with her pediment neck, or Miss Keyes with her wafer lips just as easily could have brought the message that I was timetabled to travel on a certain train to be met by Marcus at Central Station for this special weekend, during which I read through teary eyes that a party was planned. A party minus me!

At Aunt Billie and Rudi's request, Faith was to go to them at Clifton that weekend, and by mid-week with nothing arranged, desperation set in. I couldn't ring my parents up; permission to use the telephone—black with its rounded dial—prohibited unless the need was rated an emergency. And a dire emergency call made with either Mlle or Sweetie present, that was the fixed rule.

Another day passed...I glowered; I would never forgive them. Resentment should have made me feel better, but it didn't; instead it layered into an ache that corrosively began to gnaw into my bones—Marcus and Nina didn't want me home. Was 'family' something shed like skin...even as in a far-off future I was to confront the monumental issue of where Sony Jagoda fitted into my family?

A non-church goer at my parents' insistence, deprived of religion, should I defy them? With no experience, pray to God? Halo-headed, seated on HIS throne in the sky—which may or not be heaven—HE was rumoured to have the power to bring anything off.

Faith considered it worth a try. Not that given her experience she fully trusted God.

'What do I say? How do I begin?'

'Like a letter. Dear Sir,' Faith frowned, clasping her hands as she went on. 'Yep, Dear Sir, try that. Or maybe make it holy.' Hands clasped, fingers pointing under her chin, she made a sweet smile.

'Dear God?'

'My dear God,' Faith boosted.

'HE's not mine. I'm not supposed to have one; not before I'm a thinking adult.'

Faith was practical. 'You can't wait. Besides HE loves us all—well Mr. You-Know-Who says so—from the sparrow in its nest to the ...'

Yet I was grubbily mortal; fearful of fire and brimstone, if I encroached on HIM would the earth hurtle into the sun? I was filled with a rage to live but if HE was generous and deigned to send a sign, HE might want me meek, like a twittering bird in a cage.

My cage! Tensions winched tightly in my head. From tight to bursting, then, whoever hurled it, I was struck by a thunderbolt. *Run away, run away* ... suddenly ticked in my head. Caught between excitement and desperation, teeth clenched, I broke out in a cold sweat. 'I'll run away.'

## A Secret Grief

Speechless, Faith recovered enough to gasp out: 'Did HE tell you? Did HE?'

'NO!' edged by certainty, I shouted. 'NO!' again, and louder, I was unable to credit HIM with so much pull. I didn't understand but I was no tiny sparrow, had HE planted 'run away' in my head? Was I in HIS presence, subject to HIS influence, HIS will? I shook all over. Humans were supposed to have a streak of common sense but had HE—rumoured to be divine as well as to see all—pierced my skin and read my pagan heart?

'You won't, will you?' her eyes incredulous, Faith was squeaking. 'Run away?'

With no hesitation, what came scuttling out was: 'Yes, I will.' What other chance was there to get home? Families weren't perfect, so who else was to take steps to put right the damn cock-up they'd caused. Left me to repair.

Practical again, Faith was determined I couldn't go all that way on my own. All that way! Sydney! I couldn't, wouldn't, let myself reckon how far; all I could figure out was that I must get going on Friday night, at the latest, to arrive in time to shake them awake.

Barely able to believe what I'd said, I rammed hands into my pockets, and desperately ached to adjust to this turn of events. If only I had some talisman, a lucky charm like a rabbit's paw—or something—to clutch. 'I'll get going Friday night.'

'You can't. Not by yourself.'

'I can,' but Faith was tenacious, she wouldn't let it go.

'Amelia's forever on about running away,' and if Faith pronounced this defiantly, I accepted that she was uneasy for me; her face an expression of care. It's not always what's said that counts, and I grabbed her hand, squeezed it, and swung it back and fro. What seemed to be never-ending obstacles in our lives were forever appropriated by people who believed they knew best. It was becoming crystal clear that I must act for myself.

'What's up, you two?' Speak of the devil, Amelia rounded the corner, hair scraped back, from hockey, and guiltily we jumped apart. 'What's going on?'

Faith stood beside me impassively, loyal, and with Amelia turning up like destiny. I made the decision to ask her if she'd join me.

'You bet,' Amelia, the bookmaker's daughter, grinned. There was no holding back to calculate the odds; the thought of running away matched her mood. The timing was right. Sent off from the hockey field for kicking one of the sly Bradleys, a detention hung over her from the previous week. And reprimanded by Sweetie for an overdue essay, she'd been ordered to clear up the art room as well.

Remarkably adaptable for someone thoroughly spoilt and demanding, she was fired up. 'Not one second has gone by today when I haven't wanted to be out of here. Anywhere,' she shouted, 'anywhere else in the world.'

'You sure?'

'I'm sure,' she answered, sounding sincere.

I hadn't been sent off from the hockey field but sweaty, my eyes went to Amelia in her gym slip, then lifted to focus over her shoulder. On a fast trajectory, I could have been away on a direct flight path. Headed down the gravel drive, bordered by trees, then through the small exit to the left of the school's high iron gates.

They were less towering than when I was barely eight, if still intimidating. Beyond the gates was a landscape of trees, while cradled between hedges of bush was the ribbon of the road which curved away to freedom!

'How do I get away from Princes, and you from Kings?'

'On knotted sheets from the bathroom window between your dorms,' came Faith's ready reply.

Shot through with alarm, open-mouthed I scowled at Faith. She was tangling a finger in her hair, concentrating in her attempt to help. Then a burst of optimism: 'I'll help you knot them. Tight,' she emphasised. 'Rudi won't be collecting me for Clifton till mid-morning Saturday.'

'We'll be gone,' Amelia interrupted matter-of-factly, followed by laughter from me before I sealed my mouth, praying there were no kids nearby with flapping ears, gloating at our drama. Not of course praying to HIM.

Faith shot me a complicated look.

It was settled. With four days to fine tune, if I experienced doubts connected to point one—the knotted sheets from a bathroom window upstairs—it was best to think of this as the most hazardous point to be over and done with first. Ages ago, hadn't Faith and I discussed that maybe she led two lives: one with everyone who loved her, the second a strange life with her parents entrusted to eternity? But having initiated the jump-start to my escape, she came over gloomy. Tearful too.

'What if?' All three of us inspected the landing patch; a freshly dug garden bed where surreptitiously we laid soft boughs and leaves.

Autumn leaves in abundance. Despite our blood and adrenalin coming to the boil, we decided we must wear thick clothes. Thick to provide another layer of safety on impact should the sheets fall short of the ground.

'I'm taking a hockey stick,' Amelia threw in.

'Why?'

'For protection.' Feisty, and I believed bravely, Amelia came back at me, radiating reliability, so why object?

'If you want,' answer a shrug, and I refused to explore what she might need to protect herself against.

## 42

A grapevine, like unwired electricity, ran among us boarders. While we guarded our secrecy and judged it safe, guesswork and a few friends uncovered the plan. Should we trust them? We had misgivings, but they banded together to help.

Who would have believed it; there was no lingering spite towards me. Due to leave at the end of the year, and bent on becoming a great scientist or a great doctor, Hanzi Lazar kicked in with food—biscuits, bananas, and bars of Nestlé chocolate were to be lowered in a pillow slip. No; Hanzi argued for a bag slung from my shoulder to ensure we had rations if, somehow, the pillow slip got left behind.

'For the journey,' she concluded and moved close, a Hanzi who thankfully now gave attention to personal hygiene.

The journey! Is it conceivable that at twelve I was so breathtakingly cretinous? Mindless, when term-end reports stated I was imaginative and bright? Cautious and level-headed would have been better; leading me to acquire a compass and learn to read it, as well as a map.

Long-suffering Madelaine Brown came closer to the truth: 'You've got everything but sense.' Prescient Madelaine.

Eunice Caswell, with whom I had been lost in the mountains along with the scabrous Janet Bradley, hardly helped with her awful story depicting frostbite. Now Eunice—a big reader—came up with an episode from a book about escaping kids who walked all night over the Yorkshire Moors. Within sight of a village, they were waylaid by a lunatic who, forcing one of them to witness the killing, strangled the other, then chopped the tongue out of the first so he could never be denounced to the police. She provided lurid details about severed tissue and gushing blood.

Eunice may have devoured books, but if tempted to hit her, Felicity let her have it. 'You vomit-making little creep.'

'What, what's wrong with you?' she had the gall to stutter out. 'I... I ... was only ...'

Eunice, no sensitivity, managed to irritate us with everything she did or said, but as I curled my lip, I was scared. I should have been directing every thought to the escape.

Then cocoon-like, I wrapped myself in another probability: a banner spangling 'Welcome' strung across our front door, accompanied by streamers, kisses, hugs and praise for my initiative, my parents' guests taking an avid interest in me.

On Friday night, clouds paled in the sky. Dusk closed in, and it was soon black. My stomach tight, sure I'd throw up; not just disgrace myself if I ate the macaroni cheese, the last thing I needed now. Hard to dispose of, I sneaked most of it into a hanky and Justine Straffe leaned forward to shield me. Wise to the excitement, she helped me out. Meanwhile, at the next table, nerveless Amelia was tucking in, her composure complete when she turned my way with no more than medium interest.

How did I feel? Like me, and not me. Swarming in my head was a hope that tonight—then tomorrow—might never come.

End-of-week-Friday-nights meant that study was often shortened, discipline more lax and prefects less nosey. Minutes dragging through treacle, agitated, I put a cheek down to the desk and began to smell all that was wrong with my world. To my knowledge, no one in this school's history had ever scratched 'scotophobia' among the initials, hearts, dates and patterns of words on the scarred pine. Like me, 'scotophobia' ... the fear of darkness ... would have been unknown to them.

Then Faith tapped my shoulder and I lifted my head to her rigid smile. 'You don't have to. Not if you don't want to.' Her words pulsed through me, but I had to brush off our affection and our togetherness. Weren't we, each of us, on our own? Forced into inner worlds where, unravelling in my head, families cast shadows?

'I have to.' Thump: it hit me. Somehow, this expelled the doubt and let me pitch into imagined safe arms to hold back the terror.

A bell—a bell of doom?— rang. Or did it toll? Night swooped down and the time came for Kings and bed.

'Good night, Natasha, sleep well,' pediment-necked Miss Boskie hummed as we passed on the stairs; me *en route* to Kings. And beyond.

'Good night', beamed idiot me. 'Good night!'

Routines included brushing teeth in the bathroom—a sort of base camp—where the knotted sheets were to be fixed to big brass taps over the sink in an alarmingly short time. Would they hold? Would the sheets split? Would my weight, or Amelia's, yank the taps from the wall, splitting and crumbling, pipes cracking then water flooding the floor and corridors?

'Scared?' someone was lousy enough to ask.

'Lights out.'

Like me, Amelia had to peel off her pyjamas to fumble into thick clothes. Flicking torches, a candle in a jar and a forbidden cigarette lighter ... our escort led the way to the bathroom where Faith was testing the sheets over and over, time and again. Behind her, the window seemed to be framing darkness. Then the window was eased up. Brrrrh. Night rushed in, cutting down to my bones.

I supposed I would go first, followed by Amelia. Water creaked through the pipes. They spluttered and dripped.

'Where's Amelia?' Faith was demanding. Someone examining her tongue in an ill-lit mirror scuttled off to Princes before she was back, pushing Amelia through the door.

Hugging arms to her ribs, in her mouth wet strands of her sucked hair. *Not good.*

'You bloody little funk. Faith spat out. 'Funk, funk, funk.' susurrated in chorus from surrounding lips.

'I…I…I…'

'You, you, you! Amelia Hanlon the gutless wonder! Sneaky and a cheat. The bets all off? Are they, are they?'

Someone interjected: 'A soul in crisis,' and if I'd understood what she meant, she might have meant me.

'Shut up!' said Hanzi Lazar. She then turned to me, kissed me on both cheeks before slinging the bag of food over my shoulder. 'Good luck, brave one.' She made an odd salute. What's more, she'd organised a collection, though where and when we were to spend the money was a mystery. Two pounds! A fortune of pennies, half-pennies and silver coins.

Amelia flickered eyes towards me, and with no attempt to brave it out, she was muttering at the floor. Was she justifying herself to herself? While appalled by her treachery, I choked up and, hollow, Faith was imploring me not to go.

'Ssssh.' Discovery and all that meant could come at any moment. Fingers pushed hard to lips in warning, and urged to get going, but if any one of them so much as put a finger on me, I'd bite it off.

'Bon voyage,' came the hoarse whisper.

Clumsy in all my clothes, clamps of hands were hoisting me up onto the window sill. Everything was happening too fast!

'Please don't go …' was whispered.

Then, 'just go, don't look down,' came the advice, but I did. I looked down to a black void!

'Please don't go,' again, but washed by waves of panic, my one word was taut.

'Goodbye.'

Goodbye? God be with you? Was there a jittery flash of sorts? A supernatural disturbance in the night? Because across vastnesses and datelines, what I heard was Celia shout: 'HE'd bloody better be or it's the biggest damn lie I've ever heard.'

Rubbed raw by fear, and loathing the snivelling Amelia Hanlon, running away could well bring on unstoppable consequences. But I'd had enough. With each tug of breath forced from my lungs, I screwed both eyes shut, then opened them to slits and looked down.

How would I look down on this sight from the distance of years?

## 43

A moonless dark. Massed trees stood black and bare. Buoyed by relief at touching down, hiccupping convulsively, then up off my elbows and knees, unhurt, I forced myself to walk to the gates, not run. Outside my rage against Amelia deflated. I had to forge ahead. MUST. There was nothing else to do. The night air was alarming, charged, different from school air.

Looking back was useless, no help. Looking forward, I was terrified and I felt for Faith's little torch. NO! It must have dropped out. Lost.

Accustoming to the dark, I unlatched and passed through the small gate. The large gates loomed gallows-like, which against all common sense made me bolt, but not far before I halted and backed into a bush where leaves rasped my cheeks as I hid among them. I needed to be certain no one was about, no one was following me and I had no risk of being caught. WHAT! What was that? I ducked back, flattening against strands of something that bounced—a wire fence.

Nooo! I lurched, shrinking into my skin. Shaking, I wanted to be sick. A swish of bicycle tyres whipped past, leading my way, then was gone. The darkness pricked by the wink of red from the tail light, then nothing but darkness. I hated whoever rode it.

Running away for a week, the direction had to be to The Village, then on through it. But here and now it was a stark, night village; alien to me, even as I tried to imagine the staff of Mrs. Jenkins asleep behind the shop in narrow beds, their cat warming one or other of their feet. Or tiger-like on the prowl in long ragged grass; stalking a trail to chicken coops, marauding small bush burrows, whiskers beaded with blood.

Miserable, I sniffed, shuddered. On reaching The Village—the straggling streets, the jumble of outbuildings—high above the stars pricked between clouds, intermittently lighting the sky. Next came the unfenced and indistinct outskirts before I was well away, joining the long highway against the barrier of night. The way to the city, home?

Spooky and uninviting, this was strange and untrodden territory which wound away down the mountains, with the mountain tops sinister like the turrets of an ogre's castle. Menaced by thoughts and the danger of a ghost materialising and confronting it, I was struggling not to cry. My heart beat fast. Small and insignificant in a giant landscape, I was experiencing what I'd never imagined before. Why was I here? Why hadn't I planned, properly thought 'running away' through? This wasn't how it should be—terrified of anything and everything that did and did not exist. How many long miles—short miles if I could walk faster—lay ahead of me?

Driven forward even as I peered back, teeth biting my lip, all I could do was shuffle on. Then, squinting ahead in the distance, I made out a scatter of lights. I suppose I expected to be encased in silence, but cricks of sounds set me to spurts of running, and the panting breath—my breath—was welcome. The unlit road rolled on. I went with it right and left. Soon, hot, I stopped, peeled off Hanzi's shoulder bag, then my coat. A middle-class child and well-provided for, I had no second thoughts as I threw it into the bush and, faster without it, I moved on.

Round a bend, I pulled up to burrow into the sack for a chocolate bar. Head thrown back, sky above, the grainy darkness appeared to lighten with the mix of earth smells and whiffs of vegetation. Minimally less afraid, there was emptiness everywhere but I was going home. Tomorrow , everything would be sooo different. When I arrived. I could see Marcus gape with surprise before he reached for me, Nina's beautiful face clownish, then delighted as she gulped one of her slow breaths which would end in a sigh. Aunt Annya could be counted on to jump with joy, when, one arm thrown over the back of the sofa, she turned and saw me. Michael was unfamiliar but, who knows, he might scoop me up in a sailor's hornpipe, with everyone's eyes on us, which, having orchestrated my entrance, I'd lap up like cream. I imagined being truly welcome; their arms madly waving 'hello' like flags.

Less reckless now, I pressed on, stumbling when the road banked and quickly righting myself. If I passed any milestones, I didn't see them. Nor crippled trees, stunted bush or shrubs, let alone the sheer drops from sections of the highway at either side. Under my feet, the road simply went up then down. Alternating between flat, smooth, and bumpy with pot holes, I didn't stop, except when a stitch pulled me to a halt. It was essential to arrive before the party started. Besides, the cold seeped into me if I didn't keep moving.

Cloud cleared from a frowning sky, the moon rose and somehow looked sad. A bit giddy with so much still ahead of me, gradually I began to feel a bit less anxious, instead a bit sure. I shouldn't have.

Hearing the tick of an engine and tyres squealing on gravel, I swung about, fell down, and hoisted myself up. Dread shot through me. Face scrunched against oncoming headlights, they blinded me; then with hands to my eyes in the middle of the road I stood shouting before I slewed to one side, and felt my palms sting on the rough surface of the road.

'Jesus Christ, girlie!' the voice boomed in the mountains like a storm at sea. The engine cut, the lights dimmed, and with an onrush of fear I lay paralysed and spread-eagled on the road.

'Girlie. What the...?' His voice calmed and became more measured as he began to question me. 'What are you doing here? Where have you come from? Where do you belong?'

I was struck dumb.

I think he watched my lips for what I might say, before in a grave way he pronounced. 'I won't hurt you, girlie. There's nothing to be afraid of...'

Teeth on edge, one of my knees hurt and even though I was afraid, I believed him. Suddenly, inexplicably, I felt no menace under a ledge of mountains in the middle of the night. All I felt was cold.

'Girlie,' he gave a quiet cough and up-close, I saw his eyes were watery in a blunt but kind face. 'You give me one heck of a scare,' he said, shouldering out of his coat. 'Put this on.'

I did, and the warmth it held from his body heat felt like a radiator switched on low. Next he was guiding me to the car to step up its running board and into the passenger seat, before another quiet cough. 'Now, quick smart, we gotta get going; get you to where you belong.'

The door needing a slam, he slammed it, before rounding to his side behind the wheel.

Where did I belong? It was a question which had a familiar itch to it like unscoured wool.

'Well?'

I opened my mouth, then closed it. It was impossible to find the sounds to scrape through and answer him.

He was patient; there were no abrupt words or gestures, and his expression was composed under lifted eyebrows in the beam of light reflecting back to us from the headlamps he'd switched on again against the blue-black darkness that enveloped us beyond their range. Night sounds weighed heavily, birds or things with fright in their voices. Instinctively, I inched towards him and he was telling me his name. Perhaps in the hope I'd offer mine, which did not occur to me.

'I'm Mr. Abbey, Ted Abbey,' he paused, with no reciprocation from me. 'Me and Mrs. Abbey live back a coupla miles,' he jerked a thumb, then sucked his teeth and sighed. 'Girlie, best I get us going there.'

The car seemed older than any car Marcus had owned, with Mr. Abbey soon out front cranking to fire its engine which took round after round to vibrate and finally take. Frightened again, I wanted him beside me in what seemed a wilderness on either side with boulders and matted bush.

'Right,' he pronounced and we rattled away into a valley, then up out of it, with trees tall on the horizon. When we swerved to the right to slow with a series of jarring thuds, Mr. Abbey bent to the brake, then straightened. Overhead the moon was high, streaming down almost as bright as day. Ahead was a gate to a clearing and soon through it a compact building appeared, a shed. A dog barked. 'Only me, Rastus,' he yodelled, which set it cavorting in circles with yelps.

The house was small with a single middle door. Brightness showed from a window. Soon enough, the door was opened; a solid-framed figure stood beside it, a Tilley lamp held waist-high.

'That you Teddie?' a woman called, certain it was Teddie as the engine sighed and expired. But if not alarm, concern painted her voice. 'You got someone with you?'

'Yes dear,' and I was shepherded out, Rastus sniffing at my knees, hung with his master's coat, then Mrs. Abbey was stepping towards me, disturbed.

'What?'

'Let's get inside and then …'

'Then you tell me and you're to eat, Teddie, you've missed your tea.'

'Yes, yes.'

Inside a fire sputtered in a grate. Furnished simply, a sofa stood between two armchairs, with one sagging seat topped by cushions. There was a treadle sewing machine on a square rag rug, and beside it a table was set with a cup and saucer, a loaf of bread, cheese, pickles, a jam jar and a dish of cream.

'Agnes, heat up milk for cocoa for Girlie here, and I'll explain.'

'Poor little pet,' Mrs. Abbey said. With dark bright eyes and a curve to her spine, she was as mild as her husband. However, more observant. Soon enough, *sotto voce*, she was to inform him that I was from The Ladies' College, having immediately noted the crested pocket of my uniform when she exchanged Mr. Abbey's coat for a thick-knitted bed jacket. Pink. It's difficult to recognise people when they're not where they belong, but, if not second-sighted, she was well conversant with uniforms. There were two soldiers in uniform in separate frames, another with a girl wearing a sailor's hat on a shelf beside a mantle wireless.

Mrs. Abbey smoothed my hair, patted my cheek with her papery hands, and assured me I'd come to no harm with them. After an effort by Mr. Abbey to orientate her to the facts of him discovering me, it was decided I be put to bed.

Mrs. Abbey planned that I would have breakfast and be returned to school early; 8a.m. at the latest. With first light breaking over the spine of the ridge above their farm by 6a.m., this would allow sufficient time to get me back. She declared that I may or may not have been missed by that hour. I was, she said, to be returned to the 'Froggy principal', whom somehow, somewhere, they'd heard was a responsible woman, even if foreign. With no telephone to connect them to an outside world, they considered this to be the proper course in my interests, uppermost in their minds.

Ushered to a narrow bed where the sheets were warmed by a hot water bottle, lent a flannelette nightgown sprigged with roses, their easy kindness of: 'Good night, my dear,' followed by: 'Sleep tight, girlie,' lapped round and assured me.

Looking from one to the other, my eyes began to fill with tears. I didn't know what to say but Mr. Abbey did.

'Sleep tight, girlie,' he repeated before adding with a silly grin: 'You can be sure as bloomin' pigs don't fly that our bugs don't bite.'

'That's enough Teddie. Come along,' his wife chided.

My head to the pillow with its scent of lavender after they left, with the door comfortingly ajar I could hear their murmuring tones discussing me. Then, with moonlight sliding in and onto the ceiling, my lids as heavy as lead, I curved away into sleep.

## 44

I'd never seen Mlle wearing a hair net. Or seen her lips colourless, unadorned by her usual 'Bonjour Paris—Carmen Red'. If it was true that people brought their country with them, she was far from chic that morning. None of us would have ever seen this Mlle, and I didn't look, I stared. The flannelette nightdress may have been sprigged with roses like Mrs. Abbey's, but it was covered by a khaki greatcoat. Her slippers mauve and flimsy, I noted corns and calluses on her feet the colour of dough.

'*Quel heure est-il?*' she was demanding of Matron who insisted on delivering me to her in person with my flaming cheek. Shortly after leaning into Mrs. Abbey and with Mr. Abbey squeezing my shoulder in farewell, Matron had slapped me. Hard. With blood pulsing behind my eyes, her expression had been foul. All I heard were her snorts before saying, 'wicked child', then further snorts. She was a sharp-tongued woman who saw no reason to behave kindly. 'Follow me,' she had said, which I did with breath bubbling in my throat.

Mlle drew back her heavy sleeve to her watch. '*Il est sept heures et demi! Samedi!*' she proclaimed. '*Et je ne dorm pas bien!*'

I'd slept very well, but might have slept on another planet as well as eaten sumptuously in comparison to a school breakfast of lumped porridge and bullets of eggs. Savagely, I'd rejoice if a bullet was fired to hit Matron and kill her, who if not a thorough sadist, was as near as I'd ever met. Twinged by fear of what lay ahead, I tried not to think.

'*Sept heures et ...*' Again Mlle consulted her watch and above it I saw a tarnished bangle that she circled with her other hand. '*Merci*, Matron, that will be all.'

'But,' And there was a hardness to the 'But'.

'That will be all,' and somehow Mlle communicated to me that maybe I could expect to be treated with a bit of kindness and care with her words and intonations from her other world, France. I knew I respected her, unlike some of the mistresses with their stagy enthusiasms, let alone Matron, who was a barbarian under a surface cover of duty.

'Natasha?'

Suddenly, time folded in on me; I remembered—as if it was yesterday— the first time I was summoned to her private rooms as a small girl aged just eight. The easy chair with the mud-coloured cushions fashioned to her shape, a sofa covered, then as now, with books, her desk where she sat spearing papers with a stiletto-sharp pen. Being told to sit on a tapestry stool alongside her, but not too close. The reason back then? My non-religious life.

Now, this morning, in addition I saw her academic gown on a dressmaker's dummy in a corner by a bag of golf clubs half covered by a rug. Half expecting to be directed to sit and wait while she went to dress, instead she touched my arm. I felt it jerk. Then she was reaching for my hand; hers cool against the clammy of mine.

'Come Natasha,' and she led me to the sofa, pushing books to the floor, stirring them away with one mauve slipper, seating us side by side. A wall clock chimed eight. Waxy sunlight gleamed at the window. I sniffed, smelling something like peppermints, and needed to scratch my nose, but didn't dare.

'You do cause trouble, you know. Both for yourself and me. What's more, you took a high and inadvisable risk.'

Tongue on lip, I hung my head. 'But first, Natasha ...' and with a finger she raised my chin. 'The welt on your cheek?'

I felt the rest of my face hot and red to match it while my bowels turned watery with dread. 'I ...I can't ...'

'You can and you must,' now her finger was an arrow aimed at my nose and she frowned. 'Who hit you and when?'

Any refusal to answer was out, so I stuttered the facts. And with what I later came to learn was a Gallic shrug, in time rumours spread that consequences ensued for that matron. But first, Mlle was set to deal with me.

'Do you wish to tell why?'

'Why, why I caused trouble?' I whispered before my tongue turned treacherous. 'If I do?' slipped out involuntarily.

'That I think may be too difficult for either of us to answer at present. But yes, you do cause me trouble.' She turned, paused and the light showed fine hairs on her chin. 'I aim for my girls to be fearless, never reckless. So the question is: why did you run away? What was your need to bolt?'

Uncertain and intimidated, I glanced up and saw her lips curve to smile, which sent me reeling with relief. And disbelief.

'Do not answer with anything you do not mean,' she said, acknowledging something that I didn't understand. I was in a spin, and tempted to try to scramble away to another place, but Mlle Durand was not to be ignored.

She was implacable. 'Natasha?'

My eyes fell as hers met mine and all at once, knotted as it was, I fully knew what it was to contain a secret. My breath burned. The most secret thing in my life.

'I want my mother.'

'That, of course, is understandable, but ...'

'I want my mother to want me,' I wailed. Inconsolable, I wailed on. Swept by something I'd never named, I had no way to take back those words and bury them, while Mlle Durant's walls hung with sepia photos, black-and-whites, personal mementoes, framed certificates, and little portraits, far-off French landscapes. They could have yawned to a lunar emptiness.

Nina was eternally out of reach. Above every word I'd ever spoken.

'Come back,' I frantically ached to call to my mother as she was wandering in her life, her migraines and her unreadable thoughts. Even now, not daring to go as far as saying, 'Come back to me.'

For her own reasons, Nina had chosen to withdraw. Too often shadowy, flimsy and still as air, or floating, diaphanous, as if the wall behind her could be seen through her. Being but not being. But somehow given to emerge, substantially, when Marcus was present. With many shades of meaning to the word 'parent', never knowing what she thought—artless, heartless?—did I belong in spaces between spaces for her?

'My dear child ...'

Had I plunged to the bottom of my need? I baulked. Yet 'somewhere' was not 'nowhere', and I'd learned to live to the rhythm of other people's time.

'*Je ne comprends pas les parents. Jamais,*' Mlle concluded and telephoned my father. It was an emergency.

## 45

Midday when he arrived, I was dripping with tears, from which my father seemed to take comfort; uneasy perhaps that we shared a complicated obstinacy, a personal network for two. His face seemed older than when I saw him last.

'Come here,' he motioned, putting his knuckles to my cheeks, then led me out to a verandah where I was instructed to sit on a bench and wait while he was engaged with Mlle. I wasn't to join in this talk. Tears dried on my face; my best friend, good friends and ordinary friends. None were allowed to come near me. Marcus closeted with Mlle for a very long time.

With birds chirping and banging my ankles together while I waited, I refused to think what Nina might be doing. Or Annya. Or Michael, who maybe—the image crept in—was rolling about like a drunken sailor getting his land legs following life at sea.

'Natasha,' my father then led into the garden. The sun in my eyes, I suppose he put on a smile especially for the occasion. This unsought occasion, when he jumped into a borrowed Humber to travel faster after filling the tank with his petrol ration for months, discarding any reason or excuse not to come.

'Natasha,' he bent down, and I yielded to his hug before he held me from him, stroking the fading welt on my cheek. If in his head he ran through calamities that might have happened, they didn't occur to me. Few parents are rigorously objective. And anyway, aren't parts of life about concealing things from other people and ourselves?

'Am I going to be expelled?'

'No.' My father's mouth widened to an odd grin that seemed to last too long. 'We're lucky she's French; she believes that food is socially and parentally cementing.'

'What?'

'At Mlle's suggestion, I am taking you out to lunch.'

He took me all the way to Katoomba and The Carrington, where, unknown to me, my parents had honeymooned! Wind snapped at my hair from the wound- down windows and whipped my eyes wet, but I wasn't crying. Marcus was behind his driving goggles, concentrating on the bends and careening down hills. He turned often to sniffing me as I took in the different smells of the mountains; eucalyptus, burning wood, and a curious whiff of isolation. Mile after mile flew by, while tentative if anxiously happy with my father, I wondered what sorts of lives rattled past us in faster cars. It felt, but I couldn't put it into words, as if we could be taking an irreversible journey together, which we were.

'I intend to write to Mr. and Mrs. Abbey; thank them for their kindness,' Marcus said quietly to the steering wheel, and nothing more, when we circled the drive to park at The Carrington. Splendid with its ornate iron railings, stained glass and marble statues, in the huge vestibule there were banks of flowers in Ali-baba sized urns, a palm court trio, and a renowned dining room.

Ushered to a table laid for four, two places were deftly removed. Marcus shook his head to coffee and had his wine glass with its spiralled stem refilled. He steadily watched me over the rim as he sipped.

'Your mother ...' my father solemnly introduced Nina.

I jerked straight to screw the damask napkin laid on my lap by the Maitre'd into a knot.

'She doesn't care,' I finished his sentence.

'Doesn't care? You're wrong,' he leaned forward. 'You're wrong,' and pressed fingers against his lips where he might have pressed them to mine.

I huddled away, and wanted to believe him, but resisted; pangs of jealousy knifing through me as I pictured her. Then smelled her, the smells of The Carrington evaporating, and *'Joy'* to perfume the room. But I felt none. I felt betrayal, with Nina deep in preparations for her party and her guests. Then more. What could have been a murderous resentment, my desire for what was forever out of reach was overwhelming as I sat straight at the table in the high-backed chair.

If Marcus was angry, baffled and irritated, he kept his voice controlled. 'Baby,' and I heard his hurried breathing, 'you must tell me why you ran away.'

Baby! I was hit by a bolt of blind rage. Where was the 'baby' who swung down on sheets from Kings, the 'baby' who ran for miles, without Amelia, who didn't blubber and cry?

'I hate you, hate you!' I lived in a world of absolutes, unaware of how thin a partition divided love and hate. 'Hate you, hate you.' Again: 'hate you.'

'Stop that at once!' came the order.

I stopped, but the venom didn't vanish; it was only submerged for seconds waiting to resurface. Face flattened, I threw myself up and out of the chair. Somehow I walked as if I was balancing a cup on my head to reach double glass-etched doors, before I stepped through and sped. I hotfooted past Carrington guests and dodged the open arms of a man in a checked sweater and plus fours. Through doors and down the entrance flight of stairs, I hurled on to where I expected to find the Humber, but I didn't. I snarled at a dog tied by its lead to a post. My heart raced, though not for long. What shot round in my head, erupted. What I wanted was my father to bring me out of the mess and confusion that was today. To revalue me, and tell me where I could find what had to be Nina's natural love and care for me. To hand me a passport into whatever made up her world, which he'd never done. There seemed to be a loneliness in everything.

I thumped down on a garden seat hidden behind a matted hedge. It faced a fountain of cherubs and nymphs, with water splashing down from an upturned shell.

'Found you,' Marcus stood over me.

I pressed both feet down hard so that I wouldn't shake, and stared at the gravel under my shoes.

'Look at me,' he said, but evasively, all I did was nod NO. 'Natasha ...'

I said nothing. Nothing I'd say could be adequate.

'You see everything too brightly, too fiercely,' he said, and for brief moments his chin sank to his tie. Sullen now, if I waited, he didn't elaborate.

The clock in my head felt too tightly wound, squeezing my brain.

Maybe I was winning, but maybe this was the wrong game. Here in the Hotel Carrington's grounds, scents from flower beds merged with the exhaust from an ancient car and a frangipani tree in the cooling light.

What is fated, and what is freely chosen? A shift of perception and memory can be bent into any shape of who I was, and why I was who I was. But do we only remember scraps? How long did we stay where we were?

From The Carrington, Marcus took me to Echo Point, where the Three Sisters had drawn sightseers and coachloads of visitors for years.

'They're three sandstone turrets. Massive rocks formed millions of years ago,' he said, speech low, his words considered, taking on an educational role. 'With a tectonic history ...' Then a run down on simple geology which I didn't want to hear, wanting instead to assert myself, rightly or wrongly.

'Three sisters?' I glared at and quizzed him, followed up with a startling sort of question. 'Could they be us?'

'Us?'

'You and my mother and me?'

Light flared in his eyes but he didn't laugh. He didn't ask if we were massively formed and strong; 'bonded' in the new-age term of today. Together forever. Pulling tall, instead what my father imparted was the fragility of love, but in enduring terms. And if some circumstances had made him seem cruel to me, he was emphatic that this was never the case.

Gulping, my fist came up to my chin of its own accord when I asked him if there was something that would never be right between my mother and me. Slowly and affectionately, he suggested that one must love a mother. He ruffled my hair. 'And a father. But not too much.' What's more, he went on, we were cornered by a biological compulsion which in time I'd come to understand.

But inside Nina was there another Nina who was much nicer to my father than me, who one day would emerge to me if I held on?

'This is important,' Marcus was saying, and I was irritated before a happiness of sorts began to seep through. This happiness was irrational and shaky, but with a staying power and certainty that Marcus was a wonderful man, strong enough to support minor and major disappointments, as well as catastrophes.

'Sometimes,' he was saying, husking out sounds that could have been coming from his boots, 'your mother can have nightmares without plots. Horrid things.' In all probability, unsaid: private disasters she suppresses while awake. 'Then we just wait and be patient ... because there's no one in the world who can have more beautiful dreams.'

'Dreams,' stiff-lipped I heard myself echo, and he coaxed me back to impress on me that it was necessary never to close our minds to causes and remedies. What's more, I must promise to remember that Nina's smile—which sometimes may look like an effort and grudging—was a smile. She didn't always show all her feelings, but he said that I would understand this one day.

I watched him and listened with an acute sense that what my father said next he was not saying to me; instead, privately to himself: 'Depressions ... storms that just blow in from nowhere.'

Nina, Nina! Did all mothers—or only mine—have a darker side? With her conflicting demands, was this the moment when, with a new awareness of her, along with mistrust and envy, I was roused by a puzzled urge to safeguard her, this mother unable to share her life with her child? Our levels of need were different. I squirmed; was she some sort of second child who, with his personal code, my father too must protect?

'Happiness is what you think it means, Natasha. No one else can really know.' My father laid out these words like a treasure before he grinned. 'When you're older, just think of me, baby, as your uncomplicated father to whom complicated things have occurred.'

'But?'

'Mystifying, yes,' he gave a sigh, 'this won't make a lot of sense to you today.'

'But?'

'But try to remember,' Marcus smiled. And when my father smiled, I was sure anyone who saw him felt better. I felt better.

'The ho-hum things we do day to day are the key to survival,' he said, stretching his legs and arms, and reaching for my hand. 'There are times when all our lives can be difficult—a mess—but we manage. Yep, we do, and a word exists for this.'

'What word?'

Grateful, I let myself be folded into his mood. 'Optimism.'

# 46

Engaged with our own history—the actual world that surrounded us— the war was not the defining crisis of our lives.

Until, tinged an unnameable colour, the morning arrived when Sweetie took a telephone call, and stared at the wall to which the phone was attached as though it was a movie screen—and screamed. She screamed as if the blood surging round in her head would burst through.

Sweetie—our co-principal, Miss Sarah Batton-Browne—was never shrill.

Patient, sensitive, reliable Sweetie, determinedly fair and determinedly serene with her English spirit and porcelain skin, and possibly her English soul, on whom we would have done well to model ourselves, continued to scream. In outrage, in disbelief; then her legs folded under her and she fell to the floor. The nightmare was real.

Was there—is there—some sort of group nerve that's removed from the vagaries of time? Every one of us, wherever we were, swore we heard Sweetie. Or was it that immediately, Sweetie's screams were relayed one to another throughout the school, which set up a mad reaction? Hysterics built into pre-pubescence, our antennas forever quivering in any breeze, adolescents permanently attuned, and with Sweetie's harrowing call from London affecting us all?

The walls of our minds were stretched and rearranged; this was my first first-hand connection to the misery war generated. Her mother, widowed during World War I and her brother—a naval man on leave—his wife and their two young children, bedded down in the cellar of their Greenwich house. Gone. A direct bomb; Greenwich of 'Greenwich Mean Time', the meanest time on earth for the Batton-Browne family that night.

Unquantifiable, our grief for Sweetie kept changing shape.

Vengefully, we swore we'd get back at THAT enemy pilot who'd dropped THAT bomb. Somehow. THAT pilot who had rained down his destruction under a cruel and illuminating bomber's moon.

In an angry web of connections—a sub-world of hate and retribution—we thirsted for nothing but his death. Even better, his horribly mutilated flat face, high forehead and skull pulped. Or outwardly unscathed to suffer the hell of the damned with each breath he, the enemy, took. Every guttural sound.

Then with glances flickering between us, even small enemies—our day-to- day enemies—grudgingly became friends. Together, Faith and I took the decision to sidle up to the pig people and smile a bit. Even so, we kept alert. Experience had taught us to shut off expectations.

But with a moping face, which I suppose meant she was sad, the dreaded Corrine Bradley offered her form of a nicety: 'Gee, it's too bad.'

With lips locked, we swallowed the replies we might have said. Full of contradictions and puzzled, I shuddered and shrugged. If I'd previously harboured a certainty that burying the hatchet with Corrine Bradley could only mean burying it in her head, then that thought seemed to vaporise, leaving no connection between then and now.

Subdued, and with hot tears scalding cheeks, we were at a collective loss as to what to do. Daylight had taken on a gloom of night. Kneeling at Sweetie's side, Mlle, with a twitching face, insisted she take a sip from the glass she shakingly held to Sweetie's lips. Later, a prefect circulated that when the glass was returned to the kitchen, it had a sharp, malty smell.

At assembly, Mlle was forced to repeat that this was a cruel day for our beloved co-principal, so it was a cruel day for us all. Lessons were cancelled and she appreciated that such tidings were not the joyful tidings they may have been under other circumstances.

We were to keep the level of noise down. Arrangements were being made for all boarders to walk—in an orderly crocodile, hatted and gloved—to the celebrated gardens of a nearby artist, Norman Lindsay A famous artist, his paintings not Miss Clarke's style, Mlle's tongue sagging with the weight of what she edited as she went on.

'Whose works some among you may appreciate later as worldly women, but decidedly not as young girls. Young ladies,' she was emphatic to add: 'None of whom it is to be hoped will aspire to the role of artists' model.'

But with his paintings and sculpture widely recognised as 'erotic', Norman Lindsay, among other literary works, wrote the classifc for children, *The Magic Pudding* with Bunyip Bluegum, a koala, Bill Barnacle the sailor, and Sam Sawnoff, the Emperor penguin.

The day girls were to return home. Food—she refrained from the fun connotation of saying 'a picnic'—was being prepared. It was to be consumed in the shade of an avenue of grandiflora; the creamy magnolias to provide both solemn beauty and a memorable perfume. We were each to select a book from the library, a room of dark panelling and suitable titles. Quietly.

Sombre in grey pleated skirt, grey blouse and grey cardigan, Miss Frampton appeared to surge with sorrow, sigh after sigh. 'No noisy games,' she said. 'However, if restless, which is to be expected of schoolgirls, you are free to roam the many paths.' We were to avert our eyes from unsuitable outdoor statues, and if her vocal cords thickened, she'd alerted us to something. 'For those eight years or younger, hopscotch will be marked out on an area adjacent to the kitchen garden, where there will be no squealing, no squabbling, no undue rowdiness.'

Permitted ample time in the library, voices lowered to a murmur,

Faith made her choice after we discussed that we'd take stories we already knew—stories we relished at this age. She went straight to 'National Velvet', having made up her mind that one day, she'd name a daughter of hers 'Meredith', after Velvet's older sister.

I was torn between two books. First, Georgette Heyer's 'Corinthian' because it was so English and therefore had a sort of connection to Sweetie. But more probably because of Pen, the girl-heroine dressed as a boy who fell into Sir Richard's arms from a rope of knotted sheets hanging out of a second-story window. The other was James Hilton's 'Lost Horizon', dream-like with what followed after the arrival of a party of Westerners in a monastery in Tibet. I baulked. Was 'Lost Horizon's' guarded secret of Shangri-La and life forever out of place today?

Onwards alphabetically: H...K...M ... R...to Thackeray, Tolstoy and Tolkien. I snatched 'The Hobbit' from the shelf.

'What are you taking? What do you want?' a senior asked two others. They were not about to hurry us up, they were just bent on choices of their own.

'Not that there's likely to be a copy of 'The Kama Sutra' here, but ...'

'The what?'

'The Kama Sutra.'

One of them seemed knowledgeable. 'Go to Poetry; it might have just slipped in there under 'Sonnets on the Kama Sutra."

'You wouldn't want sonnets would you?' She struggled to focus through thick glasses. 'Anyway, what's it about?'

'The eight attitudes and sixty-four ingredients of love.'

'Like spells?' The senior's springy hair looked sprung up and electrified.

'Na.'

'Howja know?'

Her posture slumped. 'Because my Grandad's got a copy he keeps locked away.' She simpered. 'With pictures of men and women. Naked. Explicit. Doing things to each other, you know THINGS. With penises. Don't look so shocked, silly.'

'Nasty! '

'Not always. Well, that's what some girls say.

'Like dirty postcards! But Sweetie ...'

'Sweetie's a lovely person, a loving person so ...' She squinted, shot a look in our direction, and noticed us agog. Faith's cheeks and mine had turned red. 'Who do you think you two are staring at?' Her shoulders straightened, war-like. We hung our heads. 'Don't you two know it's rude to stare?'

## 47

A memorial service for Sweetie's family was to be held at St. Barnabas. Jointly celebrated by the Rev. Whitehead and Bishop Clintart, whose wife forever pipped Mrs. Whitehead at the ecclesiastical posts. Interestingly, Mrs. Whitehead plank-breasted while Bishop Clintart's wife's breasts always swung like a pair of church bells.

The whole school was in grief, with someone reporting she'd seen Sweetie with eyes that looked like under-shadowed plums. Sweetie's grief was our grief, and of course everyone was to attend. Or was I to be excluded?

'No,' said Faith, who persuaded me that I was equally entitled to attend, coming up with the initiative: 'Ask your parents, they can hardly refuse this once.'

Often helpless and always vulnerable, with Sweetie's tragedy, I was not prepared to remain passive. My body stiffened.

'I'll ask Mlle,' I said, and the enormity of this struck us speechless, though not for long. Huddled together, we rehearsed and re-rehearsed my approach to this formidable woman who had what seemed like life and death power over us. Mlle Durand's face floated in front of me, alternatively benign or closed. Hadn't I caused her enough trouble?

Enough fuss and embarrassment to make her rate me some kind of hairshirt?

'Well?' Faith prompted.

I quailed and rolled my eyes. 'I can't, can I?'

'You sure can,' Faith agreed.

If it wasn't Sweetie's own tragedy, she would have been more approachable.

Faith started with me down the impossibly long corridor, leaving me when we reached the green baize outer door. I passed through to where I must knock on the panel of Mlle's door. My knees began to rattle.

'*Entrez.*'

Mlle had acquired a gramophone with a trademark squat little dog —HMV. His Master's Voice. It stood on its own table near Mlle who sat enthroned at her desk as she had on each occasion I'd been in that room.

Occupied with papers, she did not raise her eyes. '*Alors.* Who do I have here? And why? Speak up, speak up.'

'Natasha Ross.'

'Aaaah,' she said, as open-mouthed as she might have uttered from a dentist's chair. And I smelled a smell between disinfectant and toothpaste, not the scent from the bowl of roses which divided us on her desk.

Yes?'

Nervous, there was nothing to do but plunge in. 'No one will notice me. I'll sit at the very back. Of the church. St. Barnabas ...' I went on unnecessarily. Her jaw firm, something about that set my resolve. I mustn't beg. 'I won't sing, won't join in the 'Amens'. I won't worship.' What was worship? How did 'worship' find a way into my mouth? 'Besides, I don't know how and ...'

'Why do you want to come? '

'To help God help Sweet ... Miss Batton-Browne.'

'Miss Batton-Browne,' she repeated, and in her sadness, straining Sweetie's name. Even so, her presence was not in decline.

'Yes.'

'How could you help, Natasha?'

I was stumped. Put down and mocked, any composure I had gathered up spilled over and ran off from my shallow little pool of hope. I pulled at deep breaths then locked my eyes on my feet, and out of nowhere remembered long ago, when nearly eight, standing on an x-ray machine in the shoe department at David Jones to see through shoe leather, socks, skin and flesh to my skeleton feet. If those bones were still in place, I hoped they'd hold me upright.

'Natasha?'

Cheeks burning, my eyes were gritty and dry. Hung in suspense, I waited for a punishment to be meted out.

'Natasha?'

Schooled to directly face whoever addressed us, especially a teacher, especially Mlle or Sweetie, this was impossible. With my heart knocking enough to crack my ribs, my stomach groaned. I didn't hear her stand up from her desk—her fortress—and move to me.

Mlle Durand raised my chin. 'God will be pleased to have you attend the memorial.'

## 48

Ordered and disordered sweeps of time—two years—hurricaned by and I was fourteen.

Seven years short of official adult status, then set at twenty-one. Someone who accepts that everything in life isn't necessarily pleasant. Yet it was evident that some of the adults in our school lives did not meet this definition.

Miss Jorgen, a perambulating bottle of vinegar. Miss Underwood, with reduced horizons, suggesting that if we tried to camp outside the fence we'd be mauled. Miss Drummond, infatuated with trivia, but sarcastic and fierce. Miss Gunton, heartless, stupid, and eaten up by envy, inane enough to squawk that Marlene Dietrich wore a mink coat and a mink stole at the same time!

Our nurturing may have been haphazard, yet it wasn't all bad luck. At an elevation of 1,250 feet above sea level *'making its climate a superb one, rivalling the far-famed winter climate of Southern France.'* The Prospectus declared as it offered English, History, Geography, French, Latin, Mathematics and Physiology to matriculation. At ground level, the mosaic of our everyday life was repeatedly patterned; plus special attention paid to *'correct speaking of English and cultivation of a good accent.'* In addition to Literature, Music, Current Events etc., we were subjected to Physical Culture,

Musical Appreciation and Folk Dancing. Games included swimming, tennis, basketball and riding. Optional extras included piano, violin, music theory, singing, dancing, elocution, eurythmics, etc. Founded in the dark ages—1897—the architects of our education appeared intent on building *'first and foremost the training of good citizens'*. Inevitably, there were slip-ups.

The past? Uncertain where it begins, one certainty remains: it is never over. Irrefutably, it moves back through the folds of memory and the pleats of time.

Dis-remembering could make us conspirators in our own lives and above all in the shifting frontiers between child and young adult. With an awkwardness and ferocity to adolescence, one fold of memory was contradictory—both harsh and tissue-soft.

At fourteen, I was home for the final holidays of the year before I sat the Intermediate Examination. There were two further years until the official Leaving Certificate, when school ended before university began if that was your bent.

'I don't want to go,' I said with disdain when Nina suggested I spend a day with her in town at her exclusive dressmaker in the St. James' Building. Her appointment was made for a fitting from fabric given to her by Annya, my delicious aunt who acquired stuff for them both, no questions asked, with rationing still in force. There were also books to be changed at my mother's library, and why not choose a birthday present for Faith? And an early Christmas present to post to Celia in Tanganyika?

Located on the fourth floor, Madame Beryl's rooms were pre-war and plushly furnished, with a cornucopia of gladioli by the reproduction French boudoir table which doubled as the desk. The appointment book was jacketed in velvet, and her assistants wore 'good' black, with tape measures their sole accessory. Madame Beryl, whose hair was an architectural feat, wore black with looped pearls. There were no mismatched colours, stripes or spots at Madame Beryl's.

'My dear Mrs. Ross, I'd no idea you had a daughter.' How did she know I was Nina's daughter, we'd not been introduced? 'You've never mentioned her,' Madame Beryl chirruped and established their long-standing dealings, her enthusiasm producing more problems than it solved. I'll look forward to creating lovely garments for ... '

'Natasha,' Nina supplied, her tone indulgent.

'Ah, Natasha,' and I was inspected, Madame Beryl passing over my face to my scrawny body which, thankfully, had begun to grow appropriate lumps. They were beyond my control to have worked out as they should. Nina had done little to inform me of periods other than post me a book, but Faith had superior knowledge and, late-developers, we were spared alarm. Anyway, in the gulag that was school, with its rumours, advice and misinformation were rife about the pins and things we needed to wear.

'Celeste,' Madame Beryl's voice coincided with her snapping a long-nailed finger to her thumb. A willowy assistant appeared with Nina's garment draped over one arm and an armoury of pins attached to a pad on her wrist, and toothy Celeste smiled.

Next, a fragile gilt chair was provided for me which sent me reeling back six years to David Jones' and the Miss Smithers who outfitted me for school. With her cylindrical kiss curls, rouged cheeks and tape in hand, after seating Nina on a gilt-legged chair Celeste was all attention to the list my mother drew from her snakeskin handbag. It was a match for her snakeskin shoes. Why do I have such photographic recall? I closed my eyes in a sort of misery that day.

Madame Beryl withdrew, leaving us in Celeste's care. Spotlighted by a subdued but telling light, she was turned—gently but decisively—this way and that. Nipped in here, murmured over there, my mother could have been a perfect woman. Not just flesh and blood with her winning ways, her brown to black moods, her beauty, and her neglect—as I saw it—of me. Together with her charm, her bits of distress which turned into headaches, blowing in from nowhere! While unmoving, I perched on the ridiculous chair, my knees together, and hands folded one over the other in my lap.

'Aha,' Madame Beryl returned. 'Aha,' and she double-checked the fitting before Celeste, the acolyte, was down on her knees, rotating the goddess until the hem was pronounced straight. Next, a further muted instruction for Celeste, who left to reappear with a green dress between careful hands.

'Mrs. Ross,' the voice might have been water purling over river stones as she angled her head, 'I would so much like to try this on your lovely daughter.'

Lovely! Me! My voice went creaky. 'I...I... don't want ...'

Was it my objection that swung the balance as Nina fingered the dress, brushing it lightly, while I wondered who owned it? Expecting her to refuse, before I knew it I was unbuttoned and, staggeringly gauche, stripped to sensible undies, my skinny arms then lifted above my head. Hair freed, cool to my flaming cheeks, silkily the dress slithered down to form over the surface of my body like green moss.

Madame Beryl exchanged her 'Aha' for an attenuated 'Aaahh ...' Then, taking my shoulders, she revolved me to the wall-sized mirror, gilt-edged like the chairs.

What did I see? Not me, because beyond my reflection, who I saw was my mother. In what felt like years but were only seconds of acute embarrassment, I stared. Electrified, I could have poked a finger into a light socket and set sparks surging through my skin, while Nina stared at me.

Stiffened fingers pressed hard to her mouth, she blinked her widened eyes. And again, as if she was chronically short-sighted, which she was not.

'Isn't she lovely?' Madame Beryl effused; off and away, expanding on mother and daughter's similar colouring, etc. She thought it 'divine' that this shade of green suited us both. It was a slippery claim to my ears. Affronted, I wished I was covered in mud. 'Well?' she questioned, her balls of tennis eyes swinging from mother to daughter.

Yet Nina's eyes were locked on me. Why? IT WAS AS IF SHE WAS SEEING ME FOR THE FIRST TIME! ACTUALLY SEEING ME!

What did I feel? Had it been possible to melt into the mirror, vanish and leave her daughter-less, I'd have jumped at it. Disappeared; left Nina, Madame Beryl, and Celeste aghast as shock rippled through the fitting room.

But doomed to remain me, a pain ran round my heart. I felt real, was real; but real and alive and diminished. At fourteen years of age, I was finally visible to the woman who'd borne me!

'Well, Mrs. Ross?'

A vein fluttering above one eye, it seemed my mother didn't object to what she saw. Me ... a boiled egg, peeled, and wrapped in a 'divine' shade of green. Nina's hand came down from her mouth and mine flew up, panicky that I'd be sick—throw up and spatter the dress, the mirror, the pale carpet and my shoes.

'Yes,' stunned, my mother spoke almost in a voice of wonder, and lowering herself to the chair, she crossed one leg over the other and smoothed her skirt. 'Yes,' and inexplicably, this confirmed me as an oddity, an aberrant and with helping hands, the green moss was creeping up then over me in reverse, tangling my hair.

'Natasha?'

Stretched tight, I couldn't answer; I didn't dare. Eyes sliding sidelong, it seemed impossible to link up my ideas and think. Except one loony thought: that if I had a body joined with a soul, would it leak away?

## 49

'You're almost hatched,' Marcus said, sighing. 'Fourteen.'

'Am I?' I was struggling to preserve something—but what?—as well as developing a policy not to argue.

'Yep, no longer our grub but our butterfly,' he replied. Across the table, Nina directed her gaze to me, said nothing and my throat went dry.

The burned-out end of a summer day, with Nina Simone murmuring a background from the gramophone, tailed away as my father rose to lift the needle before it scratched. Swivelling towards the window, I saw there was still blue in the sky. Blue like the sky when he'd take me kite-flying with the kite he made, setting it off to sail up and become part of a blue universe. Pulling but attached to me, I almost felt it tug away as the string unfurled from the ball of string I clutched in both hands. What took me back? A wish to regress to a small girl who in her subconscious must have questioned why Marcus picked sides?

Stroking Nina's lightly clad back as he passed her chair, he resumed his seat between us, with the light from a lamp accentuating a silver spoon in a bowl from which Nina ladled sliced white peaches and passionfruit.

'Natasha, we've something to tell you,' Marcus began and I blinked back to the present, my eyes fixed on the movements of his mouth. Distinctly, the grandfather clock struck in the hall: five, six, seven, eight.

Then equally distinctly, Nina was precisely enunciating words. Lots of words, her voice suffused with cautious care? The gist of it? Educated, but in a backwater, the time had come to bring me back to Sydney. Home. With wartime dangers mercifully minimal, I was to spend my final years as a day girl. Enrolled again in a Ladies' College, friends there would, in the main, be accessible. Geographically and socially accessible. A smile nibbled at her lips and Nina revolved her wrists: 'Tennis, debating, dancing classes, dances partnered by the boys from the brother school, more cosmopolitan,' she concluded.

'What!' I exclaimed. Unstrung, I almost couldn't comprehend it.

'You're coming home.'

You're coming home! A statement oddly curious with meanings of regrets, alarms and happiness.

'Yes, you're coming home,' My father chortled. 'How do you rate that as a surprise?'

I stared. 'Don't stare,' he said, watching me, and broke the ice. 'It strains the optic nerves.' Then a long pause: 'Baby, you're coming home.'

Home! It rolled off his tongue. My life was to be rearranged and not just in my head. Home! Where there had to be fewer rules. Things never again to be as they were!

'A day girl.' I felt a fleeting pause of reluctance, then disbelief. I hugged myself and marvelled. I was free to take the world in from the outside to those poor things—the boarders—cloistered away in high-ceilinged, sparse rooms where their autonomy was strictly curtailed. Marginalised. They were flowers in bud confined by crabby soil, where everything was dominated by bells, bells and more bloody bells.

My father pushed back his chair, stood up, faced the open window, watched the sky where the moon was due to rise, then turned to me with a crinkled grin. 'And my girl, you'll have to work harder. Scholastically.' Then Marcus, ever the indulgent father, was saying: 'Yes, you're clever, bright ...'

Me! 'Nooo!' Alarmed, I sat on both hands.

'Yes,' he contradicted, and if there was a second person in everyone, he had become the rationalist. 'Except for maths.'

Even with Mr. McMannus' help, I'd not done well at maths, but did remember how I'd come to be impressed by his old-man grace. And more than that, his forward-thinking; he was not a man who would consider ambition an unfeminine trait.

'So,' Marcus went on, 'it stands to reason you'll need a career outside multiplications, divisions, equations.'

'Geometry, trigonometry ...' I blurted.

'Yes. Next year you'll face more competition and ...'

'And?'

'There are choices to be made. Your choices. Yes, yours.'

'Yes, choices,' from my mother, so at some unknown crossroad, I must have grown out of being a child, but it was impossible to take in more. Evening was coming down with its sweet smells and small night sounds: bumping leaves and chirping birds. It was coming down from a younger world I'd left behind.

Whatever life I was living, it was the one I had. Waiting to engage with the present, and waiting for what was to come. Fourteen-nearly-fifteen, I was on the verge, poised to step out into the rest of my life.

With no distress and cucumber-cool, that night I wiped away the many faces of mine that I'd stared at in this bedroom mirror over many years. Doubtless, I'd scrutinise more in the years to come. And I re-heard Mlle Mimi Durand's parting words, astonished that they were delivered with a peck to each cheek: 'Natasha, surviving is an art.'

Still awake when our clock in the hall struck midnight, I lay staring at shifting patterns of light on the ceiling from a full moon. Too young to accept that life was short, on the edge of what could be boundless, I was bursting to get on with it. For this night sky to peel back to another day.

When the sun would shine over the world ... and me.

# EPILOGUE

My memory is the proof of the existence of a girl who once was me, who no longer exists. All too often formidable to keep in focus and then follow the thread, memory now can become interchangeable with mice nibbling in my head. What to preserve? What to jettison?

Deceptions attach to nostalgia, and non-reality tends to make certain things bearable when we scramble back to images in another place and probe the mystery of our backgrounds. We carry a secret grief just out of view. But we manage. We blunder along. And like the ghost of a heartbeat, Marcus—arguably not always the most judicious of men—retells me: 'Optimism.'

Nina's gone, and so is the mother I can't defeat. I can't continue to blame her for a muddle that's me—even if that's what mothers are for.

Never convinced that I lived in the worst of all possible worlds, I bore no apparent signs of neglect or abuse. It is well past the time to take my thumb out of my mouth.

Life was, and is, this thing, then what comes next, which makes us all stories that have not happened yet.

# ABOUT THE AUTHOR

Born and educated in Sydney, Natalie Scott was a freelance writer before her acclaimed novels, short stories, non-fiction, books for children and audiobooks were published internationally. A columnist for *The Sydney Morning Herald* and *The Australian*, she also wrote for television and radio and has contributed to many literary magazines, including *The Griffith Review*, *Southerly*, *Westerly* and *Meanjin,* and ran courses in creative writing at the University of NSW and Macquarie University.

# SOME OF OUR OTHER BOOKS

## Pepper Press

My Business Is Now North—Grief and Love (Anthony Sobb)

Just Because—Loss, Love, Renewal (Lisa Gallate)

Shirley's Story—A Tale of Strength, Courage, and Hope (Emily Eklund Power)

Tales of Wagging Tails—Canine Short Stories (Jim Fraser)

The Bipolar Runner (Jacqui Louise Swallow)

## Popcorn Press (Fiction)

Abebi (Texi Smith)

High Heels and Low Blows (Jill Valentine)

Light and Shadow (Candida Baker)

RIPPA! (P.J. Laverty)

Rosemary Boy (Amy Coomer)

The Bunny Club (Blanche d'Alpuget)

## Fair Play Books

"Get Your Tits Out for the Lads" (Sally Freedman)

Hell for Leather—The World of a Sporting Journalist (Phil Wilkins)

Ladies First—Australia's First Olympic Hockey Gold Medal (Ashley Morrison)

Radicalised by FIFA—Football, History and Feminism (Jean Williams)

The Natural—Richard 'Dick' Thornett (Brendan Morris & Stephan Wellink)

Turning the Tide (Michelle Ford with Craig Lord)

www.fairplaypublishing.com.au

www.ingramcontent.com/pod-product-compliance
Lightning Source LLC
Chambersburg PA
CBHW071153070526
44584CB00019B/2775